IN THEIR OWN VOICES

IN THEIR OWN VOICES

Building Urban Aboriginal Communities

by Jim Silver
with Joan Hay, Darlene Klyne, Parvin Ghorayshi, Peter Gorzen,
Cyril Keeper, Michael MacKenzie and Freeman Simard

Fernwood Publishing • Halifax

2nd printing January 2008

Editing: Jane Butler
Cover Art: Jackie Traverse
Printed and bound in Canada by Hignell Printing Limited

Published in Canada by Fernwood Publishing
Site 2A, Box 5, 32 Oceanvista Lane
Black Point, Nova Scotia, B0J 1B0
and and #8 - 222 Osborne St., Winnipeg, Manitoba, R3L 1Z3
www.fernwoodpublishing.ca

Fernwood Publishing Company Limited gratefully acknowledges
the financial support of the Department of Canadian Heritage,
the Nova Scotia Department of Tourism and Culture and
the Canada Council for the Arts for our publishing program.

Library and Archives Canada Cataloguing in Publication

Silver, Jim
In their own voices : building urban Aboriginal communities / Jim Silver.

ISBN10: 1-55266-191-1 ISBN-13: 978-1-55266-191-8

1. Native peoples--Urban residence--Manitoba--Winnipeg. 2. Community development--Manitoba--Winnipeg. 3. Native peoples--Manitoba--Winnipeg--Social conditions. I. Title.

E78.M25S59 2006   305.897'0712743   C2006-900312-2

To my daughter Zoe Silver

Who in so many ways has been the inspiration for this book

CONTENTS

ACKNOWLEDGMENTS

First, we want to express our great appreciation to all of the people, and especially the approximately 165 Aboriginal people in Winnipeg's inner city, who agreed to be interviewed for the various chapters in this book. We have agreed to keep their names confidential. Without their insights and their generous commitment of time, this book would not have been possible.

We are happy to acknowledge the generous financial support of the Social Science and Humanities Research Council (grant # 538-2002-1003) and the Manitoba Research Alliance on Community Economic Development in the New Economy, the research consortium headed by the Canadian Centre for Policy Alternatives-Manitoba, which secured and administered the grant.

In particular thanks to John Loxley, Principal Investigator for the Manitoba Research Alliance on Community Economic Development in the New Economy, who read and provided thoughtful and helpful comments on each of the chapters in this book, and the two external reviewers, Peter Kulchyski and David Newhouse, who also read the manuscript in its entirety and provided very useful comments.

For the important contributions made to this book we thank Wayne Antony of Fernwood Publishing, Shauna MacKinnon, Director of the Canadian Centre for Policy Alternatives-Manitoba, and Todd Scarth, former Director of the Canadian Centre for Policy Alternatives-Manitoba. We owe a debt of gratitude to Jackie Traverse, an Aboriginal artist from Manitoba, whose painting was chosen for our cover because it suggests people spreading their wings, transforming their lives, and that is a central theme of the book. Thanks also to those involved in the production of this book: Jane Butler, Debbie Mathers, Beverley Rach and Brenda Conroy.

For their various contributions to the preparation of this book we are grateful to each of the following people: Inonge Aliaga, Sarah Amyot, Beatrice Barahona, Elspeth Campbell, Kim Cooke, Phyllis Crow, Darlene Daniels, Yvette Daniels, Lawrie Deane, Lorraine Desmarais, Philip Evans, Brenda Foster, Ken Funk, Val Gorlick, Joan Grace, Janice Greene, Carol Hawkins, Wayne Helgason, David Henry, Josie Hill, Heather Hunter, Bob Jones, Ed Keeper, Benita Kliewer, Garry Loewen, Darren Lezubski, John Lussier, Kathy Mallett,

Crystel Marion, Liz Merrick, Claudette Michel, Rachel Mitchell, George Munroe, Ruth Murdoch, Linda Parker, Colleen Robinson, Sid Rogers, Erica Ross, Tim Scarth, Helen Settee, Byron Sheldrick, Leon Simard, Tom Simms, Jo-Anne Spence, Leslie Spillett, Bev Thiessen, Eleanor Thompson, Darlene Wheeler, Erica Wiebe, Matthew Wiebe and Barbara Wynes.

We are grateful also to the following organizations for their contributions to the book: Spence Neighbourhood Association; Inner-City Aboriginal Neighbourhoods; West Broadway Aboriginal Residents Group; Ma Mawi Wi Chi Itata Centre; the Province of Manitoba's Aboriginal Education Directorate, Research and Planning Branch of the Department of Education and Youth, and Adult Learning and Literacy Branch of the Department of Advanced Education and Training; CrossRoads Learning Centre; Horizons Learning Centre; Portage Learning Centre; Urban Circle Training Centre; Project Opikihiwawin; and Aboriginal Council of Winnipeg.

The lead author especially wants to thank Loa Henry for her constant love, support and encouragement.

Chapter One

BUILDING A PATH TO A BETTER FUTURE

Urban Aboriginal People

Jim Silver

The urbanization of Aboriginal people is a process long underway, especially but not only in Western Canadian cities. Approximately one-half of Aboriginal people in Canada now live in urban centres, more than live on reserves. Those in cities are faced with a host of difficulties — inadequate housing, shortage of work, unsafe neighbourhoods, racism in various forms. Aboriginal people in cities experience higher rates of unemployment, a higher incidence of poverty and lower levels of income, on average, than do non-Aboriginal people. At the same time, however, a wide variety of exciting urban community development initiatives are underway or planned as a result of the efforts of urban Aboriginal people. Remarkable creativity and energy are growing out of the hard urban lives of Aboriginal people. In this book we provide examples of both the hardships and the creative energy of contemporary urban Aboriginal life. In particular, in the final chapter of the book, we outline a very attractive and distinctly Aboriginal form of community development that is emerging out of Winnipeg's inner city and that has the potential to bring with it both positive changes for Aboriginal people and an alternative way forward for all of us.

The focus of this book is on Aboriginal people in cities. The research on which it is based took place in Winnipeg, and in particular Winnipeg's inner city. And, for good reason. Winnipeg has the largest urban Aboriginal population in Canada — 55,755 according to the 2001 Census of Canada — and arguably has the largest and most vibrant set of urban organizations created by, and run by and for, urban Aboriginal people of any city in Canada. A reasonable argument can be made that it is in Winnipeg in particular that urban Aboriginal people will carve out and create for themselves a new and better future, rooted in Aboriginal cultural beliefs and practices and forged and shaped by their struggles with harsh inner-city realities. There is much of importance to be learned from the experience of Aboriginal people in Winnipeg — for Aboriginal and non-Aboriginal people alike.

Table 1-1: Population of Aboriginal People in Canada, 2001

Aboriginal origin	1,319,890
Aboriginal identity	976,305
North American Indian	608,850
Métis	292,310
Inuit	45,070
multiple Aboriginal identity	30,080
Registered Indian	558,175
First Nation/Band membership	554,860

Source: Siggner 2003: 21

We use the term Aboriginal to mean North American Indians, Métis and Inuit people. In the Census of Canada a distinction is made between those people who have Aboriginal ancestry and those who identify as Aboriginal. In most cases we use the numbers for those who identify as Aboriginal. The legal status of Aboriginal people is complicated and has added considerably to Aboriginal people's woes, as have differences over which level of government is responsible for which categories of Aboriginal people. Registered, status or treaty Indians are those who are registered under the *Indian Act of Canada* and can prove descent from a band that signed a treaty, and they have particular rights as a consequence. Some Aboriginal people are band members, some are not, and there is not necessarily an overlap with those who have treaty status. The numbers of Aboriginal people in each of these categories, according to the 2001 Census of Canada, are set out in Table 1-1.

These distinctions can and do create difficulties in urban settings. The federal government has held that it is only responsible, under the *Indian Act*, for registered Indians, and even then only those on reserve, and that non-registered Indians and Métis are the responsibility of the provinces. The large political Aboriginal organizations, the Assembly of Manitoba Chiefs for example, have traditionally seen their responsibilities as confined to Aboriginal people living on reserve — although this may change with the 1999 Corbiere decision, which recognizes the right of all band members, those living on and those living off reserve, to vote in band elections — while effective urban Aboriginal political organizations have been slow to emerge. The major Aboriginal political organizations, like the federal government, have traditionally seen Aboriginal people in urban settings as the responsibility of "someone else." For many years, no "someone else" has stepped forward to address in any meaningful way the needs of urban Aboriginal people. "For their part, provincial governments contend that *all* Aboriginal people are the primary responsibility of the federal government. In short, each order of government continues to deny that *it* holds responsibility for urban Aboriginal policy" (Hanselmann 2003: 171).

Faced with this vacuum, urban Aboriginal people have been forced back upon their own creativity to build an organizational infrastructure — usually "status-blind," i.e., available to all Aboriginal people regardless of their legal status or particular Aboriginal ancestry — to meet urban Aboriginal needs. The critical nature of this work has increased with the process of urbanization and constitutes an important part of a holistic and culturally rooted form of urban Aboriginal community development.

This book is about the urban Aboriginal experience and the innovative forms of urban Aboriginal community development that are emerging from that experience. Urban Aboriginal people face a vast array of problems, all of them, in one way or another, a product of the experience of and the effects of colonization. In response, urban Aboriginal people are engaged in a process of decolonization — of struggling to remove themselves, as individuals and as communities, from the adverse consequences of colonization, but doing so in their own ways. There is no template for decolonization. The way forward is being discovered and developed by urban Aboriginal people themselves. A part of this process, an important part, is the particular form of Aboriginal community development being created by urban Aboriginal people themselves as they struggle to forge a path to the future.

THE URBANIZATION OF ABORIGINAL PEOPLE

The urbanization of Aboriginal people is a post-Second World War phenomenon. In 1901, approximately 5 percent of Aboriginal people lived in urban areas; by 1951 that percentage was still less than 7 percent; but by 2001 almost half — 49 percent — of Canada's Aboriginal people lived in urban areas (Peters 2006: 1). If we use Winnipeg as the example, we can see from Table 1-2 that the process of urbanization became significant in the 1960s and 1970s. In 1971 Aboriginal people comprised just over one percent of Winnipeg's total popula-

Table 1-2: Aboriginal People Resident in Winnipeg, 1951 to 2001

1951	1961	1971	1981	1991	1996	2001
210	1082	4940	16,575	35,150	45,750	55,755

Source: Census of Canada, various dates. (These numbers are not strictly comparable due to changing Census definitions. Figures for 1991, 1996 and 2001 are for those who self-identify as Aboriginal.)

Table 1-3: Aboriginal Identity Population, Selected Census Metropolitan
Areas (CMAs), 2001

	Number	Percentage CMA Population
Winnipeg	55,755	8.4
Edmonton	40,930	4.4
Vancouver	36,860	1.9
Calgary	21,915	2.3
Toronto	20,300	0.4
Saskatoon	20,275	9.1
Regina	15,685	8.3
Ottawa-Hull	13,485	1.3
Prince Albert	11,640	29.2

Source: Statistics Canada 2001: 23

tion; by 2001 they comprised 8.4 percent of Winnipeg's population (Census of
Canada, various dates).

Winnipeg now has the largest urban Aboriginal population in Canada,
at 55,755, the next largest being Edmonton with an Aboriginal population of
40,930, followed by Vancouver, Calgary and Toronto. The concentration of
Aboriginal people in Winnipeg is, among large urban centres in Canada, behind
only Saskatoon, where Aboriginal people comprise 9.1 percent of the population.
The concentration in other major cities is much lower: Regina (8.3 percent) is
almost the same as Winnipeg. In Manitoba and Saskatchewan, Aboriginal people
constitute 13.6 and 13.5 percent of the population respectively, with approximately 150,000 Aboriginal people in Manitoba and 130,000 in Saskatchewan
in 2001. In Canada as a whole there were just under one million people who
identified as Aboriginal, or 3.3 percent of Canada's total population, according
to the 2001 Census of Canada.

Across Canada, the Aboriginal population has been growing and urban-
izing rapidly. Both are phenomena of the second half of the twentieth century.
During the first fifty years, the Aboriginal population in Canada grew by only
29 percent, while the total population grew by 161 percent; from 1951 to 2001,
the Aboriginal population in Canada grew sevenfold, while the total Canadian
population only doubled. Put another way, in the first half of the century the
Aboriginal population grew at one-fifth the rate of the total population; in the
second half of the century, the Aboriginal population grew at three-and-one-
half times the rate of the total population. The Aboriginal birth rate continues
to be higher than the overall Canadian birth rate, although not as high today, at
one-and-a-half times, as in the 1960s, when it was four times the Canadian birth
rate. And since 1986 there has been a trend in the Census to increased report-

ing of Aboriginal origins and identity, a process sometimes known as "ethnic mobility" — i.e., more Canadians are identifying themselves as Aboriginal (Guimond 2003).

At the same time, only 31 percent, or less than one-third, lived on what Statistics Canada describes as "Indian reserves and settlements" (Statistics Canada 2001: 5–7). In other words, and contrary to popular perceptions, more Aboriginal people in Canada live in urban centres than on reserves. Particularly large proportions of non-status Indians and Métis people live in urban centres (Norris and Clatworthy 2003: 54). The urbanization process is a disproportionately Western Canadian phenomenon. Two-thirds of the urban Aboriginal population in 2001 lived in Western Canada, and seven of the nine cities with the largest urban Aboriginal populations are in the West.

Further, the growth of the urban Aboriginal population is less due to an exodus of Aboriginal people from reserves to urban areas — in fact, there is a net movement the other way (Guimond 2003: 42; Norris 2003: 58–59) — than it is to the relatively high birth rate of urban Aboriginal people and, since 1986, to the increasing numbers of people in urban centres identifying as Aboriginal people (Guimond 2003; Siggner 2003). In fact, there appears to be a great deal of movement back and forth between urban and rural communities, in circular fashion, as opposed to a one-way flow (see, for example, Clatworthy 1996, 2000), a pattern that seems to be consistent with the international experience (Portes 1991).

The Aboriginal population in Canada is younger, on average, than the non-Aboriginal population. In 2001 the median age of Aboriginal people in Canada was 24.7 years, while the median age of Canada's non-Aboriginal population was 37.7 years. The median age of Aboriginal people in Manitoba is 22.8 years. While Aboriginal people comprise almost 14 percent of Manitoba's total population, Aboriginal children comprise 23 percent of Manitoba's children (Statistics Canada 2001: 7). Based on these numbers, the Aboriginal population is expected to continue to grow relatively rapidly in the foreseeable future.

This is important for the future of Winnipeg, and for Western Canadian cities generally, because, in addition to other reasons, Aboriginal people will comprise a growing proportion of the working age population at a time when skilled labour shortages in selected industries are anticipated (Loewen, Silver et al. 2005). Mendelson (2004: 35 and 38), in his study of Aboriginal people in Canada's labour market, found that in both Manitoba and Saskatchewan "the Aboriginal workforce will climb to about 17 percent of the total workforce over the next decade and a half." He added that, "To no small degree, the Aboriginal children who are today in Manitoba and Saskatchewan homes, child care centres and schools represent the economic future of the two provinces," and concluded by saying, "The increasing importance of the Aboriginal workforce to Manitoba and Saskatchewan cannot be exaggerated. There is likely no single more critical economic factor for these provinces."

Alongside these processes is the spatial distribution of Aboriginal people in urban centres, and their mobility within urban centres, and between urban centres and rural communities. In Winnipeg — although this is somewhat less the case in other Western Canadian cities — Aboriginal people are disproportionately located in the inner city (Hanselmann 2001a; Kazemipur and Halli 1999), attracted there by lower housing prices and by the presence of other members of their family and community. Peters' (2006) *Atlas of Urban Aboriginal Peoples* points out that there were three Census tracts in Regina and four in Saskatoon in which Aboriginal people comprised 30 percent or more of the population in 2001. In Winnipeg at the same time, there were ten Census tracts in which Aboriginal people comprised 30 percent or more of the total population, plus one in which they comprised 50 percent or more. The concentration of urban Aboriginal people in Winnipeg's inner city — i.e., in poor neighbourhoods — may not be as high as that of African-Americans in some large U.S. cities, but it is high, and higher than the concentration of Aboriginal people in other Canadian cities (Maxim, Keane and White 2003: 86; La Prairie and Stenning 2003: 185). A recent study found that 80 percent of recent arrivals to Winnipeg located in the inner city (Distasio et al. 2004).

Inner-city residents, and in particular Aboriginal residents, experience lower incomes, higher rates of unemployment, higher rates of poverty, a higher incidence of single parenthood and domestic violence, and lower (although rising) levels of educational attainment than is the case for cities as a whole (Lezubski, Silver and Black 2000; Hanselmann 2001a; Mendelson 2004; Statistics Canada, June 13, 2005). The considerable majority of Aboriginal households live in rental accommodations, in Canada and to a greater extent in Winnipeg. Rates of mobility are high, both between urban and rural centres as a means of maintaining contact with communities of origin, and within urban centres, often as the result of inadequate housing and the lack of affordable, appropriate rental accommodation (Norris and Clatworthy 2003; Norris, Cooke and Clatworthy 2002; Skelton 2002; Norris, Cooke, Beavon, Guimond and Clatworthy 2001; Hanselmann 2001; Norris 2000). A Caledon Institute study found that 30 percent of the Aboriginal identity population in Winnipeg had changed addresses at least once in the year preceding the 2001 Census (Mendelson 2004: 41). As well as high rates of mobility and household crowding, the recent Winnipeg-based Aboriginal mobility study (Distasio et al. 2004: 17), showed 50 percent of respondents were "homeless" and therefore forced to live "temporarily with friends and family." This is the result of the chronic shortage of housing, especially low-income rental housing, in Winnipeg. In large urban centres in Canada Aboriginal households comprise between 20 percent and 50 percent of the total homeless population (Graham and Peters 2002). Assistance for Aboriginal people arriving in the city from rural areas is inadequate. Hanselmann (2001b: 2) found that 1996–97 federal spending for immigrant settlement and transition was $247 per person, while funding for Native Friendship Centres, which perform a similar role for Aboriginal people arriving in the city, was $34 per urban Aboriginal person (see also Distasio et al. 2004).

SOCIAL EXCLUSION

The spatial distribution of Aboriginal people in cities — for example their being disproportionately located in Winnipeg's economically and socially disadvantaged inner city — parallels their spatial distribution outside urban centres, i.e., their marginalization from the mainstream of Canadian life by their historical confinement to rural reserves. Aboriginal people's move to the city is too often a move from one marginalized community to another. The reserve system facilitated "the nearly absolute geographical separation of the colonizer and the colonized"; the move to the city produces the same outcome (Razack 2002: 129). The result is the social exclusion — i.e., the relative absence from the labour market and the core institutions of society — of a large proportion of the urban Aboriginal population. Aboriginal people's being disproportionately spatially located in Winnipeg's inner city means that many non-Aboriginal Winnipeg residents, and especially those living in suburban areas, have no personal contact whatsoever with Aboriginal people. The public space in Winnipeg offers virtually no evidence that Canada's largest urban Aboriginal population resides there (Silver 2004; Peters 2002a: 67). Aboriginal people are seldom seen working in retail shops in suburban malls, or in service sector settings of any kind. In 2002, Kathy Mallett — a long-time Aboriginal resident of Winnipeg who has been involved in many community-based Aboriginal initiatives — and I conducted an informal survey. We drove along both sides of the eastern end of Portage Avenue, Winnipeg's major commercial street, and both sides of McPhillips Avenue, another major street. Kathy entered every fast food and other retail outlet to count how many employees were working, and how many of those, based on physical appearance, were Aboriginal. The result: 221 people were working at that time in those selected retail outlets, of whom only seven were visibly Aboriginal (Silver and Mallett 2002). The public face of the city is not Aboriginal to the extent warranted by the proportion of Winnipeg's population who are Aboriginal. Aboriginal people are invisible to most Winnipeggers going about their daily activities. They are disproportionately resident in the inner city, geographically, and to a considerable extent socio-economically, separated from much of the rest of the urban population; they are much less likely to be employed in settings where they are likely to associate with non-Aboriginal people; there is little socialization at the personal level across the Aboriginal-inner city/non-Aboriginal-suburban divide; they feel outside of, not a part of, the dominant culture and institutions of the city; and they are the victims of unrelenting racism, of both the institutional and highly personal kind (see, for example, Silver, Mallett, Greene and Simard 2002). In Winnipeg, Aboriginal people frequently make their choice of neighbourhood — the inner city, the North End — on the basis of its being a refuge from the racism to which they know their children would be exposed beyond the bounds of the inner city.

It is not only that Aboriginal people experience much higher rates of poverty and unemployment and much lower average incomes than the population at large. It is also that Aboriginal people feel, and are, socially excluded from the dominant culture and institutions — employment, schools, housing, particular neighbourhoods, for example. This social exclusion is a dominant characteristic of urban Aboriginal life, and it will arise again and again in the interviews with Aboriginal people in the chapters that follow. The marginalization and social exclusion of Aboriginal people, historically facilitated by the reserve system, is being replicated in urban settings as the process of urbanization unfolds. Where are urban Aboriginal people to be found? Disproportionately in low-income neighbourhoods, especially in the inner city (Maxim, Keane and White 2003: 86; La Prairie and Stenning 2003: 185; Richards 2001; Hanselmann 2001a; Kazemipur and Halli 1999); disproportionately in institutions like the penal system (Manitoba 1991; Statistics Canada, June 2001; La Prairie and Stenning 2003) and in the child and family service system — more then 70 percent of children in care in Manitoba as of March 31, 2004, were Aboriginal (Manitoba 2003/04; see also Jaccoud and Brassard 2003).

How Did This Come to Be?

It is simply not possible to understand the circumstances of Aboriginal people in Canada — their marginalized socio-economic circumstances, their social exclusion — without acknowledging the historical and ongoing impact of colonization. This process continues to cause enormous and incalculable damage to Aboriginal people. It is not a matter that is merely incidental to an otherwise positive story of Canada's historical development. On the contrary, the process of colonization is at the heart of Canadian history; its associated ideology is still a part of our Canadian identity. Europeans arrived and dispossessed Aboriginal peoples of their land. Sir John A. MacDonald's famous *National Policy* consisted of the construction of tariff barriers behind which fledgling Canadian industries could develop; the construction of a railway system across the West to Vancouver; and the promotion of European immigration to fill the Prairies with farmers whose supplies would come by rail from central Canada, and whose grain would leave by rail to the Great Lakes headwaters or the west coast. Canada was built on the *National Policy*. But it all rested on the removal of Aboriginal people from their homes, their confinement to reserves and the construction of an elaborate system of social control justified on the false grounds of Aboriginal inferiority.

The results have been devastating for Aboriginal people.[1] They were dispossessed of their lands, pushed onto reserves and thus isolated from the dominant culture and institutions of Canada, subjected to the colonial control of the *Indian Act* and the domination of the Indian Agent, and forced into residential schools. At the heart of the process of colonization was the deliberate attempt to destroy Aboriginal people's economic and political systems and their cultures and religions — some of the practices of which were literally outlawed — and to replace them with European institutions and values. This was the strategy and policy of "assimilation." It was, and for many Canadians still is, justified on the false grounds that European institutions and cultural and religious values are superior to those of Aboriginal people. The resultant colonial ideology is pervasive. As Métis scholar Howard Adams (1999: 6) put it:

> The characteristic form of colonialism then is a racial and economic hierarchy with an ideology that claims the superiority of the race and culture of the colonizer. This national ideology pervades colonial society and its institutions, such as schools, cultural agencies, the church and the media.... the ideology becomes an inseparable part of perceived reality.

Internalizing Colonialism

Aboriginal people themselves may come to believe the pervasive notion that they are inferior. This is common among oppressed people. "In fact, this process happens so frequently that it has a name, *internalized oppression*" (Tatum 1999: 6). Or as Howard Adams (1999: Introduction) puts it, many Aboriginal people "have internalized a colonized consciousness." The results are devastating:

> Once Aboriginal persons internalize the colonization processes, we feel confused and powerless.... We may implode with overwhelming feelings of sadness or explode with feelings of anger. Some try to escape this state through alcohol, drugs and/or other forms of self-abuse. (Hart 2002: 27)

The consequence of internalizing the colonial ideology, the European-based assumption of Aboriginal inferiority, is often incapacitating:

> Aboriginal people start to believe that we are incapable of learning and that the colonizers' degrading images and beliefs about Aboriginal people and our ways of being are true. (Hart 2002: 27)

A vicious cycle begins: the assumption of their inferiority is internalized by Aboriginal people themselves; in response, many Aboriginal people lash out in self-abusive ways, reinforcing in the minds of the non-Aboriginal majority the assumptions of Aboriginal inferiority that lie at the heart of the colonial ideology. The more Aboriginal people internalize the colonization processes,

> the more we degrade who we are as Aboriginal people. All of these internalized processes only serve the colonizers, who then are able to sit back and say "see, we were right." In colonizers' eyes, the usurpation is justified. (Hart 2002: 28)

It is not possible to exaggerate the impact of the internal damage and pain that many Aboriginal people carry as a consequence of colonization. Though invisible to most non-Aboriginal people — who see only the outward, behavioural manifestations of what Aboriginal people have internalized — this internalization of the colonial ideology explains much about contemporary urban Aboriginal life.

Residential Schools
Residential schools have played a vital part in this destructive process. Although there is much more to colonization than the residential schools, a consideration of this aspect of the process is instructive. The residential school was a key "instrument of colonization" (Milloy 1999: 254). Aboriginal children were taken, often forcibly, from their parents and submitted to a deliberate and systematic process designed to strip them of their culture and their Aboriginal identity. The process began when they arrived at the residential school:

> The transformation of Cree children began the moment of their arrival in the schools. Their identities were immediately physically altered as each child underwent a disrobing and received a thorough scrubbing and a haircut. Each child was then dressed in near-identical, European-Canadian-style, uniform-looking clothing that served to further strip any outward appearances of indigenous forms of individuality and cultural identity. Newly registered children were given Christian names, and the use of their traditional languages was forbidden. Behaviour was controlled by the application of numerous regulations, the regimentation of daily routines, and the administration of forms of punishment that were often unduly harsh, even for the standards of the time. Parents were discouraged from visiting their children to prevent their children from lapsing into traditional behaviour and to discourage homesickness. (Pettipas 1994: 80)

The point was to destroy Aboriginal cultures, "to kill the Indian in the child"

(Milloy 1999: 42), not only by what was done in the residential schools, but also by excluding the family and community as the means by which to pass on the culture. "Through this system, the traditional role of the parents, relatives, and elders as producers and transmitters of culture and ideology was undermined" (Pettipas 1994: 215; see also Siggins 2005: 146). The results were devastating. As one residential school survivor told us when being interviewed for Chapter Five:

> We were more or less orphans and we got punished if there was anything that we did that resembled Native spiritual culture or traditional practices. All these things were evil and had to be completely eradicated. An imposition of values on another culture, that's what it was... the havoc that Native people experienced in their early adult life... was very severe.... Two-thirds of my life have been severely affected, negatively affected, as a result of being a survivor of this system. I hated people, I hated White people, I hated churches, I hated God, I hated government. These things I hated because they destroyed my life, brought it to a standstill... no hope, a useless existence with no future in mind and all I had was bitterness and anger.

It was, as Milloy has described it, "an act of profound cruelty rooted in non-Aboriginal pride and intolerance and in the certitude and insularity of purported cultural superiority" (Milloy 1999: 302). Manitoba's Aboriginal Justice Inquiry rightly called it: "a conscious, deliberate and often brutal attempt to force Aboriginal people to assimilate," and noted that now, "for the first time in over 100 years, many families are experiencing a generation of children who live with their parents until their teens" (quoted in Aboriginal Justice Inquiry 1991: 514–16). The result was a "loss of parenting skills through the absence of four or five generations of children from Native communities, and the learned behaviour of despising Native identity" (Milloy 1999: 299). One of the people we interviewed described this as:

> lots of disconnection, no connection to the family other than you know that's your Mom and Dad... but you don't feel any connection. So at [residential] school, it was difficult as a result of being institutionalized and then being sent into a home where you don't really know people... you've been away from them for five years and you've spent a total of two months every summer... it was more stressful being at home than it was in the institution. So very young, I started running away when I got back, when we came back as a family unit.

Another added:

> Our family relations had to be repaired, they were... severed and almost

un-repairable.... The bonds that tie parents and children were severed at
the roots and there was no hugging, no loving, no closeness, no warmth.

The price for this deliberate attempt to destroy Aboriginal families is still being
paid by countless Aboriginal people.

The residential schools were, for almost all Aboriginal children, horrific
places. In addition to the loneliness that children naturally suffered when separated from their families and communities, and the deliberate and relentless
attempts to deny them their languages, cultures and spiritual beliefs, many
suffered from hunger, overwork and shockingly high rates of disease and death.
In 1903, *Saturday Night* magazine reported that: "Even war seldom shows as
high a percentage of fatalities as does the education system we have imposed
on our Indian wards," and Duncan Campbell Scott, head of the federal Indian
Department from 1913 to 1932, reported that "fifty percent of the children who
passed through these schools did not live to benefit from the education which
they received therein" (Milloy 1999: 91 and 51).

Those who survived and managed to graduate rarely got jobs. "Employment
was not readily available, indeed, one agent informed the Department: 'race
prejudice is against them [the graduates] and I am afraid it will take time'"
(Milloy 1999: 158). Another account reports the same: "For the students who
did manage to complete their school terms, there was little to look forward to
either in white society or on their home reserves. Because of the poor quality of
education and the racial prejudice of white employers, there were few employment opportunities for graduates beyond the seasonal casual jobs already open
to their parents" (Pettipas 1994: 81).

Nor is the residential school experience a mere artifact of the distant past.
The residential school experience is intergenerational and pervasive:

> Because so many generations attended residential schools they have
> affected all First Nations individuals. For example, even though I was
> raised in the city, all my family members, including my parents, my
> grandparents, uncles, and aunts on both sides of the family attended
> these schools. Most of my friends also attended the schools, including
> my husband and cousins. As well, all of the people whom my parents
> associated with during my formative years were residential school
> survivors. (Dieter 1999: 23)

In a 2002 study of Aboriginal students in Winnipeg inner-city high schools, it
was found that more than one-half of all students interviewed had at least one
parent or grandparent who was a residential school survivor, and two of the
four authors disclosed during the study that they also were residential school
survivors (Silver, Mallett, Greene and Simard 2002: 34). The experience of the

residential schools is still felt by Aboriginal people, its lasting impact forming a part of the pervasive colonial ideology described by Adams.

Resisting Colonization

Aboriginal people did not passively accept the residential schools; they resisted, just as Aboriginal people today resist, in a wide variety of ways, the all-pervasive colonial ideology. The Aboriginal resistance to the imposition of an alien, European-based educational system has also become a part of the legacy of the residential schools, passed on from generation to generation. As one Aboriginal author observes, based on her interviews with residential school survivors: "I believe the resistance stories that have filtered through these interviews embody the spirit and courage of the children who attended these schools. The resistance was so constant that many of the acts were not even recognized by the interviewees themselves" (Dieter 1999: 71). These stories of resistance included, for example, a 1962 riot by Aboriginal students at the Edmonton Indian Residential School over living conditions and the treatment of students (Dieter 1999: 4; see also Grant 1996: 216–20). The stories:

> included runaway boys trapping food to supplement their meagre meals and girls climbing out of third-story windows to freedom. They were burning schools and defiantly challenging their oppressors. There were also the passive, subversive methods of resistance. In the early part of this century, a sign language developed that became a standardized method of communication for all schools across the country. What make these stories and the people who lived them even more courageous was that these acts of resistance were carried out by children. (Dieter 1999: 73)

There is a long and honourable history of oppressed peoples resisting the control of their captors (see, for example, Genovese 1974; van Onselen 1976). Canada takes pride, for example, in being the destination of many runaway African-American slaves who were fleeing their captors by taking the "underground railway" in search of freedom. Yet Canada's police force relentlessly hunted down Aboriginal children who had escaped captivity in a residential school. Beatrice Culleton has vividly described how Aboriginal children who were wards of the state were captured and taken back to their foster homes by the RCMP (Culleton 1984). This description of a runaway being returned to a residential school sounds similar to stories of courageous slaves who ran for their freedom:

> He was eleven years old when he ran away. When he was caught, he was escorted back to the school by the RCMP on the train in handcuffs. The penalty for runaways was either a strapping, having your head

shaved, or both. It was common practice to have the RCMP bring back runaways. (Dieter 1999: 74)

During one of the focus groups for our research, an elderly Aboriginal man mentioned that he spoke Cree. I expressed surprise, since I knew that he was a residential school survivor and that the prohibition against speaking an Aboriginal language was strictly and harshly enforced. He laughed with obvious delight, and explained how, for years, he and a number of his residential school friends met secretly after the official bedtime and spoke with each other exclusively in Cree, a language in which he is proud to say he is still perfectly fluent.

The resistance by Aboriginal children and youth to their captivity in residential schools is a part of an honourable tradition of courage and determination, and ought to be *celebrated* as such. It, too, is part of the legacy of the residential school system and, more broadly, of the imposition upon Aboriginal people of a colonial regime.

This resistance is not confined to the past. Indeed, the prevalence of Aboriginal street gangs in Winnipeg's socio-economically disadvantaged inner city, as destructive as it is, is a form of resistance to the social exclusion of Aboriginal youth, to the lack of opportunities for them in the institutions of the dominant culture in which the colonial assumptions still prevail. We see the same phenomenon in the resistance of Aboriginal children and youth to, for example, schools that do not sufficiently reflect and honour their culture. Many Aboriginal students continue to resist the imposition upon them of a school system that they find alien to their values and beliefs. That resistance, that refusal to "be educated" when "being educated" means giving up so much of themselves, is expressed in a variety of ways, many of which are not immediately apparent as resistance, nor even consciously undertaken as such. The resistance may take the form of simple disengagement from school, or may be "masked as attendance problems, acting out, discipline, or even learning problems" (Fine 1997: 177). In many cases Aboriginal children are not so much failing in school, as *choosing*, consciously or unconsciously, not to succeed.

In a well-known paper in the *Harvard Educational Review*, Signithia Fordham makes this case with respect to African-American students in the U.S.: "At the heart of this paper is the struggle that Black adolescents face in having to 'choose' between the individualistic ethos of the school — which generally reflects the ethos of the dominant society — and the collective ethos of their community." This, Fordham hypothesizes, applies to all subordinated peoples: "the desire to succeed — as defined by the dominating population — causes subordinated peoples to seek social distance from the group with which they are ethnically or racially identified" (Fordham 1988: 55). For Aboriginal people to "succeed" in school, or in the dominant culture more generally, may be seen to require distancing from their Aboriginal identity, a step that many have chosen, consciously or otherwise, not to take. Aboriginal people have resisted the loss of their cultures and their ways of being for generations. American Indian scholar N. Scott Mamaday puts it this way:

> The major issues we face now are survival — how to live in the modern world. Part of this is how to remain Indian, how to assimilate without ceasing to be an Indian.... Indians remain Indian, and against pretty good odds.... Their languages are being lost at a tremendous rate, poverty is rampant, as is alcoholism. But still there are Indians, and the traditional world is intact. It's a matter of identity.... I continue to think of myself as Indian.... I think this is what most Indian people are doing today. They go off the reservation, but they keep an idea of themselves as Indians. That's the trick. (Mamaday 1991: 438)

It has been a struggle for Aboriginal people to remain Aboriginal, to resist the relentless attempts at assimilation, to tenaciously cling to their identity in the face of the constant denigration of that identity that is at the heart of the colonial ideology. Most Aboriginal people want to be a part of Canadian society in a positive and productive way, but they do not want to give up being Aboriginal to do so. Aboriginal cultures have been battered and bruised, but they still exist, albeit often in a fragmented form. As Leroy Little Bear describes it:

> Colonization left a heritage of jagged world views among Indigenous peoples. They no longer had an Aboriginal world view, nor did they adopt a Eurocentric world view. Their consciousness became a random puzzle, a jigsaw puzzle that each person has to attempt to understand. Many collective views of the world competed for control of their behaviour, and since none was dominant modern Aboriginal people had to make guesses or choices about everything. Aboriginal consciousness became a site of overlapping, contentious, fragmented, competing desires and values. (Little Bear 2000: 22)

Yet, complex and fragmented though they may be, Aboriginal cultures are still crucially important to urban Aboriginal people. As Deane, Morrissette, Bousquet and Bruyere (2002: 25) put it:

> Aboriginal culture still exerts a powerful influence on inner-city Aboriginal residents. Aboriginal culture may be a collage of jigsaw puzzle fragments, it may be an amalgam of traditional values, mainstream adaptations, and inner-city survival skills, but urban Aboriginal culture is nevertheless recognizable to those who share it, and powerful in its normative influence.

The importance to Aboriginal people of their cultures, and of continuing to live as Aboriginal people, is evident in their repeated statements about education. In their groundbreaking work in 1972, the National Indian Brotherhood, forerunner of the Assembly of First Nations, said: "What we want for our children can be summarized very briefly: to reinforce their Indian identity [and] to provide the training necessary for making a good living in modern society" (National Indian Brotherhood 1972: 3). The Royal Commission on Aboriginal Peoples (RCAP) said the same: Aboriginal people want education "to prepare them to participate fully in the economic life of their communities and in Canadian society," and at the same time "education must develop children and youth as Aboriginal citizens, linguistically and culturally competent to assume the responsibilities of their nations" (Royal Commission on Aboriginal Peoples 1996: 433–35). A recent study of Aboriginal high school students in Winnipeg's inner city found the same — Aboriginal students want to be a part of today's world, *and* they want to continue to be Aboriginal (Silver, Mallett, Greene and Simard 2002). The dominant culture, suffused as it is with a colonial mentality that denigrates Aboriginal ways of being, resists the changes necessary for this to happen; likewise, Aboriginal people resist abandoning their identity. The result is a variety of clashes that are in many important ways detrimental to the Aboriginal minority and that have their roots in the colonial character of the dominant ideology.

Self-Esteem

The result is not only the erosion of many Aboriginal people's self-esteem and sense of self-worth, but also the emergence of a racism that is deeply embedded and pervades the institutions and culture of urban centres such as Winnipeg. The Royal Commission on Aboriginal Peoples noted about education, for example, that: "the schooling system typically erodes identity and self-worth. Those who continue in Canada's formal education system told us of regular encounters with racism, racism expressed not only in interpersonal exchanges but also through the denial of Aboriginal values, perspectives and cultures in the curriculum and the life of the institution" (Royal Commission on Aboriginal Peoples 1996: 434). A recent study of Aboriginal students in Winnipeg inner-city high schools also found a high incidence of racism in the schools. Some of it is crude name-calling and stereotyping; much of it is a more systemic form that denies the value of Aboriginal people's ways of being (Silver, Mallett, Greene and Simard 2002: esp. 23–27). Racism is more than a simple and simplistic expression of prejudice; it "is a *system* involving cultural messages and institutional policies as well as the beliefs and actions of individuals" (Tatum 1999: 7).

The result can be and often is an undermining of young Aboriginal people's sense of self-worth and self-identity. Tatum's powerful analysis of African-American children and youth in the U.S. applies to the case of Aboriginal children and youth in Canada. Tatum examines the process of "racial identity development," seeking "an understanding of racial identity, the meaning each of us has constructed or is constructing about what it means to be a white person or a person of colour in a race-conscious society." She adds: "It is because we live in a racist society that racial identity has as much meaning as it does" (Tatum 1999: xviii; see also Carter 1997: 198).

> Why do black youths, in particular, think about themselves in terms of race? Because that is how the rest of the world thinks of them. When young people ask, "Who am I?" The answer depends in large part on who the world around me says I am. Who do my parents say I am? Who do my peers say I am? What message is reflected back to me in the faces and voices of my teachers, my neighbours, store clerks? What do I learn from the media about myself? How am I represented in the cultural images around me? Or am I missing from the picture altogether? (Tatum 1999: 18)

In the case of Aboriginal people, they are often entirely or largely missing from the picture. It has already been observed that Aboriginal people are scarcely represented at all in the public space of Winnipeg. To take another example, a recent, detailed study of Aboriginal people's representation in the media found that Aboriginal people are represented dramatically less than their proportion of the population would warrant, and when they are present in the media, they are often portrayed in a negative manner (MacKenzie 2002). The world around Aboriginal people says they are inferior — this is the message of colonialism; it is the very foundation of, the justification for, the process of colonization, which in turn, as argued above, was at the heart of the creation of Canada. This false assumption of the inferiority of Aboriginal people and their cultures is built into the cultural and institutional fabric of Canada. The colossal damage that it has caused and continues to cause for Aboriginal people is painfully expressed in the voices of Aboriginal people in the chapters that follow.

Aboriginal people understand this description of their reality. They see it as a description of their daily experience. Most non-Aboriginal people do not. They do not see that their assumptions about cultural superiority and inferiority — which for them are taken-for-granted parts of what they take to be "reality" — are in fact an ideological construct. This "cultural racism — the cultural images and messages that affirm the assumed superiority of Whites and the assumed inferiority of people of colour — is like smog in the air. Sometimes it is so thick it is visible, other times it is less apparent, but always, day in and day out, we are breathing it in" (Tatum 1999: 6). The same is the case with the colonial ideology. Non-Aboriginal people seldom see it. It is not, for example, taught in schools, nor is it a part of the general discourse of day-to-day life. As

Aboriginal scholar Michael Hart puts it: "the colonizer has no idea about the reality of the oppressed. It is not incorporated as part of any curriculum" (Hart 2002: 29). Instead of seeing poverty and violence and suicide, for example, as a function of the collective, historical and contemporary experience of Aboriginal people with colonialism, "Amer-Europeans reinterpret these understandings through an a-historical, reductionist stance; they break the issues down to an individual's problem and ignore the historical roots" (Hart 2002: 30).

Yet, the historical roots are to be found in the process of colonization. The assumption of Aboriginal cultural inferiority still pervades our institutions and has been internalized by many Aboriginal people themselves. Indeed, it finds expression in self-destructive acts that serve to reinforce and justify, in the minds of those who do not understand the history of colonization, the deeply rooted assumptions of Aboriginal inferiority.

The solution, it follows, is to decolonize ourselves — Aboriginal and non-Aboriginal alike. As we will see in the chapters that follow, many urban Aboriginal people are involved in just such an undertaking, in many different and creative forms. At the heart of these efforts is the attempt to rebuild Aboriginal cultures and to re-instill in Aboriginal people — or in the case of the many who have been badly damaged by the effects of colonization, to instill for the first time — a greater knowledge of and sense of pride in what it is to be Aboriginal. This is part of a process of healing, a central element in the holistic and culturally based approach to community development that urban Aboriginal people in Winnipeg are leading.

URBAN ABORIGINAL EXPERIENCE

Very little has been written about urban Aboriginal people. And very little has been written by Aboriginal people themselves. What exists dates back to the late 1960s and 1970s. The focus then was on the problems created by the movement of Aboriginal people from rural to urban centres, their difficulties in adjusting to urban life and their disproportionate experience with poverty and alcoholism (Brody 1971; Davis 1965; Denton 1972; Dosman 1972; Krotz 1972; McCaskill 1970; Nagler 1973). The overriding theme was the urbanization of Aboriginal people *as a problem*. In particular, it was argued that Aboriginal people had not yet acculturated to urban industrial life, and their traditional ways and cultural values were an impediment to the most desirable outcome — assimilation. Dosman stands out in arguing, to some extent, that Aboriginal people's culture ought to be seen as a positive thing in an urban setting. "Only forms of activity that recognize the cultural tradition and that integrate activities into a vision of the future can nurture an adequate sense of identity... the problem of identity is fundamental to an attack on poverty" (Dosman 1972: 151 and 179). Shorten (1981) adopts a similar view. Nagler (1973), by contrast, is more typical of the dominant theme in simply assuming that it is necessary for Aboriginal people to shed their cultural values, which were impeding their successful integration into urban life, and replace them with urban industrial values — the dominant culture.

In the 1980s, much of the little that was written about the urban Aboriginal experience was quantitative. It sought an understanding of the extent to which and the reasons for which Aboriginal people moved between rural and urban settings, their mobility within urban centres and their involvement in the labour and housing markets (for example, Clatworthy 1980; 1981a; 1981b; 1981c; 1983a; 1983b; Clatworthy and Gunn 1982; Hull 1983; 1984; Falconer 1990). This work was often sophisticated and valuable in deepening our understanding of some aspects of urban Aboriginal life. References to Aboriginal culture, so dominant in the 1970s literature, were infrequent in the 1980s literature, except to the extent that a sub-theme in some of this work (Clatworthy and Gunn 1982; Falconer 1990, for example) referred to the relative absence of urban Aboriginal organizations able to deliver needed services. There are now many urban Aboriginal organizations, particularly in Winnipeg's inner city, providing services to and employing significant numbers of Aboriginal people (Peters 2000: 242–43; Newhouse 2003; Chapter Five of this volume), although the historical development of these organizations has yet to be documented. Aboriginal culture, seen in the 1970s as an impediment to "successful" urbanization, was viewed in the 1980s as irrelevant. By 1993, a summary of the existing body of urban Aboriginal literature noted that: "The literature on urban Aboriginal issues in Canada is sparse, limited in scope, largely dated in relevance" (Kastes 1993: 6).

The 1970s and to some extent the 1980s saw some examination of the experience of Aboriginal people in smaller towns (Braroe 1975; Lithman 1984; Stymeist 1975). A dominant theme in the literature of the time is the exclusion of Aboriginal people from small town life and the "intense hostility" (Peters 2002a: 56) directed at them by townspeople. Aboriginal people responded to this open hostility, this social exclusion, by withdrawing. Lithman (1984: 58), for example, writing about a well-known rural Manitoba Aboriginal community and an adjoining industrial town, observed that Aboriginal people did not become involved in non-Aboriginal organizations or opportunities in the town because they wanted to avoid "the indignities of most interactions with white men." Krotz (1972: 63) found the same in larger urban centres: "overt discrimination. In every city I visited I heard over and over the stories of landlords' refusals to rent to native people. Or the resistance of white neighbourhoods to have a native family move onto the block." This theme was repeated over and over by Aboriginal people interviewed for this book. Social exclusion is a defining characteristic of the urban Aboriginal experience.

It is this social exclusion, with its accompanying racism, and the origins of both in the historical experience of colonization, that distinguishes the urban Aboriginal experience from the problems of poverty. The urban Aboriginal experience is not *simply* an issue of poverty and related socio-economic factors such as low levels of educational attainment and high levels of unemployment. Rather, it is a function of the process of colonization and the persistent and pervasive colonial ideology. Yet the issue is often treated as one of poverty. In referring to a former executive director of the Social Planning Council of Winnipeg, Krotz (1972: 51) says that he "sees most of the problems Winnipeg is encountering which involve native people as the problems of poverty, and the problems engendered by a group suffering from poverty." This approach, common in much of the earlier Aboriginal literature (Kastes 1993: 78), situates Aboriginal people with other poor people and omits the fact that they are unique in their historical circumstances, and especially in their colonization.

More recently (Peters 1996; 2000; Cairns 2000; Newhouse 2000; Newhouse and Peters 2003), colonization has come to be seen as the essential context within which to interpret the urban Aboriginal experience, and the promotion of Aboriginal cultures is seen as a central part of an urban Aboriginal strategy. Evelyn Peters (2000: 254), for example, has consistently argued that Aboriginal cultures are a major part of the solution, not the problem, in urban settings:

> In contrast to views of Aboriginal culture as either incompatible with or irrelevant in an urban environment, Aboriginal people have argued that supporting and enhancing Aboriginal culture is a prerequisite for coping in an urban environment. These perspectives recognize that Aboriginal cultures and the Euro-Canadian cultures that dominate Canadian cities are distinct in many ways, but they insist that Aboriginal cultures will enrich cities as well as make them better places for Aboriginal people.

The Royal Commission on Aboriginal Peoples adopted a similar perspective. As Newhouse (2003: 245) observes: "The Commission reports that the central issue facing urban Aboriginal peoples is one of cultural identity. It argues for measures to enhance the cultural identity of Aboriginal peoples living in urban centres." In its final report, the Commission argued that: "Aboriginal, municipal, territorial, provincial and federal governments [should] initiate programs to increase opportunities to promote Aboriginal cultures in urban communities" (Royal Commission on Aboriginal Peoples 1996: 537). In the chapters that follow, the voices of Aboriginal people in Winnipeg's inner city will repeat the same things over and over again: we hunger for the opportunity to learn more about and/or practise our cultures. We need to know ourselves and to see our Aboriginal identities valued in an otherwise alien urban setting.

This book takes the view that the promotion of Aboriginal cultures is a central part of a holistic approach to urban Aboriginal community development. Many urban Aboriginal people have been badly damaged by colonization. They are lacking in self-confidence, self-esteem and a sense of self-worth — the result of having internalized the colonial ideology — and are in need of healing. The healing has to begin at an individual level — community development is not possible without strong and healthy individuals — but it also has to take place at a community level — the creation of strong and healthy individuals requires their nurturing by strong and healthy communities. Stronger urban Aboriginal communities are being created by Aboriginal people themselves, through a wide-ranging network of urban Aboriginal organizations painstakingly created over the past thirty years. A former president of the Aboriginal Council of Winnipeg estimates that there are now more than seventy such organizations in Winnipeg. They include, among many others, the Native Women's Transition Centre, the Ma Mawi Wi Chi Itata Centre, the Urban Circle Training Centre, the Centre for Aboriginal Human Resource Development, the Aboriginal Centre, the Indian and Métis Friendship Centre, the Urban Aboriginal Education Coalition. These and other such organizations are actively working to heal Aboriginal people, and to build healthy communities, in a distinctive form of urban Aboriginal community development.

It is Aboriginal women, in particular, who are the leaders in defining and implementing this holistic and distinctive form of Aboriginal community development. Men are active, but as many men themselves acknowledge, it is disproportionately the women who are the leaders.

There is an intellectual vision and world view that is driving this process. Many of the leaders of urban Aboriginal organizations and of the holistic process of Aboriginal community development are what political theorist Antonio Gramsci called "organic intellectuals" (Gramsci 1978). They are people who are deeply rooted in the urban Aboriginal experience — they have grown up in poverty and have experienced the negative consequences, the racism and discrimination and the social exclusion, that grow out of the colonial ideology — and who are able to conceptualize that experience and articulate a way forward for marginalized urban Aboriginal people. As will be argued below, this is not a process of "development" as it is generally understood. Rather, this emergent form of urban Aboriginal community development is rooted in the distinctive value of Aboriginal cultures in personal healing and community-building, and is built around the traditional Aboriginal notions of sharing and community.

This approach to the urban Aboriginal experience is not the result of the application of abstract theory to the circumstances of urban Aboriginal people. Rather, it arises from the method adopted in this book, at the heart of which is the belief that we can best learn about the urban Aboriginal experience by talking with, and listening to, urban Aboriginal people themselves.

PARTICIPATORY RESEARCH

In each of the research projects that form the empirical case studies of this book, we listened to the voices of urban Aboriginal people. This is consistent with a participatory approach to research, which seeks to involve the local community in the hope of overcoming, to the extent possible, the gap between those doing the research and those who are the objects of the research. To do this, the interviews had to be conducted by Aboriginal people, to begin to overcome the cultural gap between Aboriginal and non-Aboriginal people in Winnipeg. We kept in mind the advice advanced by Deane, Morrissette, Bousquet and Bruyere (2002: 8):

> If researchers cannot create a relationship of mutuality, respect, and shared purpose with their subjects, then it is unlikely that they can acquire authentic information. In this study, then, it was considered highly important for Aboriginal cultural concerns to be investigated by Aboriginal persons themselves, and for them to determine appropriate methods.

For each of the studies upon which the following chapters were based, those to be interviewed were identified in close consultation with inner-city community-based organizations and representatives of the urban Aboriginal community. The interviewers for the Spence neighbourhood project (Chapter Two), for example, were selected following a meeting of a small group of Spence community people for the purpose of identifying Aboriginal people who live in and are knowledgeable about the Spence neighbourhood and who would be good interviewers. The two interviewers, Hay and Gorzen, are Aboriginal people who live and work in Spence and who know the neighbourhood and its people well. Those to be interviewed were identified at a meeting with Hay and Gorzen, the editor of *West Central Streets*, herself a long-time community development worker in Spence, and the lead author. In addition, a summary of the project was submitted to the Spence Neighbourhood Association board, the project was approved at a subsequent board meeting attended by the author, and a next-to-final draft of the paper was circulated to board members for their comments.

The interviews in Chapter Four were done by Cyril Keeper and Ed Keeper. Cyril Keeper has lived in Winnipeg's inner city for much of his life, is active in community affairs, and as a former city councillor and Member of Parliament for the area, is well known and respected by the community's Aboriginal people. Ed Keeper was, at the time of the research for Chapter Four, a youth outreach worker with the Spence Neighbourhood Association. He interviewed seven young Aboriginal people, aged eighteen to twenty-five. All live in the neighbourhood and Ed knows each of them personally. They were chosen for this reason. Most of these interviews would not have been possible — i.e., these young people would not have agreed to be interviewed — had each of them not known Ed.

For the final chapter of this book, which is based on discussions with twenty-six Aboriginal community activists, we identified interviewees based on preliminary interviews. The interviews took place in May 2003, with four Aboriginal people — two women and two men — who are well-known and respected in community development circles in Winnipeg's inner city. We asked these four people to comment on our research proposal. All responded positively. We also asked them to provide us with a list of names of Aboriginal people who are or have been active in community development initiatives in Winnipeg's inner city and who they thought should be interviewed for the project. From these lists we selected the twenty-six people eventually interviewed. We committed ourselves to making available copies of an early draft of our study, for their comments, to all who were interviewed; to holding small focus group sessions with interviewees during which the draft paper would be discussed and modified accordingly; and to making copies of the final version of the paper, which forms the basis of this chapter, widely available in Winnipeg's inner city and beyond. We have fulfilled each of these commitments.

For the study of Aboriginal learners in adult learning centres (Chapter Three), we worked as part of a research partnership with the Province of Manitoba's Aboriginal Education Directorate, the Research and Planning Branch of the Department of Education and Youth, the Adult Learning and Literacy branch of the Department of Advanced Education and Training, and with the directors, teachers and other staff of the adult learning centres (ALCs) that we investigated. The research partnership agreed upon a plan that featured open-ended interviews with fifteen Aboriginal learners in each ALC, and sharing circles at each ALC prior to the commencement of the interviews. This was done to familiarize those who might be interviewed with the project and its purposes, and with the research team.

In every case, open-ended interviews were conducted. These are a key aspect of participatory research. An "aide-memoire" — "not a questionnaire, but a topic guide that reminds researchers of the topics to cover with each informant" (Barnsley and Ellis 1992: 45) — was used. Within this framework, interviewers were instructed to allow those being interviewed to take the discussion in whatever direction they chose. Where it was appropriate, tobacco was offered to interviewees as a sign of respect for Aboriginal cultural traditions and as an expression of appreciation for their contribution to the research project.

In addition, in each of the research projects, individual interviews — we conducted in-depth interviews with approximately 165 Aboriginal people in Winnipeg's inner city, using trained Aboriginal interviewers in each case — were supplemented with organized focus groups, at which a number of Aboriginal people who had already been individually interviewed participated in structured group discussions.

The Women's Research Centre in Vancouver, describing "participatory action research for community groups," observed that:

> The questions we ask are usually open-ended. They encourage people to talk about their lives and concerns.... It's the down-to-earth questions that let people tell their stories. Asking too many questions makes people divide up their experience. Then it's easy for researchers to lose the full picture in its complexity. (Barnsley and Ellis 1992: 14 and 17)

In a discussion of oral history methodology, David Lance makes a similar argument: "questionnaires have not been found suitable.... Partly this is because no questionnaire is sufficiently flexible to accommodate, in itself, the unexpected and valuable twists and turns" that arise from allowing the interviewee to address what s/he considers to be important (Lance 1984: 120). What is more, the use of an open-ended approach is consistent with the important observation that, at the outset, "researchers rarely know the most important issues or questions" (Skelton 2002: 132). To make use of a survey-style questionnaire would require determining *a priori* what the most important questions and issues are. Using an open-ended interview format allows the person being interviewed to decide what is more and what is less important.

This approach is consistent with recent developments in anthropology that argue that what is important is to attempt to see "how people actually experience the specific issue or problem" (Barnsley and Ellis 1992: 9). This is in contrast to the traditional (anthropological) approach predicated upon a researcher observing, from the outside, a culture that is different from hers or his, and then creating a narrative about that culture based on those observations, "all of which presuppose[s] a standpoint outside — looking at, objectifying, or, somewhat closer, 'reading,' a given reality" (Clifford and Marcus 1986: 25). The gap across cultures cannot be wholly bridged, and the picture that emerges from such research is both partial, and to some extent, fictional. In the past fifteen years, critics from those cultures studied by ethnographers and anthropologists have "turned around the anthropological mirror, questioning the way they had been represented by outsiders and offering their own, more complex... representations" (Behar 1996: 162). In an insightful study of the residential mobility of Aboriginal single mothers in Winnipeg, Skelton demonstrates that the interpretation of their behaviour, when viewed through the lens of the dominant culture, is different from the interpretation that arises from interviewing, listening to and hearing the women themselves (Skelton 2002). Thus, we attempted to uncover the culture's internal perceptions of Aboriginal people's urban experience by asking Aboriginal people themselves and by having Aboriginal people do the asking.

The same logic applies to our consideration of community development.

What *is* community development? What do Aboriginal people consider urban community development to be? The way to find out is to ask Aboriginal people living in the inner city because "development begins with listening to the people" (Fernandez and Tandon 1981: 3). "It is essential that the aspirations and opinions of people subject to the processes of development or non-development be taken seriously" (Wallman 1997: 249). The poor, for example, ought to be involved in the design and implementation of development initiatives, although this is often not the case (Patel and Mitlin 2002). As Kretzmann and McKnight (1993: 5) argue: "all the historic evidence indicates that significant community development takes place only when local community people are committed to investing themselves and their resources in the effort. This observation explains why communities are never built from the top down, or from the outside in." It follows that community development in the inner city has to include the large and growing numbers of Aboriginal people. Thus the method that we have used in the chapters that follow is intended to enable us to hear the voices of urban Aboriginal people.

Another way of putting this is that we saw as our task to lay bare the "world taken for granted" by Aboriginal people: their assumptions and what it is that they themselves find problematic. Open-ended interviews and, as was used in the final chapter, a "life story" approach (Burgos-Debray 1984; Denzin 1986; Graham-Brown 1988; Sommer 1988), enabled us to gain access to the "informal" and "inside" world of Aboriginal people, and we tried to create a situation in which Aboriginal people would share their "private" views with us. Recording the life stories of urban Aboriginal people is not just about their personal experiences, but is a method that allowed us to understand their social reality. These personal stories have provided us with insights that go beyond individual experiences. By weaving them together, we believe that we have gained a better grasp of the many issues, events and histories behind them.

This approach is consistent with Edward Said's classic study, *Orientalism*. Published in 1978, it has become a source-book through which "marginality" itself has acquired the status of a discipline in the Anglo-American academy. In *Orientalism*, Said relentlessly unmasks the ideological disguises of imperialism. He understands Orientalism as an over-arching system that regulates anything that may be written, thought or imagined about the Orient. Orientalism is a discourse, intimately linked to the exercise of power, that systematically produces stereotypes about the Orient and its people. These stereotypes, Said tells us, confirm the necessity and desirability of colonial government by endlessly establishing the positional superiority of the West over the positional inferiority of the East (Said 1978: 35). The colonial discourse typically rationalizes itself through rigid oppositions such as maturity/immaturity, civilization/barbarism, developed/developing, progressive/primitive. This perception of the colonized culture, as fundamentally childlike or childish, feeds into the logic of the colonial "civilizing mission" that is fashioned, quite self-consciously, to bring the colonized to maturity.

Said's discussion of Orientalism applies to the life experiences of the participants in this study. The colonial system in Canada started by taking Aboriginal people's land and pushing them onto reserves, then taking away their political and economic systems, denying them the right to practise their culture and their spirituality. Finally, it took away their children, placing them in residential schools where they were denied the right to speak their language. All of this was justified on the grounds that Canadians were helping Aboriginal people to break out of their "backward" ways. The price that Aboriginal people have paid for this cultural arrogance has been high.

Many of the Aboriginal people who shared their life stories with us refer to colonialism, or colonization, to explain what happened to them, their families, their identities, their spiritualities, their knowledge and their communities. They are critical of state policies and believe that various state apparatuses, in the name of "civilization," were systematically used to degrade and erode their way of life. The residential schools, the educational system, the police and legal systems, and child and family services stand out as institutions that played a central role in constructing them as the "other."

CONCLUSION

The number of Aboriginal people in urban centres is growing rapidly. This is especially true in Western Canada, where Winnipeg has the largest urban Aboriginal population in the country. Urban Aboriginal people experience many difficulties and problems, and it is the image of troubled Aboriginal people that the media, and much of the population generally, focus on if they consider the presence in cities of Aboriginal people at all. The difficulties and problems of many urban Aboriginal people are real and are, as argued above, firmly rooted in the historical experience of Aboriginal people in Canada — the experience of colonization. Many Aboriginal people have internalized the still-pervasive colonial ideology, with its largely racist assumptions about Aboriginal people and their cultures. The results have been personally and collectively devastating.

Yet the focus of this book is on the ways in which urban Aboriginal people themselves are constructing a process of decolonization. This process is rooted in the promotion and celebration of Aboriginal cultures, and it is holistic. Its focus is on individual healing, community-building and the development of Aboriginal organizations run by and for Aboriginal people, in a way consistent with the Aboriginal cultural values of sharing and community. The result is a distinctly Aboriginal form of community development, one that has emerged out of the harsh inner-city experiences of urban Aboriginal people and the revitalization of traditional Aboriginal cultural values. And it is led disproportionately by Aboriginal women.

The success of this approach is not at all assured. Urban inner-city life is a struggle, for Aboriginal and non-Aboriginal people alike. But the premise of this book is that urban Aboriginal people, out of their own historical and contemporary struggles, are themselves developing an approach to inner-city problems that is attractive and progressive and that holds immense promise. It remains for the non-Aboriginal community to "walk beside" — not in front of and not behind — Aboriginal people in this exciting process of decolonization and community development.

The book is not intended to be a comprehensive analysis of the urban Aboriginal experience. Some very important issues — Aboriginal people's experience with the legal and the social service systems; street gangs; urban reserves, for example — are scarcely touched upon. Rather, we have identified some important urban Aboriginal issues and have attempted to use them as a vehicle for providing some insight into the urban Aboriginal experience. The book proceeds as follows: In Chapter Two we seek to determine whether Aboriginal people in the Spence neighbourhood of Winnipeg's inner city are actively involved with the Spence Neighbourhood Association (SNA), an energetic and effective community-based neighbourhood revitalization organization. What we found was that almost all of the Aboriginal people that we interviewed in Spence were not involved with the SNA. They felt excluded — despite the SNA's efforts to be inclusive. They also felt excluded from jobs in the neighbourhood and from ownership of the renovated housing in the neighbourhood. The reality of urban Aboriginal people's social exclusion emerges clearly in Chapter Two. More positively, arising in large part out of the participatory research approach used in the Spence neighbourhood study, a new and energetic Aboriginal neighbourhood residents group, called I-CAN (Inner-City Aboriginal Neighbours) has emerged. I-CAN is pulling previously socially isolated Aboriginal people in Spence neighbourhood together around Aboriginal cultural pursuits and other initiatives of Aboriginal people's choosing. I-CAN is one small organizational example of urban Aboriginal community development.

In Chapter Three, we enquire into the experience of Aboriginal students in four urban adult learning centres. We wanted to know whether these alternative, innovative and more community-based initiatives are successful where the mainstream educational system has not been. What emerges clearly from the interviews is the very difficult experiences many Aboriginal people have had in the regular school system; the pain that many of them carry as the result of these and other experiences with the dominant culture; and the virtues of a holistic approach, in particular, a culturally rooted approach, to Aboriginal adult education. In a fashion consistent with Aboriginal forms of community development, the small, innovative, non-profit and non-hierarchical adult learning centres are proving to be more effective in promoting formal education for Aboriginal people than their larger, more bureaucratic mainstream counterparts. The work of the Urban Circle Training Centre is an especially important example of a highly creative and effective form of Aboriginal community development with a strong decolonization emphasis.

In Chapter Four, we asked Aboriginal people in Winnipeg's inner city whether they vote in mainstream — federal, provincial and municipal — elections, and if not, why not? Again, the results of our interviews reveal the social exclusion experienced by many urban Aboriginal people. Many do not participate in mainstream elections because they see them as a product of, and exclusively beneficial to, the dominant culture. Yet, more promisingly, many said that if political parties and candidates were to reach out to them, were to invite them to participate, were to come into their neighbourhoods and meet with them in ways consistent with their cultures, and even more, if political parties were to run Aboriginal candidates, they would vote. The greater political weight that an increased propensity to vote would likely create is an important component in a successful urban Aboriginal community development strategy, since such a strategy is predicated in large part upon public investment, and public investment requires political support.

Finally, in Chapter Five, we use a "life stories" method to listen to and interpret the words of a select group of Aboriginal people active in, and leaders of, inner-city community development in Winnipeg. They describe their often extremely difficult early years: the racism; the internalized shame and the lack of self-esteem and self-confidence they experienced as the result of being Aboriginal in a colonial culture; the often self-destructive ways in which they lashed out at their oppression. We describe the paths that they took in their journeys, from being victims of colonization to becoming active agents of social change. They articulate their vision of a distinctive Aboriginal form of community development that is holistic — i.e., that operates at an individual, community, organizational and ideological level — and is rooted in the traditional Aboriginal values of community and sharing. It is an inspiring vision of a better life for urban Aboriginal people.

This book reflects an optimistic outlook for urban Aboriginal people. We make no attempt to hide the very real despair experienced by so many urban Aboriginal people. That despair is clear in the voices of many urban Aboriginal people in the chapters that follow, and it is important that non-Aboriginal people hear and understand these voices. Yet there is much positive work being done in Winnipeg's inner city, and a great deal of it is being led by Aboriginal people. Their courage and their creativity in healing and rebuilding battered individuals and communities are inspiring. There are no quick or easy solutions for Aboriginal people in Winnipeg's inner city, or in other similar urban centres. But a unique path to a better future is being built here, and creative urban Aboriginal people are both the engineers and the builders.

NOTE

1.   This section is drawn, in part, from Silver, Mallett, Greene and Simard 2002: 32–41.

Chapter Two

IN BUT NOT OF

Aboriginal People in an Inner-City Neighbourhood

Jim Silver, Joan Hay and Peter Gorzen

Aboriginal people have migrated to urban centres in growing numbers in recent decades. In Winnipeg, they have disproportionately located in older, inner-city neighbourhoods where housing values have dropped due to the age of the housing stock and the post-war exodus to the suburbs. In recent years, particularly since the mid- to late 1990s, impressive neighbourhood revitalization efforts have started in at least some of these inner-city neighbourhoods. Revitalization has generally taken a community development form, i.e., it has relied upon the involvement of the people in the neighbourhoods themselves.

We wanted to know whether Aboriginal people are actively involved in such revitalization efforts. Do they participate in neighbourhood community development initiatives? We also wanted to know whether the character of neighbourhood-based community development strategies is consistent with urban Aboriginal people's priorities. Do urban Aboriginal people have the same views as non-Aboriginal people on what community development is and ought to be? Our answers to these questions are based on a study of Aboriginal people's involvement in community development activities in the Spence neighbourhood of Winnipeg's inner city.

By community development we mean the process by which people in a neighbourhood participate collectively in solving problems that they themselves have identified. As Wharf and Clague describe it: "Community development involves people (directly or through organizations) taking democratic control by participating in planning, bottom-up decision making, and community action" (Wharf and Clague 1997: 249). By development we do not necessarily mean conventional development — for example, economic growth, or organizations from the outside coming in to "help" — but rather the collective undertaking of whatever tasks and the pursuit of whatever goals that the community itself may identify. In the past, community development has often been imposed upon communities by outsiders, and driven by the paternalistic assumption that poverty and related problems are a function of cultural inferiority. Thus community development has often meant the attempt to replace traditional cultures with more dominant ones. We use community development to mean people themselves identifying the problems that they want to solve and the ways that they want to solve them, and this does not imply the adoption of the attributes of the dominant culture.

SPENCE NEIGHBOURHOOD

Spence neighbourhood is located in central Winnipeg, in an area now considered part of Winnipeg's inner city. By almost any measurement, Spence is one of Winnipeg's most distressed neighbourhoods. The population has been in decline for at least thirty years — from 6,230 in 1971 to 3,941 in 1996 and 3,750 in 2001; average property values dropped sharply in the 1990s — from $44,100 in 1989 to $30,200 in 1997; rates of residential mobility are double that of Winnipeg as a whole; the proportion of households living in rented as opposed to owner-occupied housing is double that for the city as a whole; the incidence of poverty, as measured by the proportion of households with incomes below the Statistics Canada Low-Income Cut-Off, is three times the rate for Winnipeg as

Location of Spence Neighbourhood

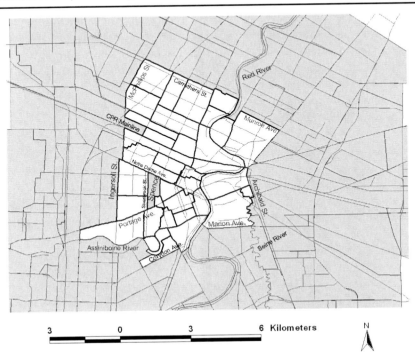

a whole; average educational levels are considerably lower than in Winnipeg as a whole (Spence Neighbourhood Council 1998). A higher proportion of homes and buildings than in Winnipeg as a whole have been abandoned and boarded up — "there are between 45 and 50 abandoned, boarded-up, vacant, or demolished dwellings and properties in the Spence neighbourhood, constituting nearly 9 percent of the homes" (Yauk and Janzen 2002: 1); sex trade workers — some in their very early teens — work the streets of Spence neighbourhood (Seshia 2005); and street gangs are more active than in Winnipeg as a whole.

At the same time, energetic efforts are now underway, led by residents of the area, to rebuild and revitalize Spence neighbourhood. Houses are being renovated; community gardens have sprouted in vacant lots; youth activities are run out of community centres; colourful murals brighten the sides of many buildings; and new lighting and fences can be seen throughout the neighbourhood. Partly as the result of these efforts, a survey of fifty-seven residents in November 2002 found that almost three in four (74 percent) plan to stay in Spence neighbourhood (Blake 2003: 16).

Spence Neighbourhood Association

The Spence Neighbourhood Association (SNA) is one of the key organizations promoting these changes. The SNA was formed in 1996/97, when residents and community groups wanting to reverse the neighbourhood's decline organized a series of neighbourhood cleanups and barbecues. The organization moved soon to initiatives aimed at improving safety and security and renovating houses. Out of these efforts, the Spence Neighbourhood Council — a coalition of individuals and fledging groups in the neighbourhood — emerged in early 1997. Several organizations branched off from the Council, one of them the Spence Neighbourhood Association. The SNA has become a leader in efforts to revitalize Spence neighbourhood.

Central to the task of neighbourhood revitalization, as the SNA sees it, is the active involvement of people in the community. The SNA Web site says in its opening paragraph that "Resident participation is the key to the approach of the organization." This is a community development approach.

In many respects the organization has been successful in promoting participation. Neighbourhood meetings called to evaluate proposed community development projects are lively and well-attended (Silver 2003); an active and imaginative youth program is run by the SNA; a host of activities, especially for women and youth, are run out of the Magnus Eliason Recreation Centre (MERC), home of the SNA; regular efforts are made to involve people in neighbourhood activities, especially by means of the door-to-door delivery of flyers.

Yet garnering involvement by residents in the work of the SNA is a struggle. As former board president Danielle Davis put it in April 2003: "We try very, very hard to get the community involved, but it's usually always the same people." Former vice-president Sue McKenzie concurred, observing that people participate "to a very limited extent… it's one of the problems that we have." When asked about the participation of Aboriginal people in SNA activities, both Davis and McKenzie offered the view that Aboriginal residents participated less than non-Aboriginal people, but that Aboriginal children are active in the youth programs, and Aboriginal mothers are active in the Mom's Support Circle program. SNA Executive Director Inonge Aliaga explains that Aboriginal people in Spence are struggling to survive and are fully occupied with family responsibilities, which is a higher priority for them than neighbourhood renewal, and that Aboriginal people, like Spence residents generally, get involved when and where they see involvement as beneficial to them.

The Aboriginal population in Spence is large and growing rapidly, as it is in the rest of Winnipeg. In Spence, the Aboriginal population was the largest single identifiable group in 1991, and this was still the case in 2001. The proportion of the total population that was Aboriginal was four times as large in Spence as in Winnipeg as a whole, according to the 2001 Census of Canada.

Historically, Spence neighbourhood has been an attractive location for recent immigrants to Winnipeg. At the turn of the century, Sargent Avenue, one of the neighbourhood's commercial corridors, was known as "Icelandic Main Street." Later in the century, the area was populated by Germans, then by Portugese immigrants, and more recently, by immigrants of Asian descent — Filipino, Vietnamese and Chinese in particular. In the past several years, large numbers of African refugees, Sudanese and Somali in particular, have settled in Spence (Madariega-Vignudo and Miladinovska-Blazeus 2005). But Aboriginal people continue to be the largest single identifiable group in Spence.

Those We Interviewed

For the study that forms the basis of this chapter, using methods described in Chapter One, we interviewed twenty-four Aboriginal residents of Spence neighbourhood. Among them were equal numbers of women and men, of a wide range of ages, levels of formal educational attainment, occupational status and years lived in Spence neighbourhood. In addition, we interviewed six people who were board members or staff of the SNA, including the executive director, and we interviewed both Hay and Gorzen in their roles as long-time Spence neighbourhood residents. Two focus groups were held in June 2003, and a total of eight people who had previously been interviewed participated.

Lack of Involvement With the Spence Neighbourhood Association

Of the twenty-four people interviewed, only one is involved with the SNA. Many had not heard of it; some had heard of it but knew nothing about what the organization does; many said they have seen very little advertising about the

Why Don't You Participate in the Spence Neighbourhood Association?

First of all, I was never extended a personal invitation.... If somebody made the personal contact to say this is what we're doing, this is what we need you for, you know, things like that... putting out posters is not really communicating.

Although they do have their monthly newsletter delivered and it does tell you about upcoming meetings and stuff like that, maybe some people want a more in-person type of invitation... personal invitation.

Sure you see a poster now and then, about a meeting, but stuff like that doesn't really work, eh?... to know that you're welcome, to know that you're being asked, you know, I don't necessarily say that you should have your hand held to go to those places, but, just posters don't really mean anything.

SNA. They made such comments as: "I don't know what that Spence Association is"; "I've never heard of it"; "I know very little about it. I know that it's a community organization but I'm not certain exactly what it's all about.... I don't even know where it's located."

There are some practical reasons for this lack of awareness and involvement. The organization promotes its activities primarily by means of flyers delivered door to door. However, most Aboriginal people in the neighbourhood are renters living in apartment blocks or rooming houses, which are not all accessible because the front doors are locked. In some cases, Aboriginal residents are not involved for reasons identical to those that keep most people from being involved: they are too busy. However, some of the people interviewed said that they were not involved with the SNA because they had never been personally invited to be involved, and they considered anything other than a personal invitation not to be an invitation at all.

The comments about not being personally invited lead us into a deeper understanding of the relative lack of Aboriginal involvement in the SNA. Our interviews have led us to believe that Aboriginal people feel disconnected from, excluded from, the dominant culture, and thus are hesitant to approach and to get involved with the institutions of the dominant culture: They see the SNA — rightly or wrongly — as a typical dominant culture institution. And they do not believe that they are welcome in such institutions, or in the city generally. One senior Aboriginal resident of Spence, who has lived in the neighbourhood off and on for twenty-five years, put it this way:

To me, I think, most of our people they come here, don't really feel part of the community. Right away, new Canadians come in and they get an awful lot of "welcome wagon" treatment, you know, they get an awful lot of help, they get guides, they get mentors, they get people who are willing to even take them shopping, it doesn't matter if they speak the language or not, they have people who are taking them around and yet a lot of new Canadians come from urban areas and they're used to urban areas. Our people come from [non-urban areas] and yet when our people come here there's nobody to show them around, there's nobody to say "hey, you're welcome." I've never heard of an Aboriginal being met by the welcome wagon yet, you know, I've heard of the welcome wagon, I've never heard of anybody getting a welcome wagon visit — an Aboriginal, you know, that's not racist, it's just the truth, and when we come here.... A lot of people they land here with no job, nothing, they come in with hope, but there's nothing for them, there's nothing, compared to the new Canadian.

A recent Canada West Foundation study confirmed this with their finding that funding for Aboriginal people making the transition from rural to urban areas was "less than five cents for every dollar spent on immigrant settlement and transition" (Hanselmann 2003: 5).

Another participant, when asked at a focus group meeting why so few of the Aboriginal people interviewed are involved with the SNA, said:

I think most of it is not feeling comfortable, or not trusting.... I think it's just part of not feeling that you're listened to or looked at different or just the usual racist feeling... that when you are surrounded, or outnumbered, by the other community members that are non-Aboriginal you sort of feel intimidated.

Another participant in the same focus group responded to this question by describing his feelings about an annual community festival in his Ontario home town, a non-Aboriginal centre:

I never felt comfortable going there because of the fact that I was native and the stereotype was, you know, drunken Indians, you were looked down upon shamefully for being drunk and not getting a job... that stigma, I think.

A young woman added:

A lot of people put down the Aboriginal people and say, oh, you're not going to do it, you're just going to go back to drinking and all that and that's what a lot of people do to Aboriginal people and that's why a lot of Aboriginal people don't go to these programs because they have no self-esteem... because of all of these other people putting them down all the time. There is a lot of discrimination in this area, for jobs… you can tell, just the way they look at you, the way they treat you and everything.

Another young woman, who had made an earlier effort to join the SNA, described the perceived gap between the Aboriginal and non-Aboriginal communities, and in so doing revealed the social class component to the gap:

A couple of my friends were talking about that the other day, how they feel, I guess, intimidated by, I don't know, non-Aboriginals, you know, like, even to job interviews and stuff like that, you know, and like even how I felt last year when I tried to join them…. I felt low class, because there was no other Aboriginals in there and they just seemed all, older, married, you know, living decent lives.

This feeling is consistent with what we know about non-Aboriginal attitudes to Aboriginal people in Canadian towns in recent decades: there has been no place for Aboriginal people in such communities, there has been "intense hostility" directed by townspeople at Aboriginal residents and visitors (Peters 2002a: 56). Aboriginal people have responded to this hostility, to this social exclusion, by withdrawing. Lithman found that Aboriginal members of a well-known rural Manitoba Aboriginal community did not become involved in non-Aboriginal organizations or opportunities in order to avoid "the indignities of most inter-actions with white men" (Lithman 1984: 58). The same is true in larger urban centres. Deane, Morrissette, Bousquet and Bruyere, in a recent study (2002: 16), observed that Aboriginal people in the William Whyte neighbourhood in Winnipeg's North End often "withdrew to avoid interactions based on values that were incompatible with, or perhaps even offensive to, their own value orientation."

This social exclusion is worsened by racism, instances of which are common in the neighbourhood. One young woman described walking with three female friends on one of the main streets in the neighbourhood, early in the evening:

There was me and three of my friends out for a walk. This was just over here, and we were crossing the street and this car drove by and he said, "Hey, you fucking Indian," you know, and it was just like, that hurt! You know, like… it really, really bothered me.

Another person, a young man, independently related a similar story: "a bunch of my friends, we were just walking… a bunch of people in a car started yelling at them calling them sniffers and drunks and everything." One of the older men described an incident in the neighbourhood in which an Aboriginal couple were leaving their apartment to go to an evening social event and were formally dressed for the occasion. The man went around the corner to hail a cab, and while he was gone the police confronted his wife on the suspicion that she was a hooker. Several participants reported incidents of racism related to jobs — we will refer to these in a later section. Such incidents serve to confirm and reinforce the social exclusion experienced by many Aboriginal people.

Many others mentioned, in various ways, this sense of social exclusion. One referred to what he perceived as the largely non-Aboriginal character of the SNA as "a bunch of white people that don't really know... they don't really know how it is inside the Aboriginal person's spirit, you know." Another said: "some people say that they feel, like, isolated, they don't feel part of the community." Another added: "The gap is so vast." A young man who attended some SNA board meetings found the formal process very alienating: "at the board level, even when I would come to meetings, I would find that they were talking around me, like I wasn't there." He added that there were very few Aboriginal people present and "after bumping my head there a few times I didn't want to go there anymore.... I didn't feel comfortable." Yet another, after revealing that "some people seem to have the idea that it [the SNA] is kind of elitist in its own way," said "I would welcome the opportunity to be treated like part of the group rather than an outsider."

The feeling of being an outsider, of not being part of the community, may be at least partly attributable to the very different sense of community in the city compared to most reserves. One person that we interviewed said:

> Growing up on the reserve, there was a community feeling there that I don't feel here. Sure you know a lot of people, you meet a lot of people, you see them every day going down the street, you say "hi," but being in a community, like on the reserve, you're basically welcome in a lot of places, you know, you go visit your relatives, your grandmother, or whatever, or your friends, you know... that to me was community, but not, like, here.

By this description, life on the reserves is lived in a more intimate, face-to-face fashion than life in the city. On most reserves, everybody knows everybody else and knows their family background. Many are related. Social interaction is frequent. In the city, by contrast, associations are more fleeting, there is a greater degree of isolation, of anomie and alienation, which adds to feelings of social exclusion.

The fact that most urban Aboriginal people are renters — all but three of the twenty-four people interviewed are renters — also sets them apart. When a participant in one of the focus groups expressed his desire to own one of the renovated SNA houses, another responded by saying: "Yeah, of course, because what you have then is you have a place that's permanent, you're not a stranger, you're now part of the community, this is yours." The point of this discussion was that Aboriginal people are not involved with the SNA because they do not feel part of the community, and they do not feel part of the community, at least in part, because they are renters and they live in apartments and rooming houses that are often very run down and poorly maintained, and they have to move frequently. They are marginalized by their housing status. If a plan were created to enable Aboriginal people who want to stay in the neighbourhood to become homeowners, then they would feel more a part of the community and would be more likely to get involved.

A senior member of the Spence Aboriginal community, resident in the neighbourhood for many years, said: "I don't know what the Spence Neighbourhood Association is doing, because we're not part of it, are we?" He offered the view that:

> Perhaps if you went to the Thunderbird House or the Aboriginal group there on Higgins [the Aboriginal Centre] and the leaders in Spence [Neighbourhood Association] if they went there and were willing to sit and listen to the native leaders there, you see, because we have a lot to teach but the thing is basically most of us here are unemployed and nobody wants to listen to an unemployed Indian, let's face it, and if you [the SNA] went to some of our leaders and listened and learned and came back with a little, you know, I hate to use the word sensitivity, it's such a buzzword [laughter] but that would work, and then you'd come back and not only would you identify with us but you'd be immediately putting us to work.

This expression of frustration arises not only because Aboriginal people do not feel fully a part of the community but also because they know that, to participate, it is they who will have to change. They know that to feel a part of the community it is incumbent upon them to become more like non-Aboriginal people, rather than non-Aboriginal people being obligated to learn about and accommodate Aboriginal culture. They are saying, let non-Aboriginal people show enough interest to learn about us, just as we have to learn about them, and this too will facilitate our involvement in the community.

We conclude that most Aboriginal people are not involved in the SNA — despite the SNA's efforts — in part because they do not feel fully a part of the community; they feel excluded from the dominant culture and its institutions. Their sense of social exclusion is reinforced by frequent instances of racism and by their relatively disadvantaged housing status. They do not feel that their own, different culture is understood or appreciated by those in the dominant culture, and they resent the minimal effort made by most institutions of the dominant culture to learn about and accommodate Aboriginal ways.

When we circulated to SNA board members a next-to-final draft of the paper on which this chapter is based, some members expressed their unease and disappointment with what they read as criticism of the SNA board and staff. We offered the view that while there are things that the SNA might do differently to encourage involvement by Aboriginal people, the problem has less to do with the specific actions of the SNA than with broader societal and historical forces — the long-term impact of colonization in particular — that have created the feeling, and the reality, of social exclusion for many Aboriginal people. The relative lack of involvement of Aboriginal people in the SNA reflects the relative lack of involvement by Aboriginal people in most of the institutions of the dominant culture. Indeed, if anything, the SNA has done more than most institutions to include Aboriginal people: at the time of the study, three of seven and a half SNA staff positions were filled by Aboriginal people, and all three of these were full-time positions; and four of eleven board members were Aboriginal. The SNA is an effective and energetic community development organization, making significant efforts to be inclusive, especially of Aboriginal people. That Aboriginal people, based on our interviews, are nevertheless relatively uninvolved in the SNA suggests that the roots of their social exclusion are broader and deeper in character.

Given this, a flyer in the mailbox is not enough to induce most Aboriginal people to attend an SNA function. A personal, face-to-face invitation would, however, be seen as a genuine attempt to reach out to Aboriginal people, to listen to what they have to say and to begin to bridge the cultural gap.

COMMUNITY DEVELOPMENT: AN ABORIGINAL VIEW

We asked those that we interviewed: "how important is Aboriginal culture to you?" We got a variety of answers and concluded from what we were told that the promotion of Aboriginal cultures is a necessary step in an Aboriginal-driven community development strategy in Spence neighbourhood.

Aboriginal Cultures

Some Aboriginal people in Spence neighbourhood are very knowledgeable about their culture. They practise cultural rituals regularly and want more opportunities for cultural involvement. For example, one woman said: "Oh, very much so, very much so. I speak my language, and I do go to sweats…. Within my household, I do smudge, I do pray." Another woman replied that she considers herself to be spiritual, and that her culture is "very important, very, very important" to her. She described taking her children to pow wow and dancing lessons at the Indian Métis Friendship Centre when they were young, putting her oldest son in Children of the Earth, Winnipeg's Aboriginal high school, and said proudly that: "now I'm working on my grandchildren." She added that what should be done in the neighbourhood is: "More spiritual components, if there was an elder, we could have sweats and healing circles and things like that, I'd *really* be interested in that."

Most of the people that we interviewed retain fragments of their Aboriginal culture and want to know more. One thirty-three-year-old man, for example, said: "I've been to… various pow wows… and I'm still not certain about the full names of the dances," but "I'm now finding in the last two years that I actually have a craving and a desire to find out more about my cultural past." Another young man said that he does not now go to traditional ceremonies. "No, I haven't done anything with that since I was a kid, when I was staying on the reserve," but "yeah, if they had something like that out here it would be good. I heard there's things like that at Thunderbird House." A young woman in her early twenties, who used to be but is no longer involved with gangs, said:

> I think ceremonies are important, like, I want to get involved with it more because I never grew up that way, I never grew up in that kind of way, when I was fifteen that's when I started getting involved with it [Aboriginal culture].… I think there should be more community centres too out here like in this neighbourhood, and maybe get some elders in here to talk to some of these youth… get some sweat lodges going on in this area, so some of the youth could try to heal themselves too, and hopefully get out of the gangs that they're in and the involvements that they're doing, like drinking and drugs, getting them into trouble.

Another woman added that "I know a lot of people have interest in it [Aboriginal cultures] but they don't know where to go to learn about it… and find out about spirituality and traditional ways." As one of the co-authors said in an evaluation session: "My feeling is that a lot of them have only bits and pieces that they've picked up through their parents or relatives… and I think that's why that interest is there." Some people are anxious for their children to learn about their culture. One young woman with two daughters said: "What about following traditional ways? I've just started learning about these and they're really interesting.… I'd even get my daughters to participate, like say in learning how to dance, the pow wows and that, like, jingle dancing." A man with two young daughters said: "Yeah, it's important, our culture, because our language is disappearing." He and his wife try to teach the daughters their language, "but they find it funny, the way it sounds." Nevertheless, he continues to believe that "it's important for our girls," and he is heartened that they have shown a real interest in jingle dancing.

Some of those we interviewed first told us that they were neither involved with nor interested in Aboriginal cultures, but then made comments that made it clear that they are not so distantly removed from their culture. One woman said: "I'm not a traditional person, I wasn't brought up that way," but when asked if she would attend if traditional ceremonies like pow wows were held in the neighbourhood, she said "Yes, I would attend that. That would be… something nice to see, like, I've seen it before… when I was younger… I've seen a lot of it back home. But that would be something nice to see." An older man, long resident in the neighbourhood, said "I've never been brought up in my culture, I've never really practised it," and then added that he goes to pow wows and believes more such opportunities would be a positive thing. A very young woman said: "I don't really bother with it, I'm not into my culture," but added "I've been to pow wows, I like those." A woman who is a Christian, when asked about her involvement with Aboriginal cultural events, said: "No, I've never been involved in that.... I'm a Christian, I'm a Pentecostal," but quickly added "well, my father was, at one time he was involved in the Sun Dance," and she added further that although she does not use it, she has an Ojibwa Spirit Name, which she told us. In short, even for those minimally involved and least interested, there is still a connection to their culture through parents and/or home communities; and in many, although not all of these cases, there is at least a vague interest, and in most cases a keen interest, in participating in Aboriginal cultural activities.

From a community development point of view, this is important, since culture can be a means of bringing Aboriginal people together. At present, as will be described at more length later, Aboriginal people in Spence are quite isolated from each other. Although they think of themselves as a community, vis-à-vis non-Aboriginal people, they do not act as a community. They are fragmented and in fact quite atomized. The promotion of Aboriginal cultural activities may be a way to begin to build community and to recreate a positive sense of identity.

Aboriginal Cultures and Healing

Many of those we interviewed are fully aware of the importance of Aboriginal cultures in healing Aboriginal people and in revitalizing the Aboriginal community. One man described the role of culture in shaping individual identity in this way:

> Neighbours come and go, people come and go, the people you pass on the street come and go, that's life, you're going to meet people and pass them on the street, but that does not take away from who you are as a person, and that is very important because if you lose that then there really is no point in living because you've lost who you are as a person and so it doesn't matter who you are, whether you're rich, poor, white, black, always maintain your culture.

He added that after a hundred years of attempted assimilation, "now it's time for us to take that back and to regain our lost customs and traditions." A young man, after saying [speaking in the third person] that "a lot of these people don't really... believe in themselves, so, that's sad but... [that's] how we got into a bunch of, like, drugs, alcoholism and what not," said about the promotion of Aboriginal cultures:

I think it's important because with it comes a sense of pride, a sense of pride as being Anishinabe. I think it's a key to changing the perception of Native people, it's the solution for the stigma that Native people as a whole... have, that low self-esteem, that are affected by the colonialism and alcoholism, would be a way out for them, to heal, not only to heal but to teach their children, ultimately the next generations, a sense of pride. It's very important, very important.

Another young man added, about the promotion of Aboriginal cultures:

It's pretty important due to the fact that there was times before like I heard people putting down my culture and stuff but in a way I wasn't too involved with it when I was younger because when I was growing up I grew up in a white community pretty much all my life, until I began to live more in the inner city and I began to see how everyone was treated.

Urban Aboriginal people have not lost their cultures but for historical reasons they are fragmented and complex, as was described in Chapter One. And a century and more of denigration has taken its toll on Aboriginal cultures. As co-author Joan Hay, speaking in an evaluation session, said:

I think that our whole culture is, like, totally fragmented and in a lot of ways people have lost their culture and probably sometimes people are grieving and they don't even realize what's going on, why they're involved in addictions and just have lost their way because there's a part of your soul that's missing, which is probably the spiritual part.

It is by acknowledging this complex cultural reality that efforts to enhance Aboriginal people's involvement in Spence neighbourhood will succeed. Aboriginal people have told us that they want more opportunities to experience and to practise their cultures. Many want to learn more about their cultures and want opportunities for their children to learn as well. This, we believe, is an integral part of an Aboriginal community development strategy.

Social Capital and Aboriginal Cultures

One way of thinking about an Aboriginal community development strategy is to connect it to the idea of social capital. One woman said about the promotion of Aboriginal cultural activities in Spence neighbourhood: "I think that's... a way for people to connect." Indeed, this is what social capital is about. Although it can mean many things, the idea of establishing connections and building networks is a common theme. Robert Putnam, the scholar most closely associated with the concept of social capital, has written that "the core idea of social capital theory is that social networks have value" (Putnam 2000: 19), and more recently that "The central idea of social capital, in my view, is that networks and the associated norms of reciprocity have value" (Putnam 2001: 1). Social capital is closely associated with lower crime rates, reduced levels of violence, improved child welfare, better health, better educational outcomes, improved economic performance and greater income equality (Putnam 2001: 12–16).

But in Spence neighbourhood, our interviews suggest strongly an absence of connections and networks in the Aboriginal community. In fact, our evidence leads us to believe that the Aboriginal community is disconnected, disjointed and fragmented at the community level.

First, Aboriginal people appear to be disconnected from each other. Many keep very much to themselves. One woman told us that "I really don't talk to too many people, I just kind of stay to myself here. My kids are my biggest priority, and that's who I deal with and I don't bother with anybody else." An older woman who has raised her family in the neighbourhood over the past twenty years said: "I never bother anybody, the only one I talk to here on this street is these people next door here, maybe every once in a while just say hi." Her husband concurred: "For all these years I've been in here, I've never bothered nobody. Nobody bothers me, I don't bother nobody." For some Aboriginal people in the neighbourhood, this has to do with fears about crime and safety. At a focus group meeting, one man, who has kept very much to himself over the past eight years that he has lived in Spence except for going to and from work in the neighbourhood, said that he is "scared because [of] everything that happens around here. You've got to be cautious who you talk to." A second focus group participant replied by saying: "with that kind of thinking, with that kind of attitude, there is no community, like the community I knew when I was growing up on the reserve." At this particular focus group, there were three men who had lived for twenty-five years, eight years and seven years respectively in Spence neighbourhood. They live close to each other but had never before met.

Second, Aboriginal people in Spence neighbourhood are for the most part not involved in the SNA or other community organizations. Only one of the twenty-four interviewees is involved with the SNA. Only four said they were involved with any other community organization in the neighbourhood, and a large majority told us they know of no other Aboriginal people involved in the SNA or any other community organization in Spence.

Third, there appears to be little connection, little networking, across neighbourhoods. We spoke with the executive committee of the West Broadway Aboriginal Residents Group, which formed in February 2002 in an adjacent inner-city neighbourhood. They told us that they would be very pleased if there were a Spence Aboriginal neighbourhood association, or a Spence Aboriginal residents group. Jo-Anne Spence, former president of the West Broadway Aboriginal Residents Group, told us that they would hope such a group would "work collaboratively with us and network, like, I see networking as a key factor for Aboriginal people no matter what community you go to so it's networking and sharing ideas and stuff like that." It is possible to imagine a network of Aboriginal community organizations forming in Winnipeg, meeting regularly, sharing ideas and co-operating on projects. Such a network could even work with and learn from similar neighbourhood organizations in other urban centres, as has been done in other parts of the world. A recent study of such exchanges involving women's community organizations in India and Africa argues that: "The exchange process is powerful in creating skills. First, community members quickly believe that they can do it. When they see professionals undertaking an activity, they may be skeptical about how easily they might take it over. When they see another community member doing it, they know it is possible" (Patel and Mitlin 2002: 132). This cannot even begin to happen as long as Aboriginal people are as atomized as our evidence suggests they are in Spence neighbour-hood. The benefits that are strongly associated with social capital are not being realized in Spence neighbourhood. This is an area where great gains could be made.

Building Social Capital by Promoting Aboriginal Cultures

There is evidence that Aboriginal people in Spence could be brought together, and social capital created, by developing more opportunities to learn about and practise Aboriginal cultures in Spence neighbourhood. Our interviews provide strong evidence that there is a great deal of interest in the Aboriginal community in doing this. Aboriginal cultural activities would connect Aboriginal people with each other and would promote pride and self- esteem.

This has been found to be the case elsewhere. In Latin America and the Caribbean, for example, there are numerous cases where "relatively small amounts of money invested in a people's expressive culture served to promote their social cohesion and enhance their self-respect" (Kleymeyer 1994: xv). People desire to maintain their cultures because:

> it is through them that they make sense of the world and have a sense of themselves. We know that when people are forced to give up their culture, or when they give it up too rapidly, the consequences are normally social breakdown accompanied by personal disorientation and despair. The attach-ment of people to their culture corresponds, then, to a fundamental human need. That is why development programs that build on cultural traditions are likely to be the most successful. (Kleymeyer 1994: xiv)

In Canada, personal disorientation and despair have certainly been the con-sequence of more than a century of attempts to eradicate Aboriginal cultures — via residential schools, the *Indian Act* and Indian Agents, and the outlawing of Aboriginal cultural and spiritual beliefs (see Chapter One). Despite this onslaught, many Aboriginal people have clung tenaciously to their cultures, although in many cases, as described earlier by Little Bear and by Deane et al. in a partial, complex and fragmented form. And there is, as seen above, a desire on the part of many Aboriginal people to learn more about their traditional cultures.

There is a growing belief among Aboriginal people that it is upon this desire that Aboriginal communities must be rebuilt. The Royal Commission on Aboriginal Peoples held a round table meeting on Aboriginal Urban Issues in June 1992. It listed the first of the themes that emerged at the round table as: "the survival of Aboriginal identity in an environment that is usually indifferent and often hostile to Aboriginal people" (Royal Commission on Aboriginal Peoples 1993: 2). Cultural concerns were raised over and over again:

- Young people growing up in the city ask: "Where can I go to learn who I am?"
- They say they need spiritual renewal and restoration of culture in order to become whole human beings again.
- One presenter at the Round Table pointed out that if he wanted to merge into the general population, institutions are already there to be used. However, if his goal is to retain or regain his Indian-ness there does not seem to be a vehicle.
- Many Aboriginal young people, participants said, are facing the same situations as their older counterparts: cultural confusion, a sense of lost identity.
- Children are confused about their cultural identity. (Royal Commission on Aboriginal Peoples 1993: 3–7, 41 and 43).

The same arguments have been made repeatedly by Aboriginal people in Canadian cities. Peters (2002a: 61) has recently summarized these: "Aboriginal people have argued that supporting and enhancing Aboriginal culture is a prerequisite for coping in an urban environment," and "In their submissions to the 1992–94 public hearings of the Royal Commission on Aboriginal Peoples, participants stressed the need to enhance Aboriginal cultures in urban areas." She quotes David Chartrand, then-president of the National Association of Friendship Centres:

> Our culture is at the heart of our people, and without awareness of Aboriginal history, traditions and ceremonies, we are not whole people, and our communities lose their strength.... Cultural education also works against the alienation that the cities hold for our people. Social activities bring us together and strengthen the relationship

between people in areas where those relationships are an important safety net for people who feel left out by the mainstream. (quoted in Peters 2002a: 63)

Deane, Morrissette, Bousquet and Bruyere (2002: 13), in their study of Aboriginal people's relationship to Winnipeg's North End Housing Project, reported that: "The community indicated that they wanted space for recreation programs for young people, and some means through which Aboriginal young people could learn their language, retain their traditions, and maintain a greater closeness to parents and elders."

As stated previously, many urban Aboriginal people identify strongly with their culture and want more opportunities to learn about their historical roots, and to experience and practise their ceremonies. Further, the deliberate promotion of Aboriginal cultures would promote relationships and connections and networking between and among Aboriginal people, and would build among urban Aboriginal people a sense of community and of identity, and thus is an essential part of a community development strategy in urban neighbourhoods.

PROMOTING ABORIGINAL
INVOLVEMENT IN SPENCE NEIGHBOURHOOD

We argue that there are at least three steps to be taken to increase Aboriginal involvement in the community. Two of these could be taken by the existing SNA, and the steps are not mutually exclusive — any or all or some combination of the three are possible. However, we believe, based on our interviews, that the third step described — the creation by Aboriginal people of a *separate* Spence Aboriginal residents group that would be organizationally affiliated with the SNA — is the preferred way of promoting Aboriginal involvement in the community, and that such an organization could best take the first two steps, i.e., the hiring of an Aboriginal community organizer and the development of an Aboriginal cultural resource centre.

Aboriginal Community Organizer

One means of beginning to respond to urban Aboriginal people's social exclusion is to hire an Aboriginal community organizer — an Aboriginal person whose job it is to personally get to know the Aboriginal people in the Spence neighbourhood, to identify their issues and concerns, and to personally invite them to become involved. The face-to-face approach, though seemingly unsophisticated, continues to be the best form of neighbourhood organizing. In his classic book *Organizing: A Guide for Grassroots Leaders*, long-time organizer Si Kahn (1991: 198) says: "Person-to-person contact is one of the great strengths of organizing" because it "carries the message that we see people as individuals...."

When we communicate person-to-person we say that each person's ideas are valuable, that each person should have control of his or her life." This applies generally in neighbourhood organizing and, we would argue, applies particularly to attempts to promote the involvement of urban Aboriginal people.

Aboriginal Resource Centre

A second response to the observed reluctance of Aboriginal people to become involved in the SNA is to develop in the neighbourhood an Aboriginal resource centre or Aboriginal cultural centre, where a wide variety of Aboriginal cultural activities and services could be offered — dance, languages, drumming, advice from elders, provision of (or access to) books and videos, for example. At one of the focus groups, participants advanced the view that there are not enough places like the Aboriginal Centre and the Indian and Métis Friendship Centre to meet the demand for Aboriginal cultural involvement, especially for adults. Those cultural institutions that exist are not in the Spence neighbourhood — "there's nothing really in this area" — and "one of our basic problems here in this end [in Spence neighbourhood] is we're damned poor," so that often it is difficult to get to places like the Aboriginal Centre or the Indian and Métis Friendship Centre.

Another woman said:

> I think it's great that they now have an urban sweat lodge at the Thunderbird House. If we had something like that over [in Spence neighbourhood] it would be good. Also, if they could have a library it would be good so that Aboriginal people know their own history from their own perspective... so that people learn a different history than you would learn in junior high or high school because they don't learn it from our perspective.... It's the whole colonization thing.

Many of the people that we interviewed expressed an interest in learning their language, and this might best be done in a non-formal or "natural" way, with Cree and Ojibwa conversational meetings, for example. Such attempts to keep alive the languages and the cultures could include youth — for example, by creating local history clubs that offer young people the opportunity to interview local Aboriginal people and record their stories, or to delve into their own family histories.

A Spence Aboriginal Residents Group

A third option to promote Aboriginal involvement in the Spence neighbourhood is to have Aboriginal people create their own Spence *Aboriginal* residents group. A significant number of those we interviewed raised and discussed this possibility. One relatively young man, speaking in one of the focus groups, said:

I think there should be a branch that is mostly [an] Aboriginal group.... I think a lot of natives have an aversion to having a group that's run by whites. If Spence Neighbourhood [Association] wants to, I don't know maybe there are Aboriginals on the Spence Neighbourhood group, but in order to be more receptive to the community, the Aboriginal community, they should have a group that is made up of Aboriginals.

An older man at the focus group carried on:

I think it would be a good thing to start that way because then we would have a sort of made-up family in a way and then we'd gain confidence, you know.... The thing is, I ran around with all these fears too, that we have, and it would be really nice to have a focus group that we could identify with, come in and just let ourselves lay back and just be ourselves, you know. Oftentimes when we go to groups where it's mixed, not only the Aboriginals but the minorities there kind of watch the way the wind blows first before we speak up, not because we're afraid of you guys or anything like that but we don't like trouble, basically, and you guys outnumber us by about thirty million to, you know... (laughter).

The younger man replied:

I would honestly prefer that an Aboriginal group be started independent of the Spence Neighbourhood Association but as part of Spence Neighbourhood Association, because what SNA is doing now, they've already got a mind-set, eh... and Aboriginals are not involved in it and they have a different way of thinking, a different way of doing things, you know, different attitudes towards things, because you know you can't come in and join a group and see the mind-set, you know, and you're kind of discouraged, you know, or you don't feel like you want to be part of it, because like I said the mind-set is already there, whereas if you start a grassroots movement amongst the people you get the ideas... the Aboriginals have a different way of doing things.... Maybe some time in the future both groups, when they learn to understand how each other works, could get together as one group.

In the adjoining West Broadway neighbourhood, Aboriginal people had already formed the West Broadway Aboriginal Residents Group. Then-president Jo-Anne Spence described why she and others got together to form the group:

I kind of recognized there was a lack of Aboriginal participation everywhere I went, because I was on many boards, any board you could possibly think of in the neighbourhood, I was involved in.... I just noticed there was a real lack of Aboriginal participation, and then I thought, well, how can

*we solve this problem? So we took the initiative from there and formed an
Aboriginal residents group.*

The West Broadway Aboriginal Residents Group offers a variety of activities,
most with a cultural component — for example, Aboriginal cultural awareness
workshops, cultural and leadership workshops, monthly gatherings and sharing
circles, and Aboriginal youth leadership programs. So far they have had some
successes and some failures, but a major part of their objective, as Jo-Anne
Spence put it, is to enable Aboriginal people "to get a sense of being part of the
community… a sense of pride in their own community." And this is happening.
One man told us that he was planning to move from the West Broadway neighbourhood, "and then I got involved with the group and it gave me some sense of
belonging, you know, you belong to something, and it's been very positive."

We believe a sense of belonging will be promoted through the creation of a
Spence Aboriginal residents group, preferably operating in a loose affiliation with
the Spence Neighbourhood Association. Again a Spence Aboriginal residents
group could hire an Aboriginal community organizer to meet with Aboriginal
people in the neighbourhood and personally invite them to become involved,
and fund-raising could start for a Spence neighbourhood Aboriginal cultural
centre.

In a study of why inner-city people become involved in their communities,
Keiffer concluded that:

> Among the central lessons of this study is the conclusion that we
> should not seek to do for others what they can do for themselves.…
> Involvement in an organization of peers appears to be the essential in-
> gredient in cultivation of rudimentary political skills. (Keiffer 1984)

This is consistent with the principles of community development and of capacity
building, which involve people learning to define and solve their own problems.
It is consistent, too, with many early feminist efforts, which established separate
organizations, or women's caucuses within existing organizations, so that women
would feel free to speak their minds without fear of male domination and so that
they could develop a sense of confidence in their own skills and abilities.

Skills and Abilities
The skills and abilities necessary to run a Spence Aboriginal residents group
are certainly present among Aboriginal people in the neighbourhood. Indeed,
we were struck by the many skills possessed by the Aboriginal people living in
Spence. We asked people a version of each of these questions: "What skills or
abilities do you know of in the local Aboriginal community that could be used
to improve the neighbourhood?" and "What skills or abilities do *you* have that
could be used to improve the neighbourhood?" Although this question was not

pursued as thoroughly as suggested in, for example, Kretzmann and McKnight (1993: 19–25), and although many people were modest about discussing their own skills and abilities, many were nevertheless identified. One thirty-three-year-old man, for example, is an amateur historian and runs a Web site. "It's not just chat lines and what not, it goes beyond that." He added: "I'm very big into history.... Everybody has a history and that is so very important in the cultural traditions that will carry us on into tomorrow." Such a person could lead a local history group, tracing the histories of local Aboriginal families and getting young people involved in interviewing elders and in creating a Web site for a Spence Aboriginal history project. Two of the people we interviewed have written for the community newspaper, *West Central Streets*, and one of the two aspires to a career in journalism. Another interviewee has been the secretary of a large public housing tenants association for many years; several say they are good at working with people with addictions; one man has experience in coaching baseball; several of the men have construction skills and experience. One twenty-year-old man told us, in response to the question about skills and abilities to improve the neighbourhood:

> One of my neighbours, his house is slowly deteriorating and a bunch of us we talked to him about, like, fixing up his yard and stuff like that, and going around and everyone helping each other... because a lot of my neighbours, they have different skills, one does fences for a living, another one's a painter, like, I can do a lot of things also.

One woman, after some prodding, told us that she is very good at sewing. "I know how to sew, like, I am an awesome seamstress, without a machine, I don't need a machine to sew, I sew by hand, I've been into leatherwork, belts, I sew pants, I make my own dresses." This woman is currently unemployed. Yet she told us:

> I can learn anything, if somebody will give me the opportunity to learn. I've had to go back to school for my GED because I quit [when she was young] but I went back and I got it and now it's just the opportunity for something to come up that would suit me.

Urban Aboriginal people's skills often go unrecognized. One older man told us:

> There is an awful lot of wisdom that's not highlighted, for instance my neighbour down the hallway here has worked many, many years in many different trades.... He has spent those years learning how to budget his money.... He had a drinking addiction, he's been free of it for many years, so he's learned how to deal with his own addictions, he has the wisdom I

think to teach younger people that. And many of our Aboriginals from up north who come here, if they had the same entry program that many of our new Canadians did, would be able to channel their hard-won wisdom to helping immediately.

He cited the case of an older woman he had known in a northern Aboriginal community, who had lived through many of life's tragedies, including seeing her children and grandchildren die. He said:

She had a heart, and when people came to her with problems she just immediately went to work and she never took a person and said "I'll fix it for you" but she said, "why don't we think of how you can fix it," and that's something that many counsellors don't think of, you know, putting the responsibility back on the person who has the problem, and this lady did, and I think we have an awful lot of these people coming into the city who could really... use their wisdom.

He added:

Our society is a paper society, if you don't have something behind your name then you're not considered a wise person, but the Aboriginal society, it's very experiential — if you have the experience and you know how to translate it to someone who has never gone through that experience, then you've got a gift that you can give, and that's I think what should be done with our elders. Many of our elders don't have the credentials to go out and wave paperwork around but they have the experience, and they have the respect to be heard by the younger people, and if they were given the opportunity, they would solve a lot of the problems that the young people have because the young people would be listening. One of the things that I find best about our culture is that we do listen to the elders.

We were given evidence of this by a young man employed by the SNA as a summer youth counsellor:

I remember one summer there we had an elder come to the community centre and the kids were very, like, even the bad ones, like, they were misbehaving, but once the elder came and talked to them they all sat and listened and they all wanted him to come back.

Two of the women we interviewed are interested and skilled in working with children. One told us that: "I'd like to be part of the ones that set up events, something for the kids to come out more, to get the community out more, like all the street festivals there [the annual Ellice Avenue Street Festival]. Just set up more, like, volleyball teams, stuff like that… for younger children to go in and have the opportunity to play instead of having them on the streets." Another woman, a young parent, told us: "I'm well involved with a lot of the children around here, like they all know who I am and you know, they see me coming and they come running up, 'hi [her name],' you know, and I like talking with the kids, you know, and I think that's a good skill." These are skills that an Aboriginal residents group could put to very good use. The benefits would accrue to the neighbourhood as a whole.

Hiring Locally
In the discussions of skills and abilities, and of involvement in the SNA and the community more generally, the issue of jobs arose frequently. Some of the Aboriginal people we interviewed expressed resentment that so many jobs with inner-city organizations are filled by non-Aboriginal people. They told us that they believe that Aboriginal people would be more likely to become involved with community organizations if more Aboriginal people were employed with such organizations. For example, one young man who is employed in construction observed that if the SNA employed more Aboriginal staff:

> *That would be better because there's times I hear people talking about, like, they don't see enough Aboriginal people doing things, like, they see maybe more white people or maybe other kind of people, they don't see enough Aboriginal people in the community. It's like, I hear some people either saying that, "oh, native people are drunks" and that, "and they don't do nothing," but I see a lot of people that have potential if they set their minds to it.*

One woman added, referring to the Spence Neighbourhood Association and what she saw as the relative lack of Aboriginal involvement there:

> *I would probably want to have at least half of the staff as Aboriginal people…. I think we've got enough Aboriginal people now that are educated enough that they could surely find some who would be qualified…. People do notice whoever is in an organization. If there's any Aboriginals or whatever, they're drawn to them right away.*

Jo-Anne Spence, former president of the West Broadway Aboriginal Residents Group and a staffer with the West Broadway Development Corporation, made the same observation:

> *When I was hired I believe I was the only Aboriginal, and that was just a stepping stone for them, and as a result more Aboriginals were hired after that, like more front-line work type staff, and I think that's really important that the Aboriginal people need to see, you know, their people up front….*

> *That's really important to them because they're a lot more comfortable talking to their own people... like a lot of people have told me that.*

One of the authors of Chapter Three, Darlene Klyne, comments on the importance to Aboriginal people of seeing Aboriginal people employed in an organization:

> *There is the perception that... Aboriginal people are accepted because there is one on staff, and the students know, "oh, they're hiring Aboriginal people," so there is immediately that perception when you're walking in there that they're a non-racist institution. When I walk into a place and see a familiar (i.e., Aboriginal) face, your comfort level immediately goes up.*

The employment of non-Aboriginal people in agencies and organizations whose clientele is primarily Aboriginal is inconsistent with the important community development principle of hiring locally, and it creates deep resentment among Aboriginal people to be subjected to what they often see as charity:

> *I went to... a Baptist Church, nothing against Baptists, nothing against those good people, we walked in and we had to wait outside for a little while and we got in and they prayed over us first and they mentioned the word S-I-N [he spells it out] a few times and then we got our food, you know. Oh, and they gave us tracts as well, gospel tracts, just in case a sinner might have gotten a bit of food, why, we had a chance to get saved, you know.*

This man, speaking in one of the focus groups, then went on to say that local Aboriginal people should be hired to run local programs and delivering services to Aboriginal people in Spence.

> *I bet you these two men [two other men at the focus group] could run a program very easily, and they'd know exactly where the people are too, and they wouldn't put on airs, you know. Some of the people, they have white shirts on and they have ties and when you walk in: "aren't we ever good people, we're helping these poor Aboriginals to a meal." My son went to a Union Gospel Mission thing and they had cameras there, would you believe, they had cameras and they were panning the tables to see the poor Aboriginals eat a Thanksgiving meal, you know. That's ridiculous!*

Use of a charity model for the delivery of services and the employment of non-Aboriginal people to do the work is inconsistent with the community development principle of hiring locally, and does little for capacity building.

There is also a good deal of racism encountered by Aboriginal people seeking employment in Spence neighbourhood. One twenty-year-old, now employed, said this:

> I hang around with a lot of my friends, we work at JobWorks, that's on
> Agnes [Street], we work there. But before that we were looking for jobs
> around this neighbourhood and it was hard for us because, like, we tried
> at the Seven-Eleven, corner stores, little businesses around here, and what
> happened was everywhere we went into, like, we went to the store to buy
> something, whatever, they accused us of, like, maybe, trying to steal some-
> thing or they looked at us different, or [we] tried to apply and one time we
> went to apply at that place and we gave them our résumés and everything,
> they threw our resumes in the garbage right away, because we walked right
> back in and we seen them right in the garbage, right? So, that's why it was
> hard for us but then once we went to JobWorks there was a lot of Aboriginal
> people working there and they gave us a chance to find a place to work and
> helped us out around here a lot because there's a lot of places around here
> that didn't give us that chance.

A young woman, speaking in a separate interview, said much the same:

> I think they should come out with more stuff for youth to do, like, even
> volunteer, or, more jobs, even, for Aboriginal youth, because a lot of people
> do discriminate, and I know that, like, there is a lot of people that discrimi-
> nate… and a lot of businesses say they're not discriminating and stuff, but
> they do it, no matter what.

That this has been the case for many years is evidenced by the story related by
a man now in his sixties. He came to Winnipeg many years ago, having recently
graduated as a teacher but was unable to secure a teaching position. "Nobody
would hire an Indian teacher… they wouldn't take a chance on an Indian…
that's the kind of welcome we got. That's why we're not part of it." In short, the
exclusion from the labour market that is a function, at least in part, of racism,
is simply a part of the larger exclusion, the marginalization, that Aboriginal
people experience in Spence neighbourhood and that manifests itself in their
relative lack of participation in the SNA.

Housing and Community Development
The same process is at work in housing. Of the twenty-four Aboriginal people
interviewed, only one woman and one couple are homeowners. All the rest
are renters, in apartment blocks or rooming houses. However, when we asked
interviewees if they had ever considered buying one of the houses renovated by
the SNA, almost everyone said that they had and that they would like to stay
in the neighbourhood.

Many people observed that the housing renovation work done by the SNA

Have You Ever Considered Buying One of the Houses Renovated by the SNA?

If we could afford one, yeah. We probably would, like, I like the area.

Yeah, but I can't afford it.

Definitely, I've seen some nice houses in this area... I like it [the area]... that's what's kept me here, because I like it.

Well, I would if I had the money. It doesn't matter to me where I live, you know, it's dangerous all over the place.

I've actually asked about it... really nice, those houses.

As a matter of fact I have, I have enquired about it.... I guess you would need some [financial] stability.

is good for the neighbourhood. One man said that the work "makes it look better, that's really a good thing." A woman relayed her mother's observations: "My mom, she lives in the North End and she would come down here to visit and she would say 'these houses are really nice now, not like before, we're really improving the area.' She's impressed. Actually, so am I."

Aboriginal people are pleased about and impressed by the housing renovation work being done by the SNA. They are concerned, however, that so few of the renovated houses are being purchased by Aboriginal people from the neighbourhood despite their obvious desire to become homeowners and to stay in Spence. One woman expressed this concern and linked it to a community development strategy for Spence — one rooted in the idea that if local people, and particularly local Aboriginal people, are hired for local jobs and are given the opportunity to become local homeowners, they *will* stay in the neighbourhood and bring to it a much-needed level of stability:

> It goes along with my belief that we can change the neighbourhood, because I have a good job but I haven't moved out of the neighbourhood and I'm not planning on moving out of the neighbourhood because I want to see people get a job and stay in the neighbourhood.... I'm hoping that we can have more actual Aboriginal and local people to own these houses that are being renovated.... [If] we could have at least a few Aboriginal owners... it might somehow give people hope that one day they could aspire to owning a home.

An older man linked the relative absence of Aboriginal homeowners to the process of gentrification and displayed the commitment to the neighbourhood expressed by many of the people we interviewed:

> *If my income were better I would think of it, I would actually buy one for a family. [But what is happening now is a process of] gentrification, which I'm really totally against... because it takes good housing that could be used by the poor and it excludes them because it puts the prices out of reach... and yeah, I would buy one if I could and I would make sure that a poor family lived in it.*

At the moment, although they would like to be homeowners in Spence, few Aboriginal people are. This adds to their sense of exclusion from the neighbourhood, as does the racism encountered day to day and when trying to find local employment and the fact that relatively few local Aboriginal people are hired to fill positions in agencies providing services in the area. Aboriginal people in Spence see themselves as outsiders in a general sense, and this adds to their reluctance to become involved with the SNA.

Promoting homeownership by Aboriginal people who want to stay in Spence neighbourhood would be consistent with the principles of community development. It would counteract Aboriginal people's sense of social exclusion, and likely promote their involvement in the community.

NEIGHBOURHOOD INVOLVEMENT AND ABORIGINAL COMMUNITY DEVELOPMENT

As stated, Aboriginal people appear to be only marginally involved in the SNA — only one of the twenty-four we interviewed is actively involved. This lack of involvement is in large part a product of a more general sense of social exclusion, of being outsiders to the dominant culture.

The sense of social exclusion was palpable in the interviews. Aboriginal people living in Spence neighbourhood repeatedly told us, explicitly or otherwise, that they do not feel part of the community. This feeling is reinforced by instances of discrimination in the job market and the ensuing resentment that so many jobs in inner-city agencies serving Aboriginal people are held by non-Aboriginal people. It is reinforced by the grinding poverty of so many in the neighbourhood, who survive on a day-to-day basis. It is reinforced by the fact that so few local Aboriginal people are homeowners and by the random, daily instances of racism. Aboriginal people in Spence feel that they are different. Referring to what he believes to be the prevailing attitude at the SNA, one man said: "Aboriginal people are not involved in it and they have a different way of thinking, a different way of doing things, you know, different attitudes towards things." Because they feel different, and excluded, and in some cases lack self-esteem and self-confidence, flyers in the mailbox announcing SNA events are not enough to overcome the deeply rooted barriers to their involvement.

The origins of Aboriginal people's social exclusion are in their history, the history of colonialization. For well over a century, Canada sought to eradicate Aboriginal cultures and languages and spirituality, as described in Chapter One. Aboriginal people's lack of involvement in the SNA is thus consistent with their more general reluctance to involve themselves in institutions of the still-dominant culture.

Yet, colonization has been unsuccessful in fully extinguishing Aboriginal cultures. Aboriginal people expressed to us — as they have in other contexts (Royal Commission on Aboriginal Peoples 1993) — a keen interest in learning more about and having opportunities to experience and engage in their cultures. This desire constitutes the basis of a community development strategy that could contribute significantly to the revitalization of Spence neighbourhood and, by extension, of other urban neighbourhoods.

The promotion of Aboriginal cultures would serve to bring Aboriginal people together, to make connections with each other and thus to build a collective strength. It would offset the deleterious effects of many years of cultural denigration and would promote a deepened sense of pride and self-esteem among Aboriginal people. As one author put it, writing about cultural expression and community development in Latin America: "there is another element to development besides change. Sometimes people must first fortify their base before they sally out to change the world" (Kleymeyer 1994: 39).

A community development approach that celebrates the expression of urban Aboriginal cultures is the foundation upon which Aboriginal people will be empowered to engage with the dominant culture. Community development for Aboriginal people means taking charge of their own affairs and deciding what they want their community to look like. It is about having the right to invent their own future. This is the way that a unique culture based on the engagement of strong and healthy Aboriginal cultures with other strong and healthy cultures will be built in Winnipeg and in other Canadian communities.

This culturally based community development strategy can best be implemented, we believe, by establishing separate Aboriginal residents groups. In the case of Spence neighbourhood, such a group would operate in loose affiliation with the SNA. Aboriginal people would then be in charge of their own community development organization and could take it in the directions they choose, and they could build their skills and confidence in the process. The result would likely be a different way of promoting community development. And in the future, when a strong and vibrant Aboriginal residents group has established itself in Spence neighbourhood — and involved large numbers of

Aboriginal people, with all the advantages that brings, and promoted many new opportunities for the learning and expression of Aboriginal cultures, and begun to "invent its own future" with all the pride and sense of accomplishment that doing so would create — then the two cultures could begin to work together to create something new and exciting.

Central to this vision is the need for *non*-Aboriginal cultures and institutions to be receptive to change. Aboriginal people in Spence stressed this, expressing their frustration at the expectation that Aboriginal people should change, rather than the institutions of the dominant culture. Such receptivity on the part of the dominant culture, together with growing numbers of skilled and self-confident Aboriginal people to engage in community development are the first steps in a process that we believe will lead to greater unity in the neighbourhood. In the long run, Aboriginal people who develop the habit of community involvement are much more likely to work with other Aboriginal *and* non-Aboriginal people in pursuit of common goals. Non-Aboriginal people who appreciate Aboriginal ways of doing things are much more likely to be a part of this process.

Indeed, partly as a result of our interviews with Aboriginal people in Spence neighbourhood, an Aboriginal residents group has emerged in Spence. Inner-City Aboriginal Neighbours (I-CAN) is now a thriving Aboriginal residents group, with more than 120 registered members, an active board, a paid community coordinator and a full program of activities. Since forming in July 2003, I-CAN has staged community feasts and cultural ceremonies; co-sponsored — with the University of Winnipeg Aboriginal Students' Association — a large urban pow wow; formed a neighbourhood softball team, the Inner City Arrows; organized a day at the beach for neighbourhood children, families and individuals who otherwise would have no such opportunity; and sponsored a lecture series on Aboriginal history and an Ojibwa language class. Former board chair Joan Hay says that many more Aboriginal people in Spence neighbourhood are now acquainted, the result of their involvement with I-CAN. And I-CAN is organizing the kinds of activities that Aboriginal people in the neighbourhood say they want. "Our group wanted to start getting actively involved in the renewal and revitalization of our neighbourhood, but most simply we wanted to get together to meet each other and participate in various events and activities, such as a community feast, local university pow wow and having a fun day at the beach." I-CAN works closely with the SNA; the association, and especially Executive Director Inonge Aliaga, have been very supportive of I-CAN. But I-CAN works at arm's length from the SNA and makes its own decisions; Aboriginal people themselves decide what to do and how to do it. This is a relatively small but nevertheless significant example of urban Aboriginal community development — Aboriginal people working together in ways of their choosing and building skills and friendships, and in more abstract language, social capital, in the process.

There is no simple solution to the problems faced by inner-city neighbour-hoods like Spence. Nevertheless, based on our interviews, we believe that the conceptually simple steps of creating I-CAN, operating in loose affiliation with the SNA, to promote Aboriginal cultural initiatives and neighbourhood strengths will ensure a strong foundation for the continued revitalization of Spence neighbourhood. There is great strength in working collectively, but Aboriginal people in Spence had not done so until I-CAN was created. Bringing Aboriginal people together in I-CAN and promoting Aboriginal cultures is a first and very important step in this direction.

Chapter Three

"THE TOOLS YOU NEED TO DISCOVER WHO YOU ARE"

Aboriginal Learners in Selected Adult Learning Centres in Winnipeg

Jim Silver, Darlene Klyne and Freeman Simard

Traditionally, education has been a way out of poverty. But mainstream education has not proved to be a good fit for many Aboriginal people. The experience of the residential schools — a process intended to "take the Indian out of the child" — has been a devastating one for many Aboriginal people (see Chapter One).

The mainstream school system continues to be a negative experience for too many Aboriginal people. The system has made relatively few concessions to Aboriginal people's different cultures and worldviews. It has proved to be, for far too many Aboriginal children and youth, a foreign place, where they and their people are not respected, where Euro-dominant views of history and life are taken for granted, where Aboriginal teachers and curricula are rare, and where racism is a common experience (Silver, Mallett, Greene and Simard 2002). This, together with the fact that disproportionate numbers of Aboriginal families live with low incomes and are engaged in a daily struggle for survival in a world from which they feel socially and economically excluded, has led to disproportionate numbers of Aboriginal children and youth leaving school before completing grade twelve.

However, within the last ten years there has emerged in Manitoba an innovative system of adult education, called the adult learning centres. Here, a "mature" grade twelve diploma is offered in a non-school-like environment and in a fashion geared to the needs and life circumstances of adults. Many Aboriginal people are taking advantage of this "second chance" system; and many are graduating with their mature grade twelve diploma. These innovative, community-based initiatives are holistic and, in the best cases, culturally rooted, and are proving to be successful where the mainstream educational system was not.

This chapter is based on our study of Aboriginal learners in four adult learning centres (ALCs) in Winnipeg. The primary purpose of the study was to determine why ALCs are as successful as they are in graduating adult Aboriginal learners. To find out, we talked with Aboriginal adult learners and ALC staff. We sought to determine what the four ALCs are doing to meet the educational needs of adult Aboriginal learners and how these learners are responding to these educational strategies and initiatives. A distinctive feature of this study, like the others in this book, is that it is based for the most part on interviews with Aboriginal people — fifteen adult learners in each of the four ALCs — conducted by Aboriginal interviewers.

The four adult learning centres — Portage Learning Centre, Horizons Learning Centre, CrossRoads Learning Centre and the Urban Circle Training Centre — were selected because they are relatively small and have a significant proportion of Aboriginal learners. This is not a representative sample of ALCs in Manitoba; it does, however, represent several different types of ALCs.

ADULT LEARNING CENTRES

Adult learning centres are a relatively new phenomenon in Manitoba. They have their origins in two inter-related developments. First, in 1994, the provincial government released *Renewing Education: New Directions*, a document that set out plans for educational change. One of its commitments was to "establish community-based infrastructures for life-long learning which provide high quality education and training for all Manitobans" (Manitoba 2001: 88). At the same time, school divisions were responding to "an emerging demand for alternative programming for adults and other students who were unable to succeed in the regular classroom" (Manitoba 2001: 89). The result was the adult learning centres. By 1996/97, ALCs were offering high school credits to adult students.

ALCs appear to have emerged in a completely unplanned way. The report of a consultant commissioned in 1999 to provide some general observations about ALCs described their emergence as follows:

> There is no evidence that the ALCs developed as a result of considered policy development by the government of the day, nor that there had been a particular identification of needs to be met. Further, no policy was considered for a local, community-driven, decentralized, flexible, province- wide array of centres designed to meet multiple adult learning needs... there was no prior discussion within government as to the concept, form, or function of an adult learning centre.... Since there was no central model or concept for a centre, centres developed very much in relation to the needs of the communities they serve, and both the range of services and the modes of delivery were largely locally determined. (Ferris 2000: 3–4)

The result is entirely consistent with a community development model. Although ALCs have many things in common, each one is unique in at least some ways. Most are relatively small, are situated in inconspicuous and rather modest surroundings, and do not look like traditional schools. They are generally storefront operations, physically located in premises not originally designed to be schools. From the inside, those that we visited had a relaxed, warm and friendly atmosphere. The number of students varies from one ALC to the next. The composition of the staff varies similarly — in some cases there are only teachers, while in others there may also be a counsellor and/or a teaching assistant, and/or an office assistant; in all cases the staff is small. The teaching styles vary: some classes are run very much as they would be in a regular high school; others are unstructured and allow complete flexibility as to what courses are taken and when. In some cases, students enter at a specified time of the year and are put through testing and interviewing before being admitted; in other cases, students may begin their studies at any time of the year, and almost everyone who is interested is enrolled. Each ALC appears to have its own character.

Adult learning centres offer the mature grade twelve diploma, which differs from the regular grade twelve diploma in that it requires that adults complete eight credits, whereas the regular high school diploma requires the completion of twenty-eight credits from S1 to S4 (or what used to be grades nine to twelve). As of July 1, 2003, all ALCs are governed by the *Adult Learning Centres Act*, which among other things requires them to operate as non-profit organizations. In the 2002/03 program year, there were forty-seven ALCs in Manitoba, and as of March 2003, there were approximately 9,300 learners enrolled, of whom about one-third (32 percent) self-identified as Aboriginal. This is more than double Aboriginal people's share of the total population of Manitoba. The total number of mature grade twelve graduates in the 2001/02 program year was 851, and the budget for ALCs during the 2002/03 program year was $12.9 million (data supplied by Adult Learning and Literacy, Manitoba Advanced Education and Training, April 22, 2003). Between July 2004 and June 2005 there were eighteen ALCs in Winnipeg, with ten (operating thirteen sites) in the inner city. Spending on those inner-city sites was approximately $4.4 million; 2,851 adult learners were enrolled, of whom 1,254 were Aboriginal; and 343 learners graduated with their mature grade twelve diploma, although the proportion who were Aboriginal is not known (data provided by Adult Learning and Literacy, Manitoba Advanced Education and Training).

In what follows, we first consider the Portage, CrossRoads and Horizons learning centres, briefly describing the operations at each, then describing some common themes. We then turn to a more detailed consideration of Urban Circle Training Centre, the only one of the four ALCs that is wholly Aboriginal in its philosophy and student body.

The **Portage Learning Centre (PLC)**, established in 1995 and funded as an ALC since 2001, is located in Portage la Prairie, a city of 14,000 located an hour's drive west of Winnipeg. The physical space occupied by PLC is a relatively small and unpretentious storefront. At the time of our study, the staff of six included the director, case facilitator, two teachers, a teaching assistant, and an administrative assistant. There is a daycare centre in the basement and the Young Parents Resource Centre on the second floor, both used by some of the PLC adult learners.

There are ninety to a hundred adult learners at the PLC in any given month, and an on-going waiting list of adults wanting to enter. Approximately 55 percent of learners at the PLC are Aboriginal. We interviewed fifteen: all but three were women; they ranged in age from sixteen to forty-three; eleven had children and eight were single parents; and thirteen had less than a grade ten education prior to enrolment at PLC. Learners at each of the other ALCs had a similar profile. Between 1999/2000 to 2001/2002, the PLC graduated seventy-eight adult learners with their mature grade twelve diploma. In the absence of the PLC, it is likely that very few of these people would have completed grade twelve.

The **CrossRoads Learning Centre (CLC)** is located in cramped quarters in a strip mall at the west end of Burrows Avenue, across the street from the Gilbert Park housing project — referred to by many residents as "Jigtown" — in Winnipeg's North End. CrossRoads has a full-time director/teacher and a full-time teacher, both experienced adult educators. Three others teach one evening course each; one person works three-quarter time, splitting her day between her roles as administrative assistant and teaching assistant. At any given time, there are ninety to a hundred students registered at the CLC, many of whom live in Gilbert Park. In 2001/02, nineteen adult learners graduated with their mature grade twelve diploma; nine were Aboriginal.

The **Horizons Learning Centre (HLC)** has three sites, all in Winnipeg. We examined the operations and interviewed Aboriginal learners and staff at the **Crossways** and **Elmwood** sites. The Elmwood site is located in a nondescript industrial strip mall off Watt Street, next door to a low-income housing development. The space is plain, utilitarian and too small. The Elmwood site had ninety to a hundred students registered in 2003. During the 2001/2002 academic year, twenty students graduated with their mature grade twelve diploma. The Crossways site is located in the basement of Crossways-in-Common, the former Young United Church, now turned into a large, multi-purpose community centre that houses a chapel, a soup kitchen and drop-in centre, community organizations' offices, housing facilities and meeting spaces. There are approximately sixty students at the Crossways site, fifteen or twenty of whom are Aboriginal. In the 2001/2002 academic year, Horizons graduated twenty-eight learners with their mature grade twelve diploma, eight from the Crossways site; at least three of those eight were Aboriginal students. Structured classes are offered at scheduled times, although there is a good deal of flexibility. This is true both in terms of students coming and going and in terms of class make-up: in any given class, students are working at different levels. For example, English classes are held at specific times, and in each English class there are students working on grades ten, eleven and twelve English. Relatively little instruction is offered to the class as a whole, although there may be an occasional lesson written on the blackboard; most instruction is of the more individualized, one-on-one or small group variety. The result is structured, but with a good deal of flexibility.

Racism

Aboriginal people confront a great deal of racism, in the community and in the regular school system. At the Portage Learning Centre a young woman told us that "It's like a stereotype thing, like, natives do nothing, I get that all the time." And in the local high school, "there was three to one... white people versus native people and they always look at you and you're nothing but trash." Significantly, adult Aboriginal learners did not experience any of this racism at the ALCs we examined. At the PLC, for example, one woman said: "Here, you're your own person, they don't care what you look like... it's great, I love it — it's non-judgemental."

Many of the adult Aboriginal learners that we interviewed referred to their shyness as a very great obstacle to their success. One said: "Like me, like I'm really shy, I can't speak in front of other people, I just get all shaky." He believes that he may have a speech impediment: "the way I pronounce the words, they don't come out right... and that's probably why, too, I'm shy, like, talking, afraid to make a mistake, a word coming out wrong." However, later in the interview, it came out that the deeper problem is his low self-esteem, which has been aggravated by instances of racism.

> When I was going to school in Thompson, eh, there was a lot of racism, well, I didn't know anybody, like I'd be alone, the first day, there was nobody else coming from my community, so I didn't have nobody... these guys, where the lockers were... they were just calling me down and I didn't know what to say, I just stood there.... I didn't want to say nothing because I didn't want to fight or anything so I just, like, kind of, like, put away my books and I just left and didn't look back or anything, or respond to them. Sometimes I think about that all the time too, why couldn't I have said something, just stood up for myself and, but I didn't want to get into trouble.

He has borne this and other pain all his life. "As a youth I went through a lot of abuse, alcohol, family violence and, like, I'm really shy and a keep-to-myself person." He still faces racism now that he is in Winnipeg, and he says: "I don't know how to deal with that, I just avoid it and run away from it.... Sometimes I would like to speak out and say something but, uh, I'm afraid what the result would be, get into a fight or something." Yet about Horizons Learning Centre, he says: it "feels safe here, I feel comfortable... nobody judging anybody, there's no racism at all... everybody seems to be friendly and the teachers are great, they help a lot."

Others at Horizons and at the other ALCs have described similarly pain-filled lives. They are in part the product of colonization and its internalization: the erosion of self-esteem and severe identity confusion are among its conse-quences. Aboriginal students come to an ALC feeling "a little bit apprehensive" about educational institutions, and it takes a while to earn their trust: they "don't trust teachers, don't trust school," said one of the teachers. Only the highly personalized, friendly, non-judgmental and holistic approach that characterizes the ALCs works.

At CrossRoads, many students mentioned racism when they described previous school experiences. Some spoke with bitterness about it, and clearly it had caused them a great deal of pain. Others, however — and this seems particularly to be the case for the men — mention racism in their previous school experiences in an almost casual way, as if to say "well, there's lots of racism but we all know about that so there's no need to say much more." They communicated this to interviewers who are themselves Aboriginal. It seems that racism in schools and in their daily lives is so pervasive that they simply take it for granted. For example, a thirty-five-year-old learner describing his previous high school experience told us that: "some of the things I didn't like was... racism, which everybody knows about, but other than that there was not too much that I didn't mind." At the ALCs we examined, however, everyone is treated respectfully and equally. One young man at Crossroads said: "teachers are excellent here, they're very respectful... they treat all of us equally... they let me know of the potential they see in me and the ability that I have... they definitely make me feel that I can do it." And a young woman added: "The teach-ers, they're wonderful, like, they're understanding... I just don't feel ashamed here."

A Learner-Centred and Holistic Philosophy

The ALCs have adopted a learner-centred and holistic philosophy, and it is put in practice by teachers who are remarkably dedicated. When asked why people stay and succeed at PLC, the director said, "we're very forgiving." The PLC is not concerned with a person's past; everyone who applies and meets the minimum academic standards is given an opportunity. It may not work for an adult learner the first, or second or even third time, but PLC continues to work with the stu-dent, and explicitly seeks to ensure that even when the student leaves, he or she does so on good terms and is fully aware that the door is open for a subsequent attempt. The case facilitator says: "We do not judge the reasons people leave."

Staff consistently exceed what might be considered "normal" job expectations. Common examples include driving adult students to class when a test is scheduled, assisting them when they have personal problems outside school, continuing to work with students who are in jail, and accompanying those who are too shy to meet with their children's teachers. As the case facilitator observed: "When you show people that you care… they don't forget that kind of thing." Students confirmed in interviews how very helpful and supportive they find staff. As one thirty-six-year-old woman put it: "If you don't have a ride, one of them will come and pick you up.… I've never encountered anything like this before so it's been very good." The same is true at each of the ALCs. At HLC, for example, a woman told us: "I really like the teachers… they don't make themselves seem like they're at a higher level than us in any way… and that's really what I like, because I don't like it if somebody acts like they're better than me or make more money and they show it, or whatever."

The philosophy is holistic, in that learners are regarded not just as students but as people with lives outside the classroom, many of which are fraught with difficulties. The adult Aboriginal learners in particular have experienced great hardship in their lives, and many are carrying the pain with them. The case facilitator at PLC spends a great deal of one-on-one time with students, and says it is "real tough looking at personal issues… a lot of our students carry a lot of wounds." This is the case at each of the ALCs that we studied. Relating to adult learners as people with lives outside the classroom is consistent with the holistic approach which, we believe, is an essential component of success in ALCs and in Aboriginal community development more generally.

At the Elmwood site of HLC, the two teachers are graduates of the Winnipeg Education Centre (WEC), which offers university-level, inner-city programs in education and social work. Their enthusiasm for their work is unmistakable. There is a "certain sort of passion in adult education," said one, adding that "nobody's here at 9 a.m. and gone at 4 p.m., that doesn't happen." The other, who estimated that she had put in forty to fifty unpaid hours in the month before we visited HLC and who stated the obvious — "I care deeply about what I do" — reiterated the importance of their WEC roots: "A lot of our best practice came from an understanding of what it is to be adult learners." She observed that for some of their students, this may well be the first time someone in a position of authority has reached out a hand to them and said they care; adult learners will say to her, "that's the first time anyone's said that to me." Like the other ALCs, the organizational structure at HLC is flat, non-hierarchical, intimate and personalized.

Much of the very considerable success of the ALCs is attributable to the energy and passion of their staff, and to their determination to run organizations characterized by a non-hierarchical structure, a commitment to equality and human dignity, and a belief in the potential that lies within each of us.

Aboriginal Cultures

Although adult Aboriginal learners feel comfortable at the ALCs we investigated, many told us that they would like to learn still more about their cultures. For example, a twenty-two-year-old woman at PLC told us: "I don't know my culture.... I'd like to learn." A young man at CrossRoads said: "more cultural awareness… youth today, they don't have an idea of their native background, like me, I've grown up not knowing about pow wows or traditional stuff like that, all my life growing up I haven't seen a pow wow." Colonization has had devastating effects on Aboriginal people's culture. As the (non-Aboriginal) case facilitator at PLC put it: "There's such an identity crisis with so many of our students," having to do with the loss of their cultures. At CrossRoads, one of the teachers, herself Aboriginal, argued that many urban Aboriginal youth "have no idea of their roots… they don't know who they are." She added: "It really saddens me, you are not Aboriginal anymore." The director, who is not Aboriginal, said the same: "They really don't know who they are"; it's a "cultural identity crisis." A Native Studies course is offered, but it is "really quite difficult because when you try to talk about ceremonies… they have no clue."

And it is worse than that. When an elder was brought in last year, "they were really afraid," said the director. Sporadic attempts to hold sharing circles have been met with suspicion by some of the Aboriginal students. This is a product, at least in part, of the long struggle between Christianity and traditional Aboriginal spiritual beliefs. A conscious attempt was made by the Government of Canada and by the Christian churches to eliminate Aboriginal spirituality (Siggins 2005). One of the young men at CrossRoads expressed a strong desire to know more about his culture — "I think it's really important, you gotta know… what Native people went through" — but his wife considers it "to be witchcraft." This is part of the "cultural identity crisis" that causes so much suffering for so many Aboriginal people. The staff at CrossRoads are proceeding with caution as they introduce Aboriginal cultural content, because they quite rightly believe that it is important to be respectful of people's beliefs.

Nevertheless, many, although admittedly not all, of the Aboriginal students at the four ALCs are curious about their cultures and in some cases are hungry to learn more. Some would come to regular sharing circles and would attend sweats and engage in smudging. Some would not, and this, of course, is their choice. But for those who did, we believe that the benefits would be great and would warrant the considerable difficulties that would arise for staff attempting to navigate these cultural contradictions. Aboriginal students have a right to learn about their cultures and about attempts to eliminate them, and to come to terms with who they are as a people and how they came to be where they are today. The benefits of gaining this knowledge are considerable and include a greater sense of personal and collective identity, and thus a stronger personal and collective foundation upon which to build academic and other success.

Transformational Learning

ALCs are making a significant difference in the lives of many Aboriginal adults. A particularly good example is three Aboriginal men in their early- to mid-twenties who we interviewed at CrossRoads. All three have had very difficult lives, including having been in considerable trouble with the law, but all are now in the process of turning their lives around. And CrossRoads Learning Centre is a central part of their personal transformations. One twenty-four-year-old told us that CrossRoads was there for him "at a time in my life when I decided to get back into school." Regular high school is not an option in such cases. A twenty-six-year-old man told us of his rough earlier life, and then added: "There's nothing that could stop me now." A twenty-two-year-old who had some particularly difficult times said that his high school experience was: "not too positive, I really don't like talking about that." The pain in his voice was tangible. He told us he was "caught up in a lot of stuff in my past, eh? Kind of changed my life around for my family... my two kids, my wife... school's really helped me out, helped me out lots, changing my outlook on life and how I used to be... it's helped me out with my family and stuff... feels good from the life style, the way I used to live." The young man expressed both determination and regret: "It's all on yourself, if you want to learn, or if you don't want to learn, sometimes people, it's not their time to go to school, they just don't want to go to school, like me when I was younger, I didn't want to go to school, now I want to go to school, I'm kicking myself in the ass, I should have went to school when I was younger."

These are remarkable personal transformations, about which several things are notable. First, these young men are motivated to improve their education. They have a sense of purpose. It is not fully clear to us what prompted their decision to make changes in their lives, but two motivating factors were advanced by the men themselves. One was their shared desire to make a different and better life for their families. Many adult learners, including these particular men, told us this. Said one: "It's my kids, mostly, my kids, my wife, really good support... my family too, my mother, my father support me lots too." Another added: "It really hurts me when I look at my kids... they need something better. I'm not going to make their lives miserable because I had a shitty life."

The other impetus, in the case of at least one of them, was the advice of an elder who counseled him while he was incarcerated and who introduced him to his own culture through sharing circles and sweats. "He's the one who got me out of where I was in, helped me to straighten out my life and look out for my kids... so I guess my elder was the biggest thing helping me out." We think it is important to emphasize that at the point that these young men decided to make a break with the past and change their lives, CrossRoads was there for them. Without CrossRoads, or another ALC, they would have been much less likely to attempt the personal transformations that they appear to be making. Adult learners must be motivated; for those who are, the ALCs are an essential part of their transformation.

URBAN CIRCLE TRAINING CENTRE

The **Urban Circle Training Centre (UCTC)** is now in its fifteenth year of operations. It started out as a program to help Aboriginal women who had been volunteering in a clothing depot prepare for jobs in the retail sector. It has grown and evolved considerably since then. At the time we did our interviews, the UCTC had moved from the heart of the North End and was located in a retail strip mall on McPhillips Street in north Winnipeg. The space included four large classrooms plus a large computer room and numerous staff offices. Since then, the UCTC has relocated to 519 Selkirk Avenue, where they have renovated the building to meet their needs and to reflect in its architecture the Aboriginal themes that characterize Urban Circle's educational approach. Urban Circle now runs a mature grade twelve diploma program, plus four additional job-specific training programs.

The UCTC's mature grade twelve diploma program is different in several important respects from the programs at the other ALCs. All the adult learners are Aboriginal, and only a limited number — usually twenty-four — are admitted each September. The intake process is rigorous: applicants must submit letters indicating why they want to be in the program, records of their previous educational achievement and letters of reference; they are tested for reading comprehension; they are interviewed; and they are asked to take part in a sharing circle with other applicants. As the UCTC co-director told us, the intake and admission processes are intended to provide an opportunity for applicants to consider whether the Urban Circle approach is the right one for them. Those admitted must have completed two high school credits; during the ten-month program they are required to complete six additional credits.

At Urban Circle, all adult learners are Aboriginal and the majority of the instructors and staff are Aboriginal. Programs are delivered, as the UCTC promotional brochure states, in "a culturally appropriate context," which includes "utilizing the philosophy of the Medicine Wheel."

We interviewed fifteen adult Aboriginal learners at Urban Circle: thirteen women and two men. They ranged in age from twenty to fifty-one years; the median age was thirty-five years. All of them have children: nine of the fifteen have more than one child; eight are single mothers; seven live with a spouse or partner. Prior to Urban Circle, eight of the fifteen adult learners interviewed

Thank goodness for this program, there was a time [she pauses, and cries], there was a time when I just thought there was nothing out there, nobody has an understanding, no help... I don't know... just like you want to give up, nobody wants to help, you know, I kept on searching where to go, what to do, I guess after all that searching I just found this place, yeah, the doors opened as soon as I came in.

Before I came here I was a quiet person, I wasn't very talkative, like I was a shy person, I guess an angry person also. I was living in a blaming life, I blamed everybody, I didn't understand why people were so cruel and I was ashamed of being Aboriginal because of seeing our own people on Main Street being sniffers... drunk, I was really ashamed of being Aboriginal, and I guess you could say Urban Circle opened my eyes to see the truth and to know the truth. That's what the Centre did for me.

Well, spiritually, I didn't know who I was and... I was kind of lost, out there, and when I came here, I found myself, like, searching, I was lost, but I found myself, I was wandering around, looking for something I couldn't find, but when I came here.... I really know where I'm going to now, because I was lost before but now I found myself.

I was working, and there was just a part of me that was empty, looking for something and not knowing what it was... not feeling wanted.... This is the place to come and search for what you're looking for, where you're coming from and stuff, and where you want to go, and a lot of people can't do that because they don't know who they are or where they've come from.... If you don't know what you're looking for, you just go out and try to fill that hole with something.

A long time ago I wouldn't actually say I'm an Indian.... I'd say, oh yeah, I'm Métis, like it was nothing to me, and now I find that I'm more proud, like you feel proud to be native, here, going here, you really feel proud.

I quit smoking pot... before I started school [Urban Circle] it was like every day, all day long.... What I was doing in high school was getting high and failing. But now, I wouldn't mind being a Native awareness teacher... to teach the younger generation about colonization and all that stuff just to let them know before they start drinking and getting high and everything else. It sounds weird but I want to be an Indian, like, my culture, I want to know it all.

It's really emotional for me, I was never given a chance. I knew right from kindergarten I was different. Everybody was up there and I was down here.... I always wanted to do this and when I came here it was like I found something, they gave me this hope that I could do it.... I got my Indian name and went to a sweat and a part of me got healed.... They help me a lot.

I swear my life's changed, for the better.... I'm getting over my shyness, a lot, a lot from here, because before I was like, I was severely shy, I'm super shy, and now it's like they're just people too.... I've gotten over my shyness to a point.... Confidence, a lot of confidence, you have to have a lot of confidence in yourself to succeed.... I had really low self-esteem for the longest time.

It has helped me a lot.... I don't put up a mask like I used to. I'm very shy but I've come a long ways.

When I started here, I was this little, like, a clam-shell, peeking once in a while, you know.

You're here to learn about yourself... it helps you come out of your shell.

I'm still shy a little bit.... It's helping me to speak up more, and not to shy away from something... because usually when that would happen to me I'd just walk away from the problem and I couldn't face it, I'd just hide my feelings.

Even the look, just going to apply for a job... the look that they gave me, that always made me scared and then not go back, and I think a lot of times people don't know that, but, you gotta fight back, you gotta look people in the eye and basically say no, you're not going to take this away from me because this is what I want.

had completed grade eight or nine; three had completed grade ten; and three had completed grade eleven.

Those attending Urban Circle go through what seems to us a truly remarkable personal transformation. Lives of pain and despair become lives of hope and pride. That was made apparent to us over and over during the interviews.

The pain carried by so many Aboriginal people is evident in their comments. It is often expressed, as observed earlier, as shyness and reflects the low levels of self-esteem among many Aboriginal people — a product of colonization and its internalization. That is the case for the adult learners at Urban Circle as well. But the Urban Circle program helps adult learners to overcome that shyness and to build their confidence, pride and self-esteem.

The experience at Urban Circle is, for many adult learners, different from and better than their previous school experiences. But their quality of life doesn't improve overnight. Many continue to struggle in their personal lives: gangs, alcohol, drug abuse. "I've been through it all," one woman told us. Poverty, racism, inadequate housing, the difficulties of being lone parents, the fear that many in the inner city feel because of the growing levels of gang- and drug-related

I've been through, oh, how would you say, through racism, and that's what really hurts me... going to a public school... that really hurts when you're called down. I learned how to shut them out, but inside, I was really, really hurting.... Here, you're not called down, you know... you're equal.

In high school I wasn't comfortable.... The way they looked at me like I was a different human being from another planet, that's the way I felt.... People were so cruel.

Well, I don't think there's anything good I liked about [a Winnipeg inner-city high school].... I wasn't comfortable.

You could just tell all the racism was there.... I just didn't like the way other people treated me.

The negative messages that were given in school, not only from the teachers but also from mainstream society itself, my peers, you know, I was a "dirty little Indian," and you know Indians don't amount to very much and that's the messages that I carried throughout my life and coming to Urban Circle they're helping me to rewrite those messages. I'm starting to find myself.... I know what I wanted to do but all the negative messages I received in the school system — I let them hold me back and it's just so different here, they help you, they give you the tools you need to discover who you are and what you want to do in life.

violence — all of these problems make life in Winnipeg's inner city difficult for many residents. And staff at Urban Circle say that in many ways the situation is getting worse. One teacher said that they now deal with "a lot of gang issues," which find their way into the classroom in various ways. "The issues are so great, and they seem to be getting greater," said another, which is precisely why the holistic approach used by Urban Circle and the other ALCs is so appropriate.

Yet despite these difficult conditions, the adult Aboriginal learners at Urban Circle are transforming their lives. How does this happen? We think that there are at least three things that are distinctive about the Urban Circle program: the life skills component in the first month of the program; the infusion into the program of Aboriginal cultural awareness; and the constant focus on job preparedness.

Life Skills

Every program at Urban Circle begins with a life skills component that continues one day per week thereafter, and each program has a life skills coach. The life skills component is structured as a course for credit and is a central part of the educational experience at Urban Circle. The life skills focus is unique in that it

I'm really struggling… paying rent and paying phone, getting groceries and he's not doing anything, and we're fighting and he's saying "well, why don't you work instead of going to school."

On the way coming from home to school on my bus ride… "oh, my hydro bill, what am I gonna do, my phone bill," you know.

is specifically tailored to meet the needs of Aboriginal people who have experienced the adverse effects of colonization. Students learn about themselves, in an introspective fashion, and then locate their personal situation in the context of colonization. They work through these revelations to develop the skills to deal with life in the dominant culture as an Aboriginal person who feels comfortable with her/himself. The pain that so many Aboriginal people carry is acknowledged, talked about and identified as a consequence of colonization. It is neither a blaming nor a shaming process. Rather, it is a healing and learning process, and it provides adult learners with the self-awareness and the self-esteem that they need to navigate their way through the dominant culture.

The life skills component, like everything at Urban Circle, is based on the holistic character of the Medicine Wheel. The Medicine Wheel has four quadrants: physical, mental, emotional and spiritual. Urban Circle stresses that all four are important. They deal with adult learners holistically, as complete people, aware that learners cannot grasp math if they are not empowered to cope with the pain they carry inside themselves. Part of this has to do with the remarkable level of commitment of the staff, who phone, talk to and counsel their learners. But also, the life skills component teaches adult learners how to cope for themselves. They learn creative problem-solving, effective communication, conflict resolution, stress, anger and time management, organizational skills and how to build self-esteem. They use sharing circles — talking with each other about their lives in a collective setting. This bonds them to each other.

In the life skills course there is what is called a "shield week." Learners create a shield — a pictorial/symbolic representation of their life story, with photos and other mementos signifying important parts of their life journey to date. Then each learner tells her/his life story to the group — as much or as little as each person chooses to share. Again, once learners have shared their lives in this way, opened up and told their stories and revealed their pain to others, there is a tight bonding that occurs. A group is built. Group support is developed. Many graduates of Urban Circle become life-long friends.

All of this is done in the context of decolonization. Built into the life skills course is a focus on the bigger reality of which each learner is, to a greater or

The shield had a big impact on me because I was able to be an adult and I was able to forgive those people the harmful things they did to me and when I learned about residential schools I guess that opened up the reasons why our people are the way they are in today's society.... So I'm not ashamed... of being Aboriginal.... Life skills and the sharing circles really opened me up, I was able to talk for myself, and I really enjoyed the sharing circle because you know you have that trust in the circle, this group, your fellow students and you can talk to them about anything, they're there to listen, so I think that sharing circle, it does really help.

With the life skills and the shield I've learned that with my pressures and everyday problems that there are people out there with the same situations and they are still trying to thrive and succeed.... Sometimes I would get down and think I was alone but I'm not alone, there are other people out there, and here at Urban Circle we are able to help each other and learn from each other in situations like that.

When we did the shield I was really scared, not scared, but shy, and I was nervous and I didn't know what to do but everybody... welcomed me... and I felt comfortable. I never had that experience before, to talk about myself in front of a whole class... all the hardships that I had from my earlier life... and it made me talk about the situations that I didn't want to talk about.... I felt relieved... when I did my shield, and to talk about my personal stuff too.

When we did our shields, it like opened the door.

lesser extent, a product. "Where we're at is the result of something greater than us as individuals," says co-director Ruth Murdoch, who developed this approach. Murdoch is referring to colonization — the deliberate attempt to strip Aboriginal people of their language, culture and spirituality, indeed, to strip them of their identity and sense of self-esteem. The life skills coach works through this revelation, and all the pain and anger, to develop the life skills to move "beyond being a victim to being a warrior." But this transformation is a process, a function of the Urban Circle approach in its totality. Simply describing what happened to Aboriginal people is not enough. For example, one of the instructors was a student of Native Studies at the University of Manitoba, but that form of learning did not have the same effect. "I could write down all the facts and it never affected me... until I came here and became part of the sharing circle and 'yeah, that's what happened to my family.'"

Part of the life skills course is immediately practical — anger management, conflict resolution and communications skills, for example. And part is deeper,

The life-skills component they have here is unbelievable. You get a sense of who you are, it helps you identify who you are… and enables you… to release some of the stuff that you've been carrying so long…. This program is so powerful, it's exactly what I've been looking for and I'd recommend it to other women, not only other women, other men.

intended to rebuild, piece by piece, the battered self-esteem and self-confidence of a people who have endured colonization and who have carried the resulting pain inside themselves for years. This is the metamorphosis that happens at Urban Circle, the truly remarkable process of personal transformation that learners here go through as they reclaim their identity as Aboriginal people, and as they then learn the skills to flourish in the dominant culture. This is the two-fold character of the life-skills course. It becomes the *foundation* upon which the process of learning math and English can take place.

The life skills coach for the Academic Education and Employment Program is herself a graduate of Urban Circle, and thus has experience from both sides. She says that when she first came to Urban Circle as an adult learner, "I just wanted to… get a job, get off assistance and become independent… but I got a lot more than an education and training. I learned about myself." She adds:

> It's the hardest thing I ever did but the best thing I ever did… it really gave me my identity after searching for years, never feeling I belonged anywhere. But now, I don't have to try to fit into the mainstream, I can be me.

And the skills learned — practical and emotional — are directly transferable to workplace and family. "Everything I learned here was transferable, when I left here I grew in every area," she says. A co-director confirms that this is the intent. "There's a skill set that they need to leave this environment," she says, and the purpose here is "to give them all the tools to facilitate their journey." In the case of the life skills instructor, the greatest benefit of the life skills learned at Urban Circle has been on her family and her four children. She became a better parent. That is "the greatest impact of my entire life. That has been my measurement of my own growth."

The approach taken at Urban Circle is holistic, starting with introspection and then situating each adult learner's personal situation in the context of an historical process that has affected Aboriginal people collectively. And everything about Urban Circle — the shield, the sharing circles, the common backgrounds, the life skills course — creates a sense of being part of a group. "We're not just a classroom, we're a group…. We're a very different kind of school…. I feel like

This way we can support ourselves as a group or mini-family to get ourselves through the week.... It's like we're a bunch of brothers and sisters when we come here.

It's like a family.

I think of them as family.

We all care for each other too, you know, like if someone's missing for two days, well, we better, where is she or where is he, you know, what's happening with her?... We don't want to leave anybody behind, we all started together, we should finish together, you know, keep this group going.

The people are great, it's just like having your own little family here.

As a group we work together and it's like a sense of belonging... every day it's, like, coming here as a family.

this is my family," says one of the instructors. And this sense of belonging is felt by all of the learners and is part of the strength of Urban Circle.

Another way in which this collectivity is achieved is through "clearing space," which can happen each morning, for ten to fifteen minutes, as opposed to the weekly sharing circles. As to the clearing space:

> It's like a buddy system, like you're comfortable with that person and you come here and you discuss your problems so that you don't have to bring it all day with you, so you try to get it off your chest, and you do that every morning, and that really helps because sometimes you come to school and you're upset about something and you're stressed and just talking to some-body helps a lot.

Related to this is the enduring support system provided to Urban Circle learners, made possible by the energy and dedication of the staff. Urban Circle is successful, says a co-director, "because of the passion of people who work here." A teacher concurs: "The staff is very dedicated to the program. For example, the participants are given unconditional, twenty-four-hour support during and long after program completion." The value of that support is reflected, as it is at the other adult learning centres being considered here, in the comments made by adult learners.

There's a big support system here.... They won't give up on you. If you want to quit they won't give up on you, they'll be right there knocking at your door and that is the reason why Aboriginal people are here.

When you feel like quitting, like giving up, they're there for you. We call [the life-skills coach] the sheriff.... She'll come at your door, you know, not in a mean way, you know (laughter)... but she'll come there to encourage you, "come on back," you know.

They're very supportive about everything.... It makes me feel so good knowing we have the support of the instructors here.... This is a challenge for me because I've been out of school for such a long time and I find that the supports here are tremendous.

ABORIGINAL CULTURE

The second distinctive feature of Urban Circle is that Aboriginal culture infuses all aspects of the program. The sharing circle is used regularly. Morning smudges are practised, along with a prayer to the Creator. As noted, all the students are Aboriginal and the majority of the staff are Aboriginal. The philosophy is based on the Medicine Wheel. "For students, it comes alive for them when they see the Medicine Wheel," says a co-director. "The wheel is so multi-dimensional... it compels us to be continually looking at where we are." And it compels a holistic approach.

The Native Studies course is distinctive in that it begins with the self — lessons are related to the learners' personal experiences. While the course outline says: "The seminars have been developed for those who seek more information about decolonization of our Aboriginal/First Nations people," the outline adds:

Aboriginal/First Nations adult learners require the knowledge to explain to the individual members of a community who they are, who their people are, and how they relate to other nations. They need to articulate how our history relates to their personal self-esteem and identity today and to the reclaiming [of] their cultural identity.... The goal of the course will be met when the student can educate the general public about the pain and oppression First Nations/Aboriginal people endured (physical, emotional, spiritual and mental) and have survived as a result of the colonizers.

Other courses have been modified to be culturally appropriate. The Career Exploration course examines workplace culture and ethics, racism and discrimination in the workplace, non-violent intervention, human rights — all important themes for everyone, but tailored and crafted to meet the specific needs of Aboriginal adult learners. And the courses interconnect and overlap in a way consistent with the Medicine Wheel philosophy. The teaching strategy is experiential, designed to get students into the community, into workplaces and post-secondary institutions, to have them develop their interviewing skills as well as their conflict resolution skills. It is "a model of living life that is different from our Western approach," says a co-director. "It's about the empowerment of a nation."

Job-Preparedness

Urban Circle staff see the adult learners' experience as only the beginning. The program is geared to learners making the transition from education to paid employment. Indeed, the Urban Circle mature grade twelve diploma program is referred to as their "Academic Education and Employment Program." Their literature states the program "includes academic upgrading for a Mature Grade Twelve Diploma," and adds: "*It also includes job preparation skills, a 6-week work placement and employment at the end of the program*" (emphasis in original).

Job preparedness is built into every program offered at Urban Circle. In courses like Skills for Success and Academic Writing and Career Exploration, students are taken to post-secondary education institutions and to jobsites. Speakers are brought in to share their insights and encourage students to feel they are part of a network. Students are required to do three informational interviews with employers and/or post-secondary institutions, which helps them build face-to-face skills and confidence and exposes them to opportunities. They also do a work placement. "The possibilities are endless in terms of work placement," says a teacher. This too develops work skills and confidence, provides exposure to workplace cultural norms and expectations (thus building on the life skills course), and adds to job networking possibilities. With respect to the latter, American author William Julius Wilson argues that inner-city unemployment among African-American youth is partly due to their not being part of personal networks, whereby they would learn of jobs by word of mouth (Wilson 1987; Harrison and Weiss 1998). Urban Circle learners also do an interview skills component in which interviews are videotaped and reviewed, and employers are brought in to provide feedback.

Job preparedness is also built into the Health Care Aide/Unit Clerk programs — job-specific training programs that are separate from the mature grade twelve program. The life skills course occupies the first four weeks and one day per week thereafter; and job placements are arranged in the city's major hospital, the Health Sciences Centre, or personal care homes. Crucially important is the fact that the employers have been involved with Urban Circle in the form of a partnership in developing these job-specific courses from the beginning. Such partnerships are "fundamental to our success," says the co-director (see also Loewen, Silver et al. 2005). Urban Circle links with the employer, arranges job placements for adult learners, works with the Health Sciences Centre staff to help them to become more culturally sensitive to Aboriginal employees and does cross-cultural training workshops "for our students to feel accepted there." Graduation from this program is "almost a guarantee that they'll get a job," says an instructor in the program, and it is a good job, at close to $14 per hour, which means that "it's worthwhile, not training for a minimum wage job, it's enough that families can get off social assistance." In the Health Care Aide program, twenty-one of twenty-four adult learners graduated in 2002, and all twenty-one are employed, at good wages. According to a UCTC instructor, twenty-one of the twenty-four had been on social assistance prior to attending Urban Circle.

From the first day Urban Circle prepares students for employment. "It's about economic empowerment," says the co-director. "Students come here wanting to get off social assistance, to get off the dependency of that horrible cycle of poverty. That is the prime motivator." And it works.

DIAMONDS IN THE ROUGH: WHAT MAKES ADULT LEARNING CENTRES SO EFFECTIVE?

On entering one of the ALCs that we investigated, visitors are unfailingly struck by the friendly, informal and respectful atmosphere that prevails, and by the remarkable energy, warmth and dedication of the staff. They exhibit a passion for adult education, a commitment to equality and human dignity, a belief in the human potential in each of us. It is impossible not to be impressed by the work being done in these unpretentious and highly effective learning centres. We agree with Peter Ferris, who, in a study done in late 1999–2000, expressed his respect and admiration for the "commitment and dedication" of the adult educators he met over a four-week period, and who said: "I could not disguise my enthusiasm for what is taking place. Adult Learning Centres are, I believe, the most innovative and progressive responses to a huge need for a range of adult education delivery that I have experienced" (Ferris 2000: 1). This enthusiasm for the work of the ALCs was reflected in our interviews with Aboriginal adult learners, a large proportion of whom are unqualifiedly positive about their experiences and about the staff.

Our second observation is that, as mentioned previously, a very large proportion of the adult learners that we interviewed carry with them a great deal of pain. Most have had hard lives; a great many suffer from lack of self-esteem. A large proportion of them faced racism in their previous school experiences, which in some cases has scarred them deeply. The roots of this damage are to be found in the impact upon Aboriginal people of colonization and the internalization by many Aboriginal people of the racist belief system that lies at the heart of colonialism. The consequences for education are clear:

Aboriginal people start to believe that we are incapable of learning and that the colonizers' degrading images and beliefs about Aboriginal people and our ways of being are true. (Hart 2002: 27)

This echoes the argument advanced by Brazilian adult educator Paulo Freire (1970: 49):

self-depreciation is another characteristic of the oppressed which derives from their internalization of the opinion the oppressors hold of them. So often do they hear that they are good for nothing, know nothing, and are incapable of learning anything — sick, lazy, and unproductive — that in the end, they become convinced of their own unfitness.

It is clear from our interviews that many adult Aboriginal learners suffer in this way. Beneath their extreme shyness lies the lack of self-esteem and self-confidence that comes from a lifetime of internalizing a colonized consciousness. The damage done to Aboriginal people by this process, and the pain that they carry because of it, make essential the warm and friendly environment that characterizes, and the respectful and egalitarian staff who work at, the ALCs that we investigated. It is particularly significant, given their countless references to racism and the negative baggage carried from previous educational experiences, that of the sixty Aboriginal adult learners who were interviewed, not a single one said that she or he had experienced racism at an ALC, and most remarked on the friendly, helpful, respectful atmosphere and staff. We are of the opinion that this is the single, most significant explanatory variable for the very considerable success of ALCs.

This view is confirmed by others, who are quite clear on the importance for adult learners, including Aboriginal adult learners, of a warm, friendly, informal and respectful environment and staff, and a non-hierarchical structure. For example, a recent survey of Aboriginal literacy programs in Canada concluded that:

It is doubtful that there is a more important consideration in sustaining an Aboriginal literacy program than the provision of a safe and welcoming environment where learning can take root and grow. (Sabourin and Globensky 1998: 239)

These authors also remarked upon "the dedication and commitment that practitioners have brought to their Aboriginal literacy program initiatives," calling them and their programs "diamonds in the rough, labouring... above and beyond the call of duty... to serve the needs and aspirations of learners" (Sabourin and Globensky 1998: 8; see also Martin 1993: 170–72). All of this is true of those adult learning centres that we investigated.

Another essential part of their success is the holistic approach taken by the ALCs that we investigated. By holistic we mean that Aboriginal adult learners cannot be treated simply as students but rather as whole people: as people whose often difficult lives outside the classroom and whose low self-esteem and lack of self-confidence are every bit as important to their prospects for completing grade twelve as their facility with math or English. This requires that instructors in ALCs be much more than "just" teachers: they are, thus, counsellors and confidants and encouragers; they are people in positions of authority who are respectful and egalitarian; they are friends who provide rides when needed, who visit when learners are absent, who help out with child care arrangements, and who respond supportively and non-judgementally to myriad real-life needs. These activities and attributes are as important as teaching — one without the other would not work for most adult Aboriginal learners. The ALC and its staff must deal, and in those ALCs that we investigated do deal, with the whole person. Focusing on the whole person is an approach to adult education, and to life, that is found in the traditional Aboriginal concept of the Medicine Wheel, which requires consideration of people's mental, physical, emotional and spiritual needs.

Support for this holistic approach and for the Medicine Wheel can also be found in other adult and Aboriginal education programs. The previously cited study of Aboriginal literacy programs concluded that:

> All Aboriginal cultures firmly believe in the power of "wholeness" and know the importance of maintaining balance within self and harmony with all things within the Creation. In order to achieve "wholeness," the four aspects of self which include the spirit, heart, mind, and body must be aligned, and the task of balancing these energies, both internal and external, is a continuous process. (Sabourin and Globensky 1998: 252; see also Graveline 1998)

Aboriginal adult educators Diane Hill and Priscilla George make the same argument. Speaking about Aboriginal literacy programs, George makes the simple but powerful observation that "literacy programs mean much more than just learning to read and write" (George 1997). Hill (1999: 12–13) argues that, given the effects of colonization on Aboriginal people, a holistic approach to adult learning is essential:

> Reversing the generational damage done to the psycho-social development of Aboriginal individuals, families, communities, and nations must begin with a more holistic model of education. In using holistic processes of learning and teaching, Aboriginal learners can be helped to explore the negative attitudes they direct against themselves, others, the educational system, and against Western culture as a whole.

All of the ALCs that we investigated use a holistic approach, and we consider this to be an essential ingredient in their success.

Also, there is a good deal of evidence supporting the view that successful adult education strategies are rooted in the experiences of learners and in the learners' culture. Brookfield (1995: 4), for example, argues that: "The belief that adult teaching should be grounded in adults' experiences, and that these experiences represent a valuable resource, is currently cited as crucial by adult educators of every conceivable ideological hue." Imel (1996: 4) adds: "Because work with adult learners begins by respecting their culture, their knowledge, and their experiences, adult literacy educators must seek to understand learners' individual and community contexts.... Only by understanding the experiences and communities of the adults they wish to serve can adult literacy educators develop viable programs." Aboriginal adult educators have made the same case. A director of an Aboriginal literacy program says: "Learning has to relate to experience, and experience relates to and reflects culture. You cannot learn unless you rely on the experiences and culture of the participant. That is why learning about and retaining our culture is such an important part of our programming" (Sabourin and Globensky, 1998: 243).

Authors like Diane Hill and Priscilla George have developed an approach to Aboriginal adult education that responds to the debilitating effects of internalizing colonialism by rooting the education of Aboriginal adults in their experiences as Aboriginal people and in seeking to replace their colonized culture with a decolonized culture.

Diane Hill works out of the First Nations Technical Institute (FNTI), located in the Tyendinaga Mohawk Territory near Deseronto, Ontario, and run by the Mohawks of the Bay of Quinte. Her starting point in developing an indigenous approach to the education of Aboriginal adults is to identify and acknowledge the damage done to Aboriginal people's culture and worldview by the process of colonization. Colonization:

> required a concerted attack on the ontology, on the basic cultural patterning of the children and on their world view. They had to be taught to see and understand the world as a European place within which only European values and beliefs had meaning: thus the wisdom of their cultures would seem to them only savage superstition. (Hill 1999: 5)

The immense psychological damage done to Aboriginal people by this deliberate strategy has been discussed above. Hill (1999: 6) argues that the solution lies in the development of "a system of education that supports the cultural revitalization of Aboriginal people."

This pedagogy of cultural revitalization then creates the foundation upon which a positive learning environment can be built. Hill (1999: 122) links this approach directly to the idea of transformational learning, by arguing that:

> a philosophy of education based on a traditional Aboriginal cultural philosophy supports a transformative process of education. It provides Aboriginal adult learners with the opportunity to transform the perceptions that they hold of themselves, others, and the very universe surrounding them by introducing them to an alternative form of knowledge that is based on a traditional Aboriginal cultural world view.

Hill (1999: 137) links this Aboriginal approach to adult education to the virtues of critical reflection and transformational learning:

> In using the learning processes associated with critical reflection and perspective transformation, I, and those who have been working with me, have been able to help Aboriginal adult learners to perceive themselves, their own culture, and the cultures of other people more broadly. In many cases, the individual transformations that have resulted from the use of these processes have led to the development of a learning community that has encouraged the building of supportive relationships and has fostered an environment where individual and cultural differences are more acceptable.

The strand of adult education theory and practice rooted in the ideas of critical reflection and transformational learning is aimed at changing the ways in which oppressed people interpret or make sense of their experiences, and thus the way they see and think of themselves and the way they are able to act in the world. This approach to adult education is important for Aboriginal people because of their experience with colonization and their internalization of colonial oppression, and the need to transform that way of interpreting the world into a decolonized interpretation of the world and their place in it. This is the pedagogy of decolonization.

The work of Jack Mezirow, for example, is predicated upon the understanding that "it is not so much what happens to people but how they interpret and explain what happens to them that determines their actions, hopes, their contentment and emotional well-being, and their performance" (Mezirow 1991: xiii). The purpose of adult education, thus, is to bring into consciousness, to subject to critical enquiry, the assumptions, beliefs and ways of seeing and interpreting that people carry with them and that shape their understanding of the world and of themselves. Mezirow's early work focused on a group of American women returning to college and undergoing dramatic changes in self-perception and self-identification after challenging culturally prescribed norms and assumptions regarding the roles of women. They underwent what he called a process of "perspective transformation" (Mezirow 1991: 167).

> Perspective transformation is the process of becoming critically aware of how and why our assumptions have come to constrain the way we perceive, understand, and feel about our world; changing these structures of habitual expectation to make possible a more inclusive, discriminating, and integrative perspective; and, finally, making choices or otherwise acting upon these new understandings.

He develops the concept of transformational learning, which involves critical reflection on existing assumptions and their replacement with a new and transformed way of seeing.

> In order to be free we must be able to "name" our reality, to know it divorced from what has been taken for granted, to speak with our own voice. Thus it becomes crucial that the individual learns to negotiate meanings, purposes, and values critically, reflectively, and rationally instead of passively accepting the social realities defined by others. (Mezirow 1991: 3)

Mezirow, like many adult educators, was influenced in his thinking about transformational learning by the work of Paulo Freire. Freire held that people had to become aware of the broad socio-economic forces that shaped their lives and their ways of interpreting the world if they were to develop the capacity to act on the world. He also held that it was the task of adult educators to develop that awareness. This process of "conscientization" is the means by which people "achieve a deepening awareness of both the socio-cultural reality that shapes their lives and of their capacity to transform that reality through action upon it" (Freire 1970: 27). In this way, adult learners come to redefine their own experiences and their sense of themselves, and are empowered as a consequence.

This tradition finds expression in the work of numerous other authors. Brookfield, for example, emphasizes the extent to which this approach to adult education involves critical reflection upon hitherto unexamined assumptions:

> Developing critical reflection is probably the idea of the decade for many adult educators.... As an idea, critical reflection focuses on three interrelated processes: (1) the process by which adults question and then replace or reframe an assumption that up to that point has been uncritically accepted as representing commonsense wisdom, (2) the process through which adults take alternative perspective on previously taken for granted ideas, actions, forms of reasoning and ideologies, and (3) the process by which adults come to recognize the hegemonic

aspects of dominant cultural values and to understand how self-evident renderings of the "natural" state of the world actually bolster the power and self-interest of unrepresentative minorities. (Brookfield 1995: 2)

This approach to adult education is consistent with the theory and the practice of Diane Hill and Priscilla George, and of Urban Circle Training Centre. By rooting their approach in the experiences of Aboriginal learners, by creating the opportunity to reflect on those experiences in a critical way and by providing a new way of thinking rooted in Aboriginal culture, these Aboriginal theorists and practitioners have been working to develop a pedagogy of decolonization for Aboriginal people.

ADULT EDUCATION AND COMMUNITY DEVELOPMENT

The ALCs can usefully be seen as a form of community development. Their personalized and holistic approach to students, warm and friendly environment, and non-hierarchical organizational structure meet the needs of Aboriginal learners who have struggled with the consequences of colonization. A process of healing can occur in an ALC, and healing is closely linked — especially in the case of Urban Circle Training Centre — with a revived sense of community and a revitalization of Aboriginal cultures. Capacity building occurs. The result is transformative, at both the personal and collective levels. This is community development at its best.

Adult learning centres are a very exciting educational innovation and an important addition to the resources available to build a better future for Aboriginal people. Given the demographic trends identified in Chapter One, such initiatives are particularly important. Their value is accentuated by the fact that, generally speaking, the regular school system has not yet made the changes needed to reflect Aboriginal educational needs, as documented in a recent study of Aboriginal education in Winnipeg inner-city high schools (Silver, Mallett, Greene and Simard 2002).

The importance for Aboriginal people of the work being done by ALCs is not just that individuals can transform their lives, as crucial as that is. It is that Aboriginal people as a whole, Aboriginal people collectively, can benefit from appropriate and effective forms of education — education rooted in an understanding of colonization and decolonization — so as to take charge of their lives. As a co-director of Urban Circle put it: "It's about the empowerment of a nation."

Chapter Four

"A VERY HOSTILE SYSTEM IN WHICH TO LIVE"

Aboriginal Electoral Participation

Jim Silver, Cyril Keeper and Michael MacKenzie

Aboriginal people have historically had little involvement in Canadian electoral processes. Colonization not only removed Aboriginal people from their traditional lands, confined them to reserves, and sought to erode their cultures, languages and the practice of their spirituality. It also removed their traditional governance structures, imposed upon them the band council, the Indian Agent and the strictures of the *Indian Act*, and denied to them until 1960 the right to participate in the dominant, European-based political system of Canada. Their own political system undermined, Aboriginal people were excluded from the colonizers' political system — yet another aspect of social exclusion, with its roots in the process of colonization. It should come as no surprise, then, that what little evidence there is suggests that, on average, Aboriginal people are less likely to participate in the mainstream electoral process, and in particular are less likely to vote in federal, provincial and municipal elections, than non-Aboriginal people. At the same time, there is evidence that voter turnout rates in many First Nations band elections are relatively high.

In this chapter we examine this issue — the relatively low propensity of Aboriginal people to vote in mainstream elections — to determine whether this is the case in Winnipeg's inner city, and if so, why?

Whether Aboriginal people should or should not vote in federal, provincial and municipal elections is a contentious issue in some Aboriginal circles, as will be shown later in this chapter. We maintain that a higher voter turnout among urban Aboriginal people, particularly those in the inner city, could help advance the emergent forms of Aboriginal community development described in this book. To thrive, urban Aboriginal community development requires increased public investment, which in turn requires government support. Those who do not vote are less likely to benefit from government support.

ABORIGINAL POPULATION BY
ELECTORAL DISTRICT IN MANITOBA AND WINNIPEG

Manitoba has a larger proportion of Aboriginal people than any other province in Canada, and as a result, Aboriginal people in the province constitute a potentially significant electoral force. In the constituency of Churchill, as can be seen in Table 4-1, almost two out of every three people (64.77 percent) are Aboriginal. In each of Dauphin-Swan River, Selkirk-Interlake, Winnipeg Centre and Winnipeg North, at least one in every six people is Aboriginal. Thus in five of Manitoba's fourteen federal ridings, Aboriginal people are a significant presence, and in every federal riding in Manitoba, the proportion of the population that is Aboriginal exceeds the national average (Statistics Canada 2001, Census). These numbers exaggerate somewhat the potential political clout of Aboriginal people in Manitoba: the ratio of Aboriginal people to total population in a riding is not, in fact, equivalent to the ratio of potential Aboriginal voters to total voters in a riding, because a much higher proportion of Aboriginal than non-Aboriginal people are under the legal voting age of eighteen years. Nevertheless, the numbers are significant and will become even more so as today's Aboriginal youth reach voting age.

Table 4-1: Proportion of the Population that is Aboriginal, by Federal Electoral District in Manitoba, 2001

Federal Electoral District	Population	Aboriginal Identity	Share (%)
Brandon-Souris	83,510	6,270	7.51
Charleswood St. James-Assiniboia	81,870	3,475	4.24
Churchill	73,420	47,555	64.77
Dauphin-Swan River	77,590	16,185	20.86
Elmwood-Transocna	78,000	6,815	8.74
Kildonan-St. Paul	77,040	3,655	4.74
Portage-Lisgar	83,385	5,495	6.59
Provencher	81,915	6,795	8.30
Saint Boniface	81,240	5,920	7.29
Selkirk-Interlake	86,550	14,935	17.26
Winnipeg Centre	80,930	13,340	16.48
Winnipeg North	79,415	13,255	16.69
Winnipeg South	77,080	3,005	3.90
Winnipeg South Centre	77,635	3,340	4.30
Average 13.69			

Source: Statistics Canada 2001 Census

At the provincial level, the numbers are perhaps more significant. According to the 2001 Census of Canada, Aboriginal people comprise a large majority of the population in Rupertsland (90.5 percent) and The Pas (69.9 percent), and in Thompson (49.7 percent) form a near majority. In another five provincial electoral districts — Interlake (41.1 percent), Flin Flon (39.4 percent), Swan River (38.2 percent), Point Douglas (34.8 percent) and Ste. Rose (30.1 percent) — Aboriginal people comprise more than or almost one-third of the population. In another nine provincial electoral districts, Aboriginal people constitute between, approximately, one in five and one in six of the total population — Lac du Bonnet (22.6 percent), Wellington (20.8 percent), Burrows (18.1 percent), Portage la Prairie (16.8 percent), Russell (16.7 percent), Selkirk (16.6 percent), Wolseley (16.4 percent), St. Johns (15.8 percent) and Minto (15.4 percent). Thus in seventeen of fifty-seven provincial electoral districts, or just under one-third, Aboriginal persons constitute at least one sixth of the total population. In another six provincial electoral districts, Aboriginal people constitute more than 10 percent of the total population. And in all but eight provincial electoral districts in Manitoba, the Aboriginal share of the total population is above the national average.

Of particular interest to us here are the numbers of Aboriginal people in the City of Winnipeg. Almost 38 percent of Aboriginal people living in Manitoba, or more than one in every three, reside in Winnipeg. Thus Winnipeg is the largest Aboriginal community in the province and the largest urban Aboriginal population in Canada. Aboriginal people make up 8.4 percent of the city's total population, and in specific areas, Aboriginal people constitute a potentially significant electoral force. As noted, there are two federal electoral districts within Winnipeg that have a sizable minority Aboriginal population: Winnipeg Centre and Winnipeg North, at 16.7 percent and 16.5 percent respectively. In nine of the thirty-one provincial electoral districts in Winnipeg, the Aboriginal population comprises more than 10 percent of the total population, and in six of those districts, approximately one in every six people is Aboriginal. These are Point Douglas (34.8 percent), Wellington (20.8 percent), Burrows (18.9 percent), Wolseley (16.4 percent), St. Johns (15.8 percent) and Minto (15.4 percent).

Similarly, Aboriginal people in Winnipeg are concentrated in specific municipal wards. Table 4-2 shows that in three of fifteen wards in the City of Winnipeg, Aboriginal people comprise more than, or almost, one in six of the total population. These are Mynarski (23.3 percent), Point Douglas (17.4 percent) and Daniel McIntyre (15.1 percent). In a fourth ward, Elmwood-East Kildonan (11.8 percent), Aboriginal people constitute more than one in ten of the total population.

The relatively high proportion of Aboriginal people in Manitoba and in

Table 4-2: Proportion of the Population that is Aboriginal, by City of Winnipeg Electoral District, 2001

Ward	Population	Aboriginal Identity	Share (%)
Charleswood-Tuxedo	32,470	785	2.42
Daniel McIntyre	43,495	6,580	15.13
Elmwood-East Kildonan	38,640	4,570	11.83
Fort Rouge	47,325	4,235	8.95
Mynarski	39,160	9,125	23.30
North Kildonan	39,190	1,710	4.36
Old Kildonan	41,340	2,360	5.71
Point Douglas	41,915	7,290	17.39
River Heights-Fort Garry	49,560	1,520	3.07
St. Boniface	45,650	3,245	7.11
St. Charles	31,730	1,725	5.44
St. James	29,095	1,935	6.65
St. Norbert	39,090	1,715	4.39
St. Vital	47,780	3,195	6.69
Tanscona	33,245	2,010	6.05

Source: Statistics Canada, 2001 Census Area Data combined with the City of Winnipeg Ward Divisions of 2002

Winnipeg presents a special opportunity for Aboriginal voices to be heard politically. There are few places in Canada where Aboriginal people make up an electoral majority, but there are many electoral districts in Manitoba and in Winnipeg, at the federal, provincial and municipal levels, where Aboriginal people make up a potentially significant minority. If we consider population numbers alone, there is a real incentive for politicians at all three levels to listen to the demands of the Aboriginal community. But politicians do not consider population statistics alone. What really matters is who votes.

PROPENSITY TO VOTE

Not a great deal is known about voter turnout rates for federal, provincial and municipal elections among Aboriginal people in Canada. Even less is known about urban Aboriginal voter turnout rates for such elections. Few quantitative and fewer qualitative studies have been undertaken.

Obtaining quantitative data about voter turnout rates for any specific group is complicated by two primary factors. First, such data are not collected at polling stations. The ballot is secret. How members of a specific group have voted is generally impossible to determine. Exit polls would provide an approximation of such information, but we know of none for Aboriginal people's voting. Second, studies in which respondents are asked, subsequent to an election, whether or not they voted in that election are not always trustworthy. The proportion of respondents who say they voted is often inflated. For example, Elections Canada and polling company Ipsos-Reid conducted a survey that targeted Aboriginal people in northern areas of British Columbia, Alberta, Saskatchewan, Manitoba, Ontario and Quebec. Seventy percent of respondents said they voted in the 2000 federal election (Elections Canada 2000: 10). This is far higher than poll-by-poll results would suggest. Similar problems arise in studies that ask whether respondents plan to vote in an upcoming election. In many cases, the number of people who say they plan to vote is greater than the number who actually vote. More generally, surveys of Aboriginal people's voting behaviour are made difficult by the fact that Aboriginal people constitute a relatively small percentage of Canada's population. The result is that general Canada-wide surveys reveal little about Aboriginal people's voting behaviour. This problem is made worse by such factors as relatively low levels of telephone access and high rates of residential mobility, which make traditional survey methodology more difficult for Aboriginal populations. Due to these and other difficulties, we do not know as much as we would like about Aboriginal people's, and particularly urban Aboriginal people's, voting patterns.

The most reliable data on Aboriginal people's voting behaviour come from polls found entirely within First Nations reserves, where First Nations people constitute an overwhelming majority. But this means that there are no reliable data on the propensity to vote among Aboriginal people off-reserve. Consequently, we know almost nothing about the voting patterns of urban Aboriginal people.

Despite this lack of data, there is a general consensus that the voter turn-out of Aboriginal people in mainstream elections is significantly lower than that of non-Aboriginal people, although there is evidence of significant variation across provinces, communities, Aboriginal nations and elections. Guerin (2003) has reported the results of a recent study of participation levels of on-reserve Aboriginal people in the 2000 federal election. He found considerable variation in turnout rates across provinces and territories. Numbers were highest in Prince Edward Island and Saskatchewan, where polling stations on First Nations reserves reported average turnout rates of 66.9 percent and 55.0 percent respectively. These rates are close to national turnout rates; indeed, the PEI rate is higher than the national turnout rate. At the other end of the spectrum, polling stations on First Nations reserves in Manitoba and Quebec reported average turnout rates of 36.6 percent and 35.3 percent respectively, much lower than the national turnout. Guerin (2003: 12–13) has reported that in the 2000 federal election: "the turnout rate for all 296 polling stations included in the study was 47.8 percent — 16 percent lower than the turnout among the general population." In an internal Elections Canada study on First

Table 4-3: First Nations Voting on Manitoba Reserves in Federal and
Provincial Elections, 1962–2003

Year	Total Votes Cast	Registered Voters	Turnout (%)
1962F	5,664	8,667	65.35
1963F	6,038	9,793	61.66
1965F	5,334	9,511	56.08
1968F	5,039	9,491	53.09
1969P	6,177	11,554	53.46
1972F	6,627	12,205	54.30
1973P	8,444	14,427	58.53
1974P	6,338	12,331	51.40
1977P	7,738	15,631	49.50
1979F	7,972	15,824	50.38
1980F	9,120	16,278	56.03
1981P	8,770	16,894	51.91
1984F	8,311	18,272	45.48
1986P	8,684	19,818	43.82
1988F	9,512	20,141	47.23
1988P	8,859	21,375	41.45
1990P	10,426	24,792	42.05
1993F	9,914	24,988	39.68
1995P	9,381	26,426	35.50
1997F	8,967	27,546	32.55
1999P	9,990	28,030	35.64
2000F	12,223	26,742	45.71
2003P	7,924	29,681	26.70

F = Federal Election; P = Provincial Election
Source: Michael Kinnear 2003: 47

Nations people's political participation in federal elections prior to the 2000
election, Jean-Nicolas Bustros reported on turnout rates at polls wholly within
First Nations communities: 41 percent in the 1992 referendum; 38 percent in
the 1993 federal election; and 40 percent in the 1997 federal election (Guerin
2003: 11). In short, where it has been possible to determine Aboriginal voter
turnout in federal and provincial elections — in most cases in their home communities — they vote considerably less, on average, than the overall population.
There is evidence that voter turnout in First Nations band elections is higher
(Bedford and Pobihushchy 1995; Guerin 2003).

The historical pattern of on-reserve First Nations voter turnout rates in

federal and provincial elections in Manitoba has been described by Kinnear
(2003). Some of his data are reproduced here as Table 4-3, which shows that
for on-reserve First Nations people in Manitoba, the turnout rate in federal and
provincial elections was quite high directly after the extension of the franchise,
in the 1960s, and has been declining dramatically ever since. In the most recent
provincial election, in 2003, the turnout rate on Manitoba reserves reached an
all-time low of 26.7 percent, less than one-half the overall voter turnout in that
election.

A similar pattern of decline was reported in a pioneering study conducted
by Bedford and Pobihushchy (1995). The voter turnout in federal elections at
polling stations on First Nations reserves in New Brunswick fell from 70 percent
in 1962 to 17.8 percent in 1988. In Nova Scotia the rate fell from 89.3 percent
in 1962 to 54.0 percent in 1988. It is unfortunate that we do not have reliable
figures on voter turnout rates among Aboriginal people living off-reserve to contrast with these results. All that we have is the previously mentioned Elections
Canada/Ipsos-Reid survey, which found that Aboriginal people living in urban
areas were three times less likely to say they had voted in the 2000 federal election than those living on reserves (reported in Guerin 2003: 13). Given that
surveys of this nature frequently over-estimate the voter turnout rate, it seems
reasonable to assume that the voter turnout rate in federal and provincial elections among Aboriginal people living in Winnipeg, and in other urban centres,
is lower than the average turnout rate. Further empirical research is needed to
determine the true extent of the difference.

Why Should Aboriginal People Vote in Mainstream Elections?
Why, indeed, should Aboriginal people vote in federal, provincial and municipal elections? And why should Aboriginal people, and Canadians generally, be
concerned that Aboriginal people, on average, vote less in such elections than
non-Aboriginal people? We believe there are several reasons.

First, governments are much less likely to respond positively to the demands
of those people who do not vote. One of the most highly regarded political sci-
entists in the U.S., V.O. Key, expressed this clearly and emphatically more than
half a century ago: "The blunt truth is that politicians and officials are under
no compulsion to pay much heed to classes and groups of citizens that do not
vote" (Key 1949: 527). A recent study of women and electoral politics in Canada
concludes that: "We can expect parties to respond to the feminist party agenda
only when that agenda is espoused by a significant electoral constituency" (Young
2003: 89). Henry Milner (2002) has developed a wealth of evidence to show that
more participatory societies are more egalitarian. From this finding, we would
argue it follows that Aboriginal people's electoral participation in Canadian
politics would be likely to contribute to the generation of policies that would
accrue to their collective benefit. Milner (2002: 175) argues that "as the data on

who votes clearly show, if turnout averages 50 percent in country or period A, and 80 percent in country or period B, then we can reasonably expect that different interests will be aggregated in A than in B: policy choices in A will be skewed more closely to the interests of people at higher levels of income and wealth." Aboriginal people have, on average, lower levels of income and wealth. C.B. Macpherson, although making the case for a form of participatory democracy that goes beyond simply voting, has observed that "low participation and social inequality are so bound up with each other that a more equitable and humane society requires a more participatory political system." And in their analysis of the general decline in voter turnout, Leduc and Pammett (2003: 25) reiterate the pointed observation of V.O. Key: "Politicians and political parties are more likely to respond to the demands of voters than of nonvoters." The socio-economic needs of Aboriginal people in Canada are considerable; the likelihood of such needs being positively responded to by governments are reduced by Aboriginal people's lower than average propensity to vote in mainstream elections.

Second, there are strong reasons why Aboriginal people would benefit from being represented in legislative bodies by other Aboriginal people. Jane Mansbridge (2000: 99–100) argues that there are at least three types of situations in which members of disadvantaged groups might benefit from being represented "by individuals who in their own background 'mirror' the typical experiences and outward manifestations of belonging to the disadvantaged group." First, this kind of representation is important for effective communication between the elected representative and members of the disadvantaged group, because "members of groups embedded in a tradition of domination and subordination often experience faulty communication: the dominant group has not learned to listen and the subordinate group has learned to distrust." Second, this kind of representation is important in ensuring that issues of particular importance to the dispossessed group can be effectively raised in the legislature, because "representatives who are not personally in touch with the typical experiences of their constituents will often not contribute adequately to the deliberation of these issues" (see Tremblay and Trimble 2003, especially 18, on the effectiveness of elected women in raising issues of particular significance to women in legislative bodies). And third, proportionate representation of members of a disadvantaged group in a legislative body... confirms that members of this group are capable of that function and expected to fill it," which then "increases the de facto legitimacy of the polity for members of these groups." In short, Mansbridge argues not only that voting is important to members of marginalized groups if their needs are to be met, but also that *electing* and thus being represented by members of those disadvantaged groups is important if their needs are to be met (for a similar argument see also Williams 2000). A non-Aboriginal Member of Parliament from northern Quebec echoed this argument in the House of Commons: "I find it extremely difficult to represent and defend the interests of the native population for a score of reasons ranging from cultural differences, languages and distances" (quoted in Milen 1991: 39). The Manitoba Keewatinowi Okimakanak (MKO), Manitoba's northern chiefs organization, has made the same case: "We need Members of Parliament who do not have to be taught who we are, what we want, and why we are important to this country.... To be effective, we have to have the capacity to elect our own representatives to the House of Commons" (Milen 1991: 40). Canadian scholars have led the way in advancing arguments about the necessity and the merits of recognizing difference, and of designing political systems so as to affirm both differences and a shared identity (see, for example: Borrows 1999; Cairns 2000; Kymlicka 1995; Taylor 1992; Tully 1995; and Young 1990).

Third, all Canadians should be concerned about the relatively low numbers of Aboriginal people who vote because their lack of participation erodes the legitimacy of the political system. Kymlicka (1995: 32) argues that "there is increasing concern that the political process is 'unrepresentative' in the sense that it fails to reflect the diversity of the population. Legislatures in most countries are dominated by middle class, able-bodied, white men." At the same time, relatively few Aboriginal people vote in elections to those legislatures. Bedford (2003: 19) argues that "the voter turnout data indicate that there is a crisis of legitimacy facing the Canadian state. A significant proportion of a group that makes up 4 percent of the total population of Canada has serious and deep-seated questions about the legitimate authority of the Canadian state and its control over their lives." The issue of legitimacy is magnified in Manitoba and in Winnipeg, where Aboriginal people constitute approximately one in ten of the province's and the city's populations. If a group of people of that size is largely excluded from and/or does not participate proportionately in the dominant political system, for whatever reasons, then serious questions arise not only about the system's ability to hear their concerns and to meet their needs, but also about the legitimacy of such a system.

ABORIGINAL PEOPLE AND THE VOTE

There are four broad categories of explanation for Aboriginal people's relatively low voter turnout in mainstream elections. All four are rooted in their deliberate exclusion from the mainstream of Canadian society, the historical consequence of colonization. The first is the "nationalist" explanation: some Aboriginal people choose not to vote because they see themselves as members of distinctive nations and seek nation-to-nation relations with Canada. Thus, to vote in Canada would undermine the logic of their position. Some Aboriginal people do not vote in Canadian federal, provincial or municipal elections for this reason, although they may still vote in band elections. Second, many Aboriginal people do not vote because they distrust and feel excluded from the Canadian electoral system. Their historical and current experience is such that many Aboriginal people, including many urban Aboriginal people, feel that they are not a part of the dominant culture and institutions of Canadian society. Third, the socio-economic and demographic characteristics of Aboriginal people are, on average, consistent with those of non-voters generally. And fourth, there is evidence that "political opportunity" and "political effort" are important factors in explaining the relatively low levels of Aboriginal political participation in mainstream politics. Political parties are not generally open to Aboriginal people's involvement, so the argument goes, and parties and politicians do not make much effort to involve Aboriginal people. These factors also appear to contribute to relatively low Aboriginal rates of voting.

The Impact of Colonization on Aboriginal Voting

Historically, Aboriginal people have been excluded from the mainstream Canadian political process. This exclusion was an important part and a consequence of the process of colonization. Efforts to act politically in the first half of the twentieth century were thwarted by the *Indian Act* of 1876. The *Indian Act* imposed upon First Nations communities the structure of elected band chiefs and councils as a means of destroying traditional governmental systems. As Patricia Monture-Angus (1995: 182) has observed: "The *Indian Act* replaced Aboriginal forms of government with non-democratic and hierarchical government institutions which were unfamiliar to the people of our communities. The imposition of the band council governments met the opposition of many communities" (see also Boldt 1993: 169). The Indian Agent came to exercise almost total control over the political life of reserves. For example, while band councils might pass bylaws, all band funds were controlled by the Indian Agent, who had the authority to overturn any decision made by the band. Intelligent First Nations people might have asked why participate in a political process such as this — an imposed and colonial political system? Revisions to the *Act* in the 1920s placed restrictions on the right to assemble, to leave the reserve without the permission of the Indian Agent and to raise funds other than from government. This made political organizing beyond the band level all but impossible from the late 1920s to 1951, when further revisions to the *Indian Act* removed some restrictions (McFarlane 1993: 29 and 243). Harold Cardinal (1969: 98) has described the impact of the *Indian Act* and the Indian Agent upon political organizing:

> The Indian Agent, dead set against any successful Indian organization, actively worked against the leaders of the day. To the autocratic agent… the development of Indian organizations was a threat to his power and potentially to his job. He had many weapons and never hesitated to use

them. Sometimes he openly threatened to punish people who persisted in organizational efforts. More often he used more subtle weapons such as delaying relief payments or rations to show the Indians which way the wind was blowing.

It was not until the *Canada Elections Act* was revised in 1960 that status Indians, male and female, were extended the right to vote in Canadian elections without having to give up their Indian status. Prior to that, First Nations people could vote at the federal level only upon "enfranchisement," which meant giving up their status as Indians. As Smith (2003: 41) put it, prior to 1960 "voting rights were a reward for abandoning one's Aboriginal heritage." Most Indians were not prepared to do that. They resisted assimilation. This resistance was expressed in a petition delivered to the King of England in 1926, which concluded by stating: "We do not want enfranchisement, we want to be Indians to the end of the world" (McFarlane 1993: 28–29). So while the Canadian state enacted measures to prevent First Nations' political organizing, First Nations people themselves came to see the vote in particular as a betrayal of their determination to live as Aboriginal people and a potential threat to their treaty rights. As a result, there has not developed among Aboriginal people the tradition of participating in the mainstream Canadian electoral process. As Kulchyski (2002: 191) has put it: "by the 1970s Aboriginal people were not interested in their Canadian citizenship for good reason: the State had spent a century trying to enforce citizenship on them at the expense of their rights." The protection of those rights — those collective, national rights — came to be the primary focus of Aboriginal political activity.

The Nationalist Explanation
A major part of the explanation for the relatively low levels of Aboriginal people's participation in the mainstream Canadian political process is nationalism. Many Aboriginal people see themselves as distinct peoples, as members of distinct nations. As Cairns (1993: 210) has put it:

> Their distrust of the federal and provincial governments is so high, and their sense of difference so profound, that they seek not to be accepted by the majority as individuals on the former's terms but to achieve institutional and constitutional recognition of a special status that will contribute to their ongoing survival as distinct nations.

Schouls (1996: 745) says the same, arguing that: "Aboriginal peoples... are less concerned about representative involvement in the governing structures of Canada and more concerned about circumscribing the extension of the Canadian government's power over their nations." It is likely for this reason that the Royal Commission on Aboriginal Peoples (RCAP) devoted only eight pages out of more than 3500 to the issue of Aboriginal people's parliamentary representation. The RCAP described the "inherent ineffectiveness of the democratic political relationship as seen by Aboriginal peoples," and added that "Aboriginal peoples seek nation-to-nation political relations, and these cannot be achieved simply by representation in Canadian political institutions" (quoted in Cairns 2003: 5). Writing in *Electoral Insight*, in a recent issue dedicated to Aboriginal political participation in elections, Ladner (2003: 24) says: "I would argue that a majority of Aboriginal people with strong ties to their communities and their history, traditions and language have explicitly decided not to participate in Canadian elections." This dismissal of Canada as an alien political system was forcefully articulated by Anishinabe scholar Leanne Simpson: "I don't vote in elections in France, I don't vote in elections in Ethiopia. Why would I vote in Canada? They are all foreign nations" (quoted in Ladner 2003: 24). Certainly the development of an Aboriginal political movement with the establishment of the National Indian Brotherhood (NIB) in the late 1960s, and its takeoff following the 1969 federal *White Paper*, came to be about advancing the collective, national rights of Aboriginal peoples. In fact, by the early 1980s, almost all Aboriginal politics had been subsumed under the "common Indian philosophy" (McFarlane 1993: 8) centred upon the pursuit of Aboriginal rights and self-government, and the winning of sovereignty for First Nations. The centrality of this nationalist definition of Aboriginal politics has largely suppressed — and among some of the Aboriginal leadership, made illegitimate — discussion of a politics directed at increasing Aboriginal people's political clout and thus improving their socio-economic circumstances, by increasing their participation in the mainstream Canadian political process. This is the case *despite* the fact that many Aboriginal leaders have developed close relations with the Liberal Party, since this appears to be, as will be argued later, an elite accommodation approach with little attempt to mobilize the vote of the mass of the Aboriginal population.

The Social Exclusion Explanation
Aboriginal people feel excluded from, distanced from and distrustful of, the Canadian political system. Writing in the special issue of *Electoral Insight* on Aboriginal political participation, Cairns (2003: 2) says: "A widespread diffuse alienation from the Canadian constitutional order crops up again and again in the literature dealing with Aboriginal issues and concerns. The leading theme in First Nations discourse, according to the sociologist Rick Ponting, is 'the untrustworthiness of government.'" Aboriginal people see the Canadian political system as representing non-Aboriginal interests. Given their history and their colonization, why would they not? Why would they trust the Canadian political system? As George Erasmus has asked: "Trust us: I mean what do you think we are, forgetful or just plain crazy?" (Cairns 1993: 207). Menno Boldt (1993: 246) has argued that: "A history of Canadian deception, theft, and betrayal has

resulted in a collective and individual Indian attitude of distrust towards the dominant society. This distrust is translated into a profound reluctance to enter the Canadian social and economic mainstream." This includes a reluctance to vote in mainstream elections.

Studies of voting generally reveal that many of those who vote are people who feel a sense of civic duty. Pammett and Leduc (2003: 38) argue that civic duty is the "feeling that participation is to be valued for its own sake, or for its contribution to the overall health of the polity." In their analysis of the 2000 federal election, they found that "there is a strong relationship between having an attitude of civic duty and having voted in the 2000 election... non-voters show a much lower level of civic duty."

Why would Aboriginal people, having been colonized by the Canadian state, have a sense of "civic duty"? Far from having the sense of duty associated with voting, Aboriginal people feel excluded from the Canadian governmental system and believe — not surprisingly given their experience — that it is a system designed to oppress Aboriginal people and to promote the interests of non-Aboriginal people. "By and large, Aboriginal people continue to see the Canadian political system as an instrument of their domination and oppression" (Ladner 2003: 23); they feel "a profound sense of distance from the mainstream political system" (Hunter 2003: 30). Elijah Harper, former Manitoba MLA and Member of Parliament who is perhaps most famous for his role in the defeat of the *Meech Lake Accord*, has described his first reaction to the Manitoba Legislature: "My first time going into the chamber, I wondered what I had gotten myself into. It was a different kind of feeling than when you go into a chief's meeting — this was not my own." His biographer adds: "He never fit into white politics, despite his efforts. 'I constantly struggled to be a part of it, whether it was caucus or cabinet. Somehow I was always viewed as an outsider. I could just feel it — even after Meech,' he says" (Comeau 1993: 87 and 207).

He could feel it because Aboriginal people are, indeed, outsiders. They *are* excluded from the dominant institutions of society, and governments are *not* "their" governments. By Cairns' definition, they are unlikely to feel they are "citizens." Cairns (1999: 4) argues that:

> Citizenship has both a vertical and a horizontal dimension. The former links individuals to the state by reinforcing the idea that it is "their" state — that they are full members of an ongoing association that is expected to survive the passing generations. Their relation to the state is, accordingly, not narrowly instrumental, but supported by a reservoir of loyalty and patriotism that gives legitimacy to the state. The horizontal relationship, by contrast, is the positive identification of citizens with each other as valued members of the same civic community. Here, citizenship reinforces empathy and sustains solidarity by

means of official statements of who is "one of us." Citizenship, therefore, is a linking mechanism, which in its most perfect expression binds the citizenry to the state and to each other.

In neither the vertical nor the horizontal sense are Aboriginal people likely to feel they are "citizens." Far from such positive feelings as loyalty and patriotism toward the state, and empathy and solidarity with Canadians, Aboriginal people are more likely to feel a sense of exclusion and distance from the state and from non-Aboriginal Canadians.

In urban areas there is a strong sense of social exclusion among many Aboriginal people, of distance from the people and the institutions of the dominant culture. In Chapter Two we showed that Aboriginal people living in Winnipeg's inner-city Spence neighbourhood, as elsewhere in Canadian cities, have felt a profound sense of social exclusion from the local neighbourhood association and from urban institutions generally. In Chapter Three, Aboriginal adult learners' comments revealed the same sense of exclusion from the regular school system. A study of Aboriginal people's relationship to a North End Winnipeg housing project — which also had made significant efforts to involve Aboriginal people — found the same sense of exclusion (Deane, Morrissette, Bousquet and Bruyere 2002). Numerous studies of Aboriginal people in rural towns have pointed to their exclusion from mainstream town life. There has been "intense hostility" directed by townspeople at Aboriginal residents and visitors (Peters 2002a: 56), to which many Aboriginal people respond by withdrawing to avoid "the indignities of most interactions with white men" (Lithman 1984: 58; see also, among many other examples: Brody 1971: 71; Comeau and Santin 1990: 39 and 47; Stymeist 1975, especially 68–75). It could be argued that Aboriginal people's marginalization from the mainstream electoral system and their lower rate of voter turnout are but a part of their broader social exclusion from the dominant culture.

Socio-Economic and Demographic Explanations
In addition to the nationalist explanation and the social exclusion explanation, there are a host of other practical socio-economic and demographic factors that are likely to impede Aboriginal people's participation in the electoral process. For instance, Aboriginal people move more frequently than non-Aboriginal people (see Chapter One) and are thus harder to keep registered on the voters' list; this causes complications when they try to vote in their district of residence.

Also, Aboriginal people have, on average, lower incomes than non-Aboriginal people, and income levels, or socio-economic status, correlates with voter turnout. According to the 2001 Census, the average income in Canada was close to $30,000, whereas the average income for Aboriginal people was just over $19,000. Among the Canadian population as a whole there was a 34 percent incidence of low income in 2000; for Aboriginal people the incidence of low income was 55.9 percent (see also Lezubski, Silver and Black 2000). There is considerable evidence that voter turnout correlates strongly with socio-economic status (Pammett and Leduc 2003). In his 1996 address to the American Political Science Association, Arend Lijphardt "noted that most studies on voter turnout have concluded that those who are socio-economically disadvantaged and have a lower overall status in society also have significantly lower rates of voter turnout, exacerbating their general powerlessness to effect outcomes" (quoted in Bedford 2003: 16). Milner (2002: 260) refers to a "study comparing voters and nonvoters in the 1996 U.S. presidential election [which] found that 33 percent of those with incomes under thirty thousand dollars voted, compared to 60 per cent for those with incomes above that amount." U.S. studies have found that "political involvement in the United States is highly stratified by socioeconomic status, with high-SES adults and their children participating at greater levels in comparison to members of low-SES families" (McDevitt et al. 2003: 5; see also Zaff, Malanchuk, Michelsen and Eccles 2003: 23). The socio-economic model of participation holds that "participation input is weighted in favour of people with higher socio-economic standing because 'the higher-status individual has a greater stake in politics, he has greater skills, more resources, greater awareness of political matters, he is exposed to more communications about politics, he interacts with others who participate'" (Burt 2002: 237). But as has been observed, "many Aboriginal persons move frequently, have low literacy levels, are unemployed, are disconnected from mainstream society and are distanced from the discussion process that attends federal elections" (Cairns 2003: 4).

Aboriginal people in Canada are also younger, on average, than non-Aboriginal people, and voting correlates strongly with age (Blais et al. 2003). The older people are, the more likely they are to vote (Milner 2002: 41). Pammett and Leduc have produced a table — reproduced here as Table 4–4 — showing a remarkable decline in voting turnout by age cohort in the 2000 federal election.

The 2001 Census of Canada shows that while 31 percent of all Canadians are twenty-four years of age or younger, approximately 50 percent of Aboriginal people are in that age group (Guerin 2003: 13). Thus their age structure alone is a factor in Aboriginal people's relatively low levels of voter turnout.

Education also correlates strongly with voter turnout: the higher a person's level of formal education, the more likely that person is to vote (Burt 2002: 237; Pammett and Leduc 2003). Andre Blais (2000: 52) has shown that "the two most crucial socio-economic determinants of voting are education and age. The gap between the least and the most educated and between the youngest and the eldest is a huge 20 points." Combining these factors, young people with higher levels of education tend to vote more — their education offsets their age. Gidengil

Table 4-4: Decline in Voting Turnout by Age Cohort, 2000 Federal Election

Age	Percent Who Voted in 2000
68+	83
58–67	80
48–57	76
38–47	66
30–37	54
25–29	38
21–24	28
18–20	22

Source: Pammett and Leduc 2003: 4

et al. (2003: 10) observe that "the more education young people have, the more likely they are to vote. Education remains one of the best predictors of turnout because it provides the cognitive skills needed to cope with the complexities of politics and because it seems to foster norms of civic engagement." The U.S. experience is consistent with the Canadian: youth decline in voter turnout is offset by education. "Among those with a Bachelor's degree or more, the downward trend in youth voter turnout has been reversed" (Lopez and Kirby 2003: 3). The correlation between levels of formal education and voter turnout is significant because Aboriginal people have lower levels of formal education on average than non-Aboriginal people, although educational levels among Aboriginal people are improving (Lezubski, Silver and Black 2000). According to the 2001 Census of Canada, approximately 31 percent of the Canadian population over the age of fifteen years had less than a high school education whereas approximately 48 percent of the Aboriginal population had less than a high school education.

In short, the fact that large numbers of Aboriginal people feel excluded and alienated from the electoral system due to their experience of colonization is, in our view, a more important causal variable for Aboriginal people's relatively low levels of voter turnout in mainstream elections. However, it is still important to add that there are also a host of socio-economic and demographic variables — low levels of income, a younger population, lower levels of education, higher rates of residential mobility — that correlate generally with voter turnout and are also likely to play a part in Aboriginal people's relatively low levels of voting in mainstream elections.

Political Opportunity and Political Effort Explanations
Finally, we believe that "political opportunity structure" and especially "political effort" can assist in explaining Aboriginal people's relatively low voter turnout. Political opportunity structure has been used, for example, in explaining varying rates of immigrant voter turnout in European countries. Togeby (1999:

667) describes the political opportunity structure as constituting "for instance the electoral system, other electoral arrangements, party system, but also the indigenous population's attitudes towards ethnic minorities. So the question is: how open are the receiving country's institutions and culture to including ethnic minorities in the political process." We could say that historically, the "political opportunity structure" facing Aboriginal people, and particularly First Nations people, was created by the provisions of the *Indian Act*, which specifically sought to *prevent* First Nations people from participating in the Canadian political process. It closed rather than opened opportunities for them to participate politically. How much more open is the political opportunity structure for Aboriginal people today? Len Marchand, Canada's first Aboriginal Member of Parliament, observed some years ago that:

> As it stands today, Parliament is the exclusive domain of the settler, a reflection, no doubt, of the fact the electoral system was designed by settlers for settlers and historically developed to exclude Aboriginal peoples…. For the vast majority of Aboriginal Canadians Parliament is seen in the distance but there is no trail to get there. The trails that do exist are made for the workboots of the settlers. The path has been too sharp and barnacled for the moccasins of our people. (quoted in Milen 1991: 42)

Political effort is a related concept: not only, how open are the institutions and cultures to others' participation; but also, do the dominant institutions make an effort to include those now excluded? Do political parties try to secure votes by informing voters; do they seek out and encourage minority candidates; do they modify their practices to encourage the involvement of those on the outside? (See, for example, Burt 2002; Milner 2002.) We know, for example, that political parties play an important role in perpetuating the under-representation of women in politics (Tremblay and Trimble 2003: 10). A recent American study found that voter turnout among Latinos is increased by targeted mobilization efforts and is particularly increased when door-to-door canvassing during election campaigns involves Latino canvassers speaking to potential Latino voters (Michelsen 2003: 1 and 3). Yet matters of particular concern to Aboriginal people are typically at the bottom of political parties' priorities, thus confirming in Aboriginal people's minds the view that the political process is not relevant to them.

ABORIGINAL PEOPLE AND VOTING IN WINNIPEG

We interviewed Aboriginal people in Winnipeg, and particularly in Winnipeg's inner city, to find out whether they participate in the political process and, in particular, whether they vote in federal, provincial and municipal elections. All interviews were conducted by two Aboriginal interviewers, both of whom are long-time residents of Winnipeg's inner city. They started by asking: "what do you think of when you hear the word 'politics'?" Interviewees were also asked if they ever vote in mainstream elections, why they do or do not, whether urban Aboriginal people generally vote in mainstream elections, and why they do or do not.

A total of forty Aboriginal people were interviewed: seven young people aged eighteen to twenty-five were interviewed by Ed Keeper; an additional thirty-three people were interviewed by Cyril Keeper. Roughly equal numbers were reached by approaching Aboriginal people involved in the Spence Neighbourhood Association and Inner-City Aboriginal Neighbours (I-CAN); going door-to-door on Agnes Street in Spence neighbourhood; approaching people at a pow wow held at the Forks, in downtown Winnipeg in April 2004; approaching people at an inner-city Aboriginal church in April 2004; approaching students at the Aboriginal Students' Centre at the University of Winnipeg; and deliberately contacting particular people known to be knowledgeable about the urban Aboriginal experience.

Those interviewed do not constitute a random sample of Aboriginal people in Winnipeg's inner city. However, we have included a fairly broad cross-section of urban Aboriginal people. Of the forty people interviewed, twenty-one were women and nineteen were men. They included a wide range of ages and educational levels, although thirteen of the forty had a university degree or community college diploma, and this is a considerably higher proportion than the total urban Aboriginal population with at least some post-secondary education.

Not Many Aboriginal Nationalists

What we found in our interviews is not completely consistent with expectations about Aboriginal voting. In particular, it appears that the nationalist explanation for low levels of Aboriginal voting may not apply in Winnipeg. Only one of those interviewed offered anything like a nationalist explanation. He referred to "the way the Mohawks and to some extent other groups look at sovereignty, and the fact that voting is in fact an action by which you give consent, and that's been the objection in some cases for some groups." He then added: "although I don't think that's widely held." His was the only explicit mention of people consciously and deliberately not voting on the grounds that to do so is to give consent — i.e., the nationalist explanation. Another respondent made a statement that sounded like a nationalist explanation. She said about voting: "I think it's a culturally foreign instrument.... They smashed our political instruments." Yet far from a deliberate rejection of voting, this person always votes and has frequently worked on election campaigns for candidates in Winnipeg. It may well be that the nationalist explanation has less resonance in urban areas than in First Nations communities.

Protecting Aboriginal Rights by Participating in Canadian Politics

In fact, a stronger theme arising from the interviews is, in effect, the inverse of the nationalist explanation — that this is the system we now live in, like it or not, and we need to participate in it. One young woman, a university student, responded to the question, "Does politics matter to Aboriginal people?" with:

> *Of course it does, yeah. This is the system that we live in, right now, and we really need to get involved if we want to change our standards of living or policies that affect us in a negative way. For Aboriginal people to become a healthier community I think you need to get involved in politics.*

Others said that it was important to be involved in politics precisely in order to protect Aboriginal rights. Those who made this kind of statement were quite knowledgeable about the political system and were at the same time involved in the practice and promotion of traditional Aboriginal cultures. Their immersion in Aboriginal cultural pursuits did *not* lead to a nationalist argument against voting, but rather to an argument in favour of voting to protect Aboriginal rights. One forty-nine-year-old woman, one of only two of our interviewees actively involved in Aboriginal women's groups, said: "if we really want… to protect what's ours then we have to get involved. We're not going to protect our treaties and protect what's ours unless we get out there and stand up for it." Another woman, a grandmother, said: "I think it's very, very important to vote now, in this day and age, it's 2004, I think it's time that people pick up their medicine bundles and come out and start voting." A young man, a university student, implied that the nationalist explanation was a thing of the past. He said:

> *I was raised in a family where Native people always thought of politicians as evil or wicked or they'll just take away our rights or whatever else, so if we don't partake in it [voting] that's just the best way to deal with it, I guess, just not to be there.*

However, the young man now votes and justifies doing so by saying: "We want to vote for the person who's least likely to do damage towards First Nations peoples." Another man in his forties, active with the Liberal Party, said: "We are a separate people within Canada," and so we vote "wherever we see people supporting our ideas and not trying to make drastic change to our rights."

It appears, based on our admittedly limited and non-representative sample, that the nationalist argument for refusing to participate in the Canadian electoral process finds relatively little resonance in Winnipeg. In fact, nationalist feelings, or at least identification with the notion that they are a distinct group with rights that need to be defended, are precisely what leads many Aboriginal people to vote. They vote to protect their identity as a separate people and to protect their specifically Aboriginal rights.

Social Exclusion and Voting

While the nationalist explanation for relatively low Aboriginal participation in the mainstream political process was scarcely mentioned by our respondents, social exclusion was frequently mentioned. A majority of our respondents said that the reason so many Aboriginal people do not vote is that they feel excluded or marginalized from the system.

A former chief, now resident in Winnipeg, told us that:

> *First Nations people don't have a sense of ownership of the electoral process. They still think it's the other guys' process, not theirs, so they're more apt to not be involved. It's not our game so they don't get involved.*

A significant number of our participants demonstrated the social exclusion explanation by telling us that they, or others of their acquaintance, do not vote because they do not know how to vote. For example, a forty-three-year-old man told us, "I don't really know where to go." One woman said:

> *A lot of people are isolated and I do mean isolated.... When they come into the city... they feel it's too much, it's overwhelming for them and they do want to get involved but they're very shy because they don't know how.*

A forty-eight-year-old woman who is now very politically active described her early years in the city, when she was a young woman: "I just didn't really know where to go.... I didn't get enough instructions about where to really go... they should have come to my door." Another woman, also now politically active and in her forties, said: "I know some people who have such low self-esteem... who are intimidated... at how to deal with other non-Aboriginal people in the voting system."

Many of the young people that we interviewed seemed particularly removed from the electoral system. One twenty-year-old, when asked by his friend Ed Keeper, "What do you think of when you hear the word 'politics'?" asked that the tape recorder be stopped in order to ask Ed: "What is politics?" When asked if he ever voted he replied: "No. There's no need for me to vote, I guess. First of all, I don't even know what's going on with the voting and stuff like that. I don't have no information, so there's no point in voting, I guess." An eighteen-year-old, when asked if he ever voted, replied: "No, never really heard about it." A twenty-five-year-old replied to the question, "What do you think of when you hear the word 'politics'?" with "Ah, don't really care. Do I vote? No, I don't. Because I don't wanna." After some additional questions, including one about

I don't believe they feel they're a part of the rest of society.

I think Aboriginal people don't feel that they belong.

Kind of being outside of the mainstream of what's happening.

They don't feel like they have anything to do with it, they feel not a part of it.

They don't feel connected in any way.*

*We have asked all of our respondents why Aboriginal people tend to vote less in the mainstream political process than non-Aboriginal people. It could be argued that only those who do not vote can explain why they do not vote. The responses of Aboriginal people who do vote could be seen as mere speculation. However, we hold to the view that urban Aboriginal people — those who do not vote in mainstream elections and those who do — have valuable insights into Aboriginal voting behaviour.

the Assembly of Manitoba Chiefs, he said in frustration: "What? Am I supposed to know about this stuff? Really? I never even voted, in my life.… I don't care about no chiefs. I don't. I care about myself, care about my friends… that's all I care about." A twenty-two-year-old woman said about many of her friends that "they don't really care, they've got other priorities in life, and that is not one of them." These young people seem to be completely removed from the political process. It is of course important to note that there has been a precipitous drop in voting among all young people, not just young Aboriginal people. And it is interesting to note that a number of our other participants, including people who are now politically active, told us that when they were young, not only did they not vote but they "didn't have a clue what was going on in the world." The fact that young people, including young Aboriginal people, are particularly distant from the political process does not necessarily mean that they will remain that way.

Some said that many Aboriginal people see the system as designed by and for non-Aboriginal people, and they feel that there is little point in their being involved. They feel a sense of futility.

Feelings of futility about voting in a system that is both alien and unresponsive are reinforced when Aboriginal people are mistreated in the voting process. One respondent, experienced in political campaigns, said: "I've been at the polls, I've taken people to the polls, and we've gotten such disrespect from the people, you know, 'who are you?'" She described the campaign of an Aboriginal woman

I guess I figure it doesn't make a difference... because we're the minority and if we all voted it wouldn't matter because it would be so small.

I guess because they feel their voice is never going to be heard, it doesn't matter, I won't make a difference.

I think they don't vote because they think it doesn't make any difference.

It's because they think, what use, what's the use? you know.

Hopelessness... what difference?

I think that they feel that their vote is not going to make a difference and just the general apathy toward the whole political process, that the government is not really working for the people.

It doesn't make any difference to them. They have a crappy life; it's never going to change; and why is my vote gonna count? That's the attitude.

running for City Council in Winnipeg's North End some years ago. "All of the poll clerks at [an inner-city school with a very high Aboriginal population] were white middle-class people, and we were taking elders to vote... and they got treated with such derision by the poll clerks, 'Speak English'. . . . I've been involved in many elections; I've seen it over and over again." In other cases this manifests itself as feelings of distrust, as described by a middle-aged woman: "people don't trust the politicians, the government, eh? We've always been mistrustful. We're still dealing with things like treaties."

Voting on Home Reserves

A number of interviewees said they never vote in Winnipeg but either do vote or have in the past voted on their home reserves. One forty-one-year-old man said: "I vote for my chief on the reserve," but when asked whether he votes in the city said "No, because I have no understanding of voting for them." A twenty-five-year-old man, who does not vote, when asked if he knows anyone who does, replied yes, on the reserve, but added "I don't know anybody who votes here, in the city." A twenty-five-year-old woman said: "I think there is a gaining of interest for people to vote *on their First Nation* [her emphasis]. They're interested in First Nations politics but when it comes to provincial and federal government politics in regards to elections and political parties, I think there is a lot less interest." This is similar to other studies that show voter participation is higher in many First Nations elections than in provincial or federal elections (Bedford and Pobihushchy 1995; Guerin 2003). Why is this? We think the reason is that many Aboriginal people do not feel excluded from politics in their home communities, because it is a more face-to-face process in which they personally know the candidates. A former chief told us that "in band elections voter turnout is usually high, and that probably can be attributed to, it's close to home and it directly affects them." A current chief, long involved in Aboriginal politics, said that in First Nations communities:

> *They know the person, and they know that they can do something if they want to. And the other thing is that they know that they're in control, that they can remove this person if they want to, as opposed to provincial or federal, they really don't have any control.*

A thirty-five-year-old woman, herself a very knowledgeable voter, reiterated the observation that some Aboriginal people who do vote on their First Nation do not vote in the city, and explained it by saying:

> *Partly it's, they might not be educated necessarily in mainstream politics. It's different in quite a few ways to First Nations politics. It operates differently, and it's like two separate political entities... for one, First Nations politics is very localized to the First Nations community. A lot of times... it's a very small community, usually, like on average say 800 people in a First Nation community. So of course you have access to chief and council, you see them possibly on a daily basis and you know them better, you grew up with those people, whereas you come to the city and you don't know the people who are running, and I guess you might feel some sense of intimidation going and trying to make an appointment with them, or find out where they're located and then going through all the red tape of having some time to spend with them. And you don't know them on a personal level.*

Those cases in which Aboriginal people vote in their home communities but not in the city in federal, provincial or city elections seem to confirm that non-voting is rooted in urban Aboriginal people's sense of exclusion from the mainstream political system.

At the same time, however, we were told that in some cases it is the experience of Aboriginal politics, both on and off reserve, that has turned some Aboriginal people off politics. Part of the problem, some people told us, is that urban Aboriginal people are largely ignored by chiefs' organizations, which see their sole responsibility as the people on reserve, "although they receive funding for people who don't live on reserve," as one woman pointed out. On at least some reserves, chief and council do not operate in an open and democratic fashion.

One woman who is active with Aboriginal women's organizations, said about Aboriginal NDP MLAs Eric Robinson, Oscar Lathlin and George Hickes: "I have respect for those men… but I know there's chiefs on reserves… they wouldn't give you the time of day." A former chief himself told us that: "I find that our First Nations governments do very little consultation… only the chief and council and staff know what's going on." Women in particular are excluded, consistent, as one woman told us, with a "male-oriented society [which] excludes women." She added that for women, and especially Aboriginal women's groups, "We're treated worse than third world countries in our own country here. It's like white male, white women, and then the minorities, and then somewhere down below there's the native women." Efforts to challenge such exclusion, we were told, are all too often met with hostility and retribution. As one sixty-three-year-old told us:

> No, no, most Aboriginal people don't follow politics… it's a matter of their experience. Even with the chiefs' organizations, very often the chief that's in doesn't always appreciate "back-seat drivers" or people who have a difference of opinion, so usually if you're quiet and do your own thing, you're better off than if you're really involved, especially if you're on the losing side.

A long-time inner-city activist in a host of Aboriginal organizations said:

> time and time again, there's retribution on the basis of your association, and we've seen people taken advantage of politically, and those who lose the political fight are dealt with harshly… a lot of people walk away from that, eh, a lot of Aboriginal people who are exposed to adversarial circumstances such as this simply don't want to be involved.

The political experience on reserves is an important contributing factor in shaping Aboriginal people's attitudes about mainstream political participation. Its impact is contradictory. In the case of many we interviewed, reserve politics, with its face-to-face character, is a comfortable experience. Those running for office are well known to them, the issues have an immediate impact on their daily lives, and the process is one with which they are familiar. They vote or have voted on reserve. But in the city, where the process is anonymous, the political contestants are unknown to them and the issues are more removed from their daily experience, they do not vote. In the case of others, reserve politics has left a bad taste in their mouths, so to speak. They told us that they had found chiefs and council to be removed from the community and secretive in their way of operating, and in some cases, to have punished those who dared to question or speak out against them. As a result, they are disaffected and disinclined to become involved in politics. In either case, the result is non-voting in the city.

Informed Cynicism

In many cases, respondents offered what we would describe as an "informed cynicism" as their explanation for many Aboriginal people not voting. One eighteen-year-old woman said: "They just never speak about Aboriginal, they'll say something, then when it comes down to it, they like to get us to vote for them, they'll just, like, don't do it, you know, they won't come through." An eighteen-year-old man said much the same: "They don't hear what native people have to say, and they just, you know, do their own thing and build their big high-rises or whatever... kind of drift off and forget about native people." A twenty-eight-year-old man who is a university student says about those Aboriginal people who do not vote in mainstream elections: "they know they've been screwed over but they don't want to get involved with it." A woman in her fifties adds: "Why should we participate in that stuff?... For Aboriginal people nothing changes, we're still on the bottom of the barrel." A fifty-seven-year-old man, long involved in Aboriginal and to some extent non-Aboriginal politics, offers the same explanation:

> It's mostly the fact that governments do not seem to be doing anything substantial for Aboriginal people, I think that's the main reason. No government actually enacts policies that really will change the conditions in our communities. That's the experience of most Aboriginal people.

"It's a system that the rich and the powerful control, essentially," concluded a politically experienced fifty-one-year-old woman. Her colleague, present at this interview, a woman in her forties, added: "I can't be bothered voting because to me it's a waste of my time. Not once in my life have I ever voted."

Among many urban Aboriginal people, there is a profound sense of futility in voting in mainstream elections. They do not believe that voting will make a difference in their lives. They know that governments are largely controlled by others, by non-Aboriginal people, by "the rich and powerful," and they know that policies are rarely enacted that accrue to their benefit. This is a cynicism rooted in their personal experience.

Surviving Day to Day

For many urban Aboriginal people, their focus is on survival, on making it from one day to the next, and the electoral experience and the possibility of voting are completely outside their daily experience. "The majority of our people are just struggling with day-to-day life and really don't have the energy or inclination for politics," said a man in his sixties. Several women described being single mothers when they were young and simply not having any connection with politics. A thirty-two-year-old woman said:

I didn't start living until my last child and that was when I was twenty-five.... I've had a kid since I was fifteen, so ten years I was raising kids and when I turned twenty-five... that's when it started, I started volunteering in the community.

A forty-seven-year-old woman offered this assessment:

When you feel disempowered, you don't feel you're worth anything and you don't feel you're making a contribution to society, so you don't participate. Your basic function in life is to survive. A high percentage of Aboriginal people are barely surviving in our society, and there are a lot of issues that they're facing on a day-to-day basis such as poverty, suicide, unemployment, addiction, which prevent them from moving forward. And I think when you have a group in society that's like that... and there's no leadership in terms of how to bridge the gap between the haves and the have-nots, then nothing really happens and the gap widens and as a result of that I believe the community looks at the system as a very hostile system in which to live.

An understanding of politics and the attitude that regards voting as a public duty develop to a considerable extent in the family. Many urban Aboriginal people have grown up in circumstances in which mainstream politics was never mentioned. Several of those who do vote in mainstream elections, however, mentioned the role of their families as an explanation. One sixty-four-year-old man said that the reason he votes is: "Probably because my grandmother and grandfather would turn over in their graves if I didn't." A sixty-three-year-old man explained his voting in mainstream elections by saying: "I was brought up by my father to be interested in politics, I remember he thought it was very important, he said he fought for democracy and it was something he felt was very important and he brought me up that way." A forty-seven-year-old woman who votes regularly said: "I remember in the 1960s and early 1970s, my parents being involved with the NDP and helping to get a person elected... they got all us kids delivering leaflets door to door." A twenty-two-year-old woman said that she frequently talks with people about politics, "especially my family, that's where I get most of my knowledge, they're kind of like my newspaper, they inform me of what's going on and they give me their opinions." She added:

Whereas a lot of families don't talk about politics as much.... I think it's a part of their upbringing, their culture, it's not something they grow up surrounded in, like I was, in politics. They haven't been giving it much thought, they haven't really been involved in it a lot when they're young and growing up. I don't know, I think it's just a repetitive cycle so they don't really hear much about it from the parents or get involved and so it

*just keeps repeating itself. And I mean, also, I mean throughout history the
Aboriginal people really haven't been given the right to vote or be involved
in the political system.*

In all of these various ways and for all of these various reasons, many
Aboriginal people in Winnipeg's inner city feel excluded from mainstream society generally and from the electoral system in particular. The social exclusion
explanation for lower levels of Aboriginal voting in mainstream elections was
a prominent theme in our interviews.

Age, Education and Socio-Economic Status

The observation that voting is correlated with age, level of formal education and
knowledge of political affairs generally — the third of the four broad explanatory
streams — was borne out in our study. For the women interviewed, seven of
the nine who told us that they always vote were thirty-five years of age or older
and had at least some post-secondary education. For the men, six of the eight
who always vote were thirty-five years of age or older and had at least some
post-secondary education. In total, thirteen of the seventeen (76.5 percent) of
the interviewees who told us that they always vote were thirty-five years of age
or older and had at least some post-secondary education. We interviewed eight
university students; six told us that they regularly vote, one does not vote for
religious reasons (she is a Jehovah's Witness), and one nineteen-year-old had
only once been eligible to vote and had not voted on that single occasion but
intends to in the future. One of the students told us that Aboriginal students
at the University of Winnipeg talk politics "all the time. Political subjects are
coming up all the time at school, and I don't think I've been more politically
aware than since I have been at school."

WHAT COULD BE DONE TO INDUCE MORE URBAN ABORIGINAL PEOPLE TO PARTICIPATE IN THE MAINSTREAM ELECTORAL PROCESS?

Many more urban Aboriginal people would vote if political parties and candidates for office were to make an effort to reach out to them. This is the fourth
broad explanatory theme discussed above, and it was borne out in our interviews.
A majority of respondents told us that politicians and parties need to connect
with Aboriginal people and need to come into Aboriginal neighbourhoods and
meet and talk with residents face to face.

Aboriginal people in urban centres feel socially excluded from mainstream
non-Aboriginal institutions. Further, because of their history of colonization,
many are reluctant to become involved. But our respondents told us that if urban
Aboriginal people were to be approached by politicians and political parties,

I think for my friends, I think they'd get more active if politicians... really tried to connect with the community more.

Well, knocking on doors and sitting down with people and talking to them.

You have to try to find people... harness those votes, on a face-to-face kind of thing.

One of the things would be for the politicians to... the more locally involved they are, the more exposure they have to the community, to the people. I think people really warm to that and people don't necessarily warm to seeing someone's face on a billboard and having no connection with them or not being able to speak with them at all.

The grassroots people are the people they should be targeting, and being out there and talking to and letting us know who they are.

and treated with respect, they would become involved. Aboriginal people need to be approached, one long-time urban resident told us, "so they feel welcome and involved in political activity." This echoes a central finding in Chapter Three. Aboriginal people want to be treated as equals, "and simply because your skin is brown or you have a funny accent, you need to be accepted as a *complete equal*" (his emphasis). Another long-time urban resident said much the same: "If there's perceived caring, if there's perceived interest, then of course people will come out to vote." People feel excluded. "Keep in contact, and let us into the workings of the political process... let us in on some of the political process."

Yet far from letting Aboriginal people into the political process, politicians and political parties, as we were told repeatedly, do not even come into Aboriginal communities to meet with Aboriginal people. One thirty-two-year-old woman, resident in Winnipeg all her life and very knowledgeable about politics, said: "I've never seen anybody [from a political party] in the community." A forty-nine-year-old woman, herself politically active, told us that: "The majority of them don't keep in touch with the grassroots people and that's where the voters are.... It's like corporations and big business, it's always them come first." A forty-one-year-old man who has not voted offered an explanation echoed by many of our respondents: "because nobody comes around to see me at election time."

It is very likely that this is so, at least in part, because of the manner in which political parties organize their election campaigns. The typical electoral strategy is for a party to identify those parts of a constituency in which its candidate got many votes in the previous election, and then work to maximize the turnout there; in those polls where turnout was relatively low, the typical strategy is to exert little effort. To the extent that this is the case, those neighbourhoods with large Aboriginal populations would likely be targeted for little if any political effort.

Yet we were told repeatedly that if they were to be approached, Aboriginal people would participate. If their opinions were to be actively sought on matters of direct importance to them, Aboriginal people would respond. "If they had town hall meetings on welfare rates, for example, you'd get hundreds of people out, if they had town hall meetings on crime you'd get hundreds of people out," and the same would be the case if such meetings were to be organized to discuss schools or children, matters of direct concern to urban Aboriginal people.

We believe not only that many more Aboriginal people would vote in federal, provincial and municipal elections if they were approached by politicians and political parties, but also that significant increases in participation would be achieved if politicians and political parties were to employ strategies specifically crafted to reach Aboriginal people. One very knowledgeable forty-seven-year-old respondent put it this way:

> Oh yeah… they need to be talking to the grassroots people. And the way you do that isn't the same way you would do it with your average person. I think we need to use a different format in speaking with a group that's disenfranchised.

This woman works with both Aboriginal and non-Aboriginal people, and when she meets with Aboriginal people she does so in a sharing circle. She adds: "I wouldn't invite them in to tell them what I thought. I would invite them in to hear what they have to say." She uses a different approach, a specifically designed approach, to meet and work with Aboriginal people. In the inner city, Aboriginal people can be mobilized by invitation to collective, cultural events. A long-time inner-city activist describes it this way:

> Typically at Friendship Centres, having a feast or something or a cultural event or a meal brings people out in great numbers, it just seems to be that it's legitimate to come out to share in a community experience, and then the voting is something that happens.

If candidates for political office in constituencies with large Aboriginal populations were to reach out to Aboriginal people in a door-to-door, face-to-face manner, Aboriginal people tell us that they would vote. If candidates were to call public meetings to hear Aboriginal people's views on matters of importance to them, hundreds of people would turn out, as we were told. And if political parties and candidates were to break from their long-established electoral campaign strategies and be creative in designing specific strategies to meet, talk with and hear from Aboriginal people, the results, we have been told, would be positive. For example, if a candidate for public office were to organize a meeting of Aboriginal constituents that featured a meal and that took place in an Aboriginal cultural context, Aboriginal people would attend. Clearly, then, with such simple solutions at hand, Aboriginal voter turnout remains low because politicians and political parties are unwilling to exert the political effort.

Even more likely to improve the Aboriginal electoral turnout would be the presence of Aboriginal candidates for elected office. Chris Henderson, candidate for mayor of Winnipeg in 2002 and now Grand Chief of the Southern Chiefs' Organization, generated considerable Aboriginal involvement. Several participants told us that they became involved politically because they heard that there was an Aboriginal candidate for mayor. Henderson himself described the effect on Aboriginal people of his candidacy:

> I meet young Aboriginal people and they tell me, like, wow, I saw you on TV or I read about you in the newspaper or I heard you on radio and I was so impressed that, you know, I've never ever voted in my life, I've never had an interest in politics, but as a result of hearing you or seeing you, I went out and voted for you, and I told all my friends to vote for you.

Henderson told us that Aboriginal people will vote, but some targeted political effort is needed. A candidate seeking Aboriginal votes should go door to door; hold neighbourhood barbecues; go to the local bingo hall; and say to Aboriginal people that she/he would "very much encourage your input and participation." Even the young people involved in the focus group session at an inner-city community centre, most of them almost completely marginalized from the dominant culture and from the political process, told us that they were delighted to be asked their opinions and if they were consulted by politicians, and especially if Aboriginal politicians were to run for office, they would become involved.

An Elite-based Strategy:
The Liberal Party of Canada and Aboriginal People

The Conservative Party of Canada appears to have made little organized effort to recruit Aboriginal voters; the Liberal Party of Canada has. The Liberal Party's is almost exclusively an elite-based approach. It is not aimed at inner-city Aboriginal people. The Liberals have established an Aboriginal People's Commission whose purpose is "encouraging the active participation of Aboriginal people at all levels within the Party" (Liberal Party of Canada n.d.). The Commission was established thirteen years ago by Paul Martin and was called a "big step forward for us" by one participant, who added: "I believe that Paul Martin is very sensitive to our needs." Although the Commission has been relatively inactive for most of that time, its level of activity has picked up lately. For example, in early November 2003, an Aboriginal fund-raiser event was held in Winnipeg for the Liberal Party. It attracted 200 people, most of them Aboriginal, most the Aboriginal elite. One respondent active in the Liberal Party described the event and in so doing revealed much of the Liberal Party strategy for recruiting Aboriginal people:

> We had the elites out, the elites being of course the current political leaders — very few business people from within the Aboriginal community by the way — but nonetheless political and organizational leaders, and young people, students often, aspiring within that political spectrum... there has been some movement in that regard, I mean, six, eight years ago there wouldn't have been such an event, so there is participation. Whether it has much effect on the overall voter turnout is yet, I think, to be seen. I expect it will influence it somewhat, but... my guess is that out of the 200 people who purchased tickets for this event, they might influence four to five others who will vote... that's a guess.

This is a traditional Liberal Party strategy, honed over the years in various immigrant communities: target the elite, the leaders within a community, and hope that their influence trickles down to others in that community. Little or no effort has been made by the Liberal Party to mobilize directly the bulk of the inner-city Aboriginal population.

The Aboriginal leadership, for example, many of the chiefs — "we have some very strong Liberals in the chiefs," one Liberal Party member told us — have responded to this strategy for purely pragmatic reasons. Two non-Liberal Party people who were interviewed, a man and a woman, each in their fifties, described the Aboriginal leadership affiliation with the Liberals in these terms:

> Well, federally, the NDP will never get into power, unless it's in a minority situation and I guess most [Aboriginal] people... they expect the Liberals are going to be in power.... It was a calculated strategy... a lot of people running for the Liberals.

> I know there are lots of the Aboriginal leadership that are Liberals but part of it is that it's not an ideological kind of commitment. It's a kind of a pragmatic commitment, you know, you have to be in those places where the power is.

This pragmatic approach has its limits, as the January 2006 federal election has demonstrated.

A significant component of the Liberal Party's Aboriginal strategy is its focus on young Aboriginal people currently in or recently graduated from university or community college. For example, the November 2003 fund-raiser was organized by young people, in return for which their $900 delegate fee to the Liberal convention was paid. Some thirty to thirty-five young Aboriginal people from Manitoba were sent to the Liberal convention by this method.

In the early 1980s, the provincial NDP government took steps similar to those the Liberal Party is now taking. They created an Aboriginal caucus, and many bright young university- and community college-educated Aboriginal people became involved. One of those people, a man now in his fifties, described what happened this way:

> Yeah, I was part of that, and again, there was some resistance by the party to that and then they used to water down our resolutions. It died out because of that. Some of the people that were committed just went.... It petered out.. It's okay to have gender policies, like women, and labour, but policies on racial grounds, or an Aboriginal caucus, there was resistance to it.

He described a similar process now taking place in the Liberal Party:

> I know some people who are involved in there and they have the same problems as we did with the Aboriginal caucus. You have to fight your own party… fight your way in, and then fight once you get in.

The Liberal Party, in other words, would have to deliver in policy terms — which means the party would have to be returned to office — to continue to attract Aboriginal supporters. However, there appears not to be much in the Liberal Party approach — even if they are returned to office — for urban Aboriginal people, a significant proportion of whom are poor. As one of our respondents, a Liberal Party and inner-city activist, put it:

> Our political system is made up of elites, really, elites who participate, elites who stand guard over what governments and what policies and what benefits are decided upon, and many people at the lower end of the income scale who can't afford the fund-raisers and can't afford the memberships and the delegate fees and the contributions don't really have a voice, and frankly are probably disenchanted by [the fact that] there's a barrier to participation in the political process.

It appears that only the elite of the Aboriginal community are being consciously targeted by the Liberal Party. Whether any party will seek to win the votes of the majority of urban Aboriginal people remains to be seen.

We draw two conclusions from the Liberal Party's Aboriginal strategy and Aboriginal people's response to it. One is that the exertion of political effort by a party can succeed in attracting some Aboriginal people into political involvement. Many of our respondents told us of their positive responses to both symbolic and tangible efforts exerted by the Liberals. A second conclusion, however, is that because this strategy is so deliberately elite-focused, it is unlikely to yield much benefit to low-income urban Aboriginal people. For that to happen, political effort — and real policy benefit — would need to be targeted not at the Aboriginal elite, but precisely at low-income inner-city Aboriginal people. How might this be done?

Political Education

Several of the people we interviewed suggested the need for educational initiatives that are both targeted at low-income inner-city Aboriginal people and focus on promoting and developing an understanding of politics. For example, one twenty-seven-year-old woman said: "First of all, education… how voting works, not just the logistics of going down on election day and voting, but how it actually works… realistic education about how democracy actually works." A twenty-five-year-old woman advocated the development of:

> some way for people in the inner city… and Aboriginal people all over Winnipeg that could really benefit from learning about politics… teaching those people about the importance of who is in power.… If there was some way you could get the regular Aboriginal person to learn and be interested, it would be very good.

And there is evidence, we believe, that low-income inner-city Aboriginal people *would* respond positively to such an initiative. Our focus group session with urban Aboriginal youth, most of whom are largely unaware of the political process, drew a very positive response. One eighteen-year-old told us that the focus group was the first time he had ever talked about political matters, and he enjoyed it. "This I like, what [the leader of the focus group] is doing, it's a really smart idea." To us, this suggests a latent and very significant potential for an imaginatively designed political education initiative. Similarly, a woman who is a university student described attending the forum at which the City of Winnipeg's urban Aboriginal strategy was released, an event attended by large numbers of Aboriginal people, many of whom lined up at two microphones to speak. She said: "It was great and I just wish it could have gone on… for a couple of days.… We need more time with that kind of thing." For many urban Aboriginal people, there is no political space in which to talk about the issues that interest and affect them.

Similarly, young Aboriginal people respond well to opportunities created in their communities, and consistent with the strong correlation between young people's community involvement and their propensity to vote, these appear to lead in some cases to increased levels of political interest and awareness. An eighteen-year-old had been a participant in the Youth Opportunity Project, an inner-city program aimed at getting youth involved and exposing them to job opportunities. This led to her volunteering for Chris Henderson's mayoralty campaign: "I heard him speak once and he seemed to really want to help, and that really affected me." Another Aboriginal youth got a job with the Youth Advisory Committee associated with the Spence Neighbourhood Association (SNA). This made him aware of neighbourhood issues and gave him the opportunity to design a youth project and present it to the SNA board for approval. He is the eighteen-year-old who liked talking about political issues, which he did for the first time ever at our focus group session. Again, this suggests to us the very significant potential for increased Aboriginal involvement in the mainstream political process.

If Aboriginal people themselves were to begin to educate and mobilize the inner-city Aboriginal community around the importance of political involvement, and particularly the importance of voting, we believe — based on the evidence gleaned from our interviews — that the community would respond positively. Indeed, inner-city Aboriginal people are *telling* us that if somebody reached out to them to invite them directly and personally to participate in the mainstream political process, they *would* participate. The best way for this to happen is for Aboriginal people themselves to undertake this kind of voter mobilization, much as was done in the voter registration drives of the American civil rights movement.

Aboriginal Candidates

More Aboriginal people would vote if there were more Aboriginal candidates. This was very clearly stated in our interviews. One young woman in her early thirties told us that "last year I voted for someone because he was an Aboriginal person running for mayor and I thought that was the greatest thing." A thirty-year-old woman told us that if there were more Aboriginal candidates, "then you'd see more people… you look at Chris Henderson… a lot of people came out." A forty-five-year-old woman told us that more Aboriginal people would come out to vote "if we should be so lucky as to have an Aboriginal person run in our area."

It is our opinion that the question may soon be not "why do urban Aboriginal people not vote in mainstream elections?" but rather "who will they vote for?" Many urban Aboriginal people have told us that they would vote if someone were to ask them to vote. We believe that Aboriginal people themselves could, and should, seize this opportunity to reach out to other urban Aboriginal people on a face-to-face basis and engage them on the issues that matter to them. We believe, in short, that the urban Aboriginal vote can be mobilized with the exertion of some political effort. And to the extent that the proportion of Aboriginal people who go to university and community college continues to grow, the evidence shows that the urban Aboriginal vote will correspondingly grow. We think it likely that urban Aboriginal people are soon going to come bursting into electoral politics as education levels increase, as Aboriginal people begin to organize themselves around political issues, and as political parties and politicians realize that the demographics are such that the Aboriginal vote is significant, and that it can be mobilized if political effort is exerted.

Will Aboriginal people use the political potential available to them to advance the interests of the still very large numbers of urban Aboriginal people whose lives are consumed by the struggle to survive? Or will their politics take the elite form that many of our respondents told us characterizes all politics, Aboriginal and non-Aboriginal alike? The political effort exerted by the Liberal Party to date has certainly taken an openly elite form, aimed at attracting only those in the Aboriginal community who are economically advantaged and university-educated. Nevertheless, there are large numbers of urban Aboriginal people whose objective circumstances are such that a more egalitarian form of politics would be very much to their advantage. The form that Aboriginal electoral politics takes in the near future — elite-based, or more egalitarian — remains to be seen. Our speculation, however, based on the results of our interviews, is that in the very near future, urban Aboriginal people and the urban Aboriginal vote are going to become a significant part of the urban political landscape in cities that, like Winnipeg and others in Western Canada, have large Aboriginal populations. Whether this will benefit urban Aboriginal people, particularly the relatively high proportion of urban Aboriginal people who live in disadvantaged circumstances, is an open question.

THE ELECTORAL POTENTIAL OF ABORIGINAL PEOPLE

It appears from our interview evidence that Aboriginal people in Winnipeg's inner city, like Aboriginal people in Canada generally, vote less on average than non-Aboriginal people in mainstream elections. It is also the case, however, that Aboriginal people in Winnipeg and in Manitoba have considerable *potential* electoral power. They constitute a majority of the population in two provincial constituencies, and a significant minority — at least one in six — in another fifteen provincial constituencies, of which six are in Winnipeg. This is enough to matter: in six of the last nine Manitoba provincial elections, the winning party had a majority of three or fewer seats out of fifty-seven (Elections Manitoba data). And Aboriginal people constitute a significant minority in two federal ridings in Winnipeg, and three City of Winnipeg wards. If Aboriginal people in Manitoba and in Winnipeg were to begin to vote at the same rate that non-Aboriginal people do, political parties and candidates for federal, provincial and municipal office would find it in their interest to offer policy inducements and, potentially, other institutional changes to secure their vote. The results could be that the socio-economic circumstances of Aboriginal people would improve and the political opportunity structure available to Aboriginal people open up.

It would be a mistake, however, to over-estimate the likely political benefits to Aboriginal people, and especially low-income Aboriginal people, of increased Aboriginal voting in federal, provincial and municipal elections. Women, for example, vote in significant numbers and constitute more than one-half of the Canadian population. Yet it could not be said that women are politically powerful, nor that political parties have significantly changed their structures, practices or agendas to attract women's votes. And a disproportionate number of women continue to be found among the ranks of the poor.

As discussed, that Aboriginal people in Winnipeg's inner city do not now vote in mainstream elections as much as non-Aboriginal people appears to be attributable largely to their sense of exclusion from the dominant culture and institutions of society, the cumulative product of Aboriginal people's colonization. In addition, it appears from our interview evidence that political parties and politicians exert relatively little effort to attract the Aboriginal vote in Winnipeg's inner city, thus reinforcing Aboriginal people's social exclusion.

The results of our interviews, however, lead us to think that the voting practices of Aboriginal people in Winnipeg could soon change. We noted a strong, positive correlation among respondents between level of formal education and likelihood of voting in mainstream elections; and the numbers of Aboriginal people attending post-secondary educational institutions are growing. Perhaps more importantly, many of our respondents made it very clear that if they were approached by political parties and asked to vote, they would be likely to do so, and if Aboriginal candidates were to be running for office, they would be even more likely to do so. Given the significance of their numbers in so many electoral districts, it seems to us likely — if for no other reason than self-interest — that political parties and politicians will start to court the Aboriginal vote, and that more Aboriginal candidates will be sought and will emerge in particular electoral districts.

We can expect that Aboriginal people in Winnipeg will *not* vote as a bloc, although our interviews suggest that most are unlikely to vote for right-of-centre political parties. As one female university student put it: "the Alliance [sic] Party would not be favourable to us, there's a lot of 'Cowboy Bobs' in there." Another young woman said about the Conservative Party: "that's just money; we don't have money." Numerous other respondents expressed similar views. Some are likely to vote Liberal, and the federal Liberal Party does exert some political effort to attract Aboriginal voters, particularly the elite and post-secondary students. Others are likely to vote NDP — at least provincially — because, our interviews suggest, the NDP is deemed to be the party most likely to respond positively to urban Aboriginal people's socio-economic needs. Whichever party Aboriginal people vote for, *if* they begin to vote in greater numbers than is now the case, political parties will find it in their self-interest to vie for their vote. Aboriginal issues are then more likely to rise on parties' agendas for action, and parties may modify their internal practices to reflect and accommodate Aboriginal members. The key is voter turnout — votes are the currency that political parties trade in.

The urban Aboriginal vote in Winnipeg is likely to increase not only because of rising educational levels and parties' increased political effort, but also because there are steps that the Aboriginal community itself could take to increase voter turnout. The inner-city Aboriginal community may take these steps because it is in their interest to do so: the evidence strongly suggests that increased political participation leads to improved socio-economic circumstances. An educational effort undertaken by the Aboriginal community and aimed at making inner-city Aboriginal people more aware of and knowledgeable about the electoral process would likely increase the rate of Aboriginal voting. Numerous interview respondents told us, and our focus group with young Aboriginal people made especially clear, that many inner-city Aboriginal people would respond positively to initiatives aimed at increasing their knowledge of the electoral process.

Whether increased rates of Aboriginal voting would truly benefit urban Aboriginal people, and particularly the relatively high proportion of urban Aboriginal people who live in disadvantaged circumstances, remains an open question. The result *could* be just another form of elite politics. Alternatively, it could reflect the kinds of Aboriginal community development initiatives described in Chapter Five, in which case Aboriginal voters would lead the way in shaping a new, more egalitarian politics in urban centres.

Chapter Five

SHARING, COMMUNITY AND DECOLONIZATION

Urban Aboriginal Community Development

Jim Silver, Parvin Ghorayshi, Joan Hay and Darlene Klyne

In this chapter, urban Aboriginal people, long-time activists in their community, outline an inspiring, holistic, Aboriginal approach to community development. Rooted in traditional Aboriginal values of sharing and community, this approach to community development starts with the individual and the individual's need to heal from the damage of colonization. The process of people's healing, of their rebuilding or recreating themselves, is rooted in a revived sense of community and a revitalization of Aboriginal cultures; this in turn requires the building of Aboriginal organizations. The process of reclaiming an Aboriginal identity takes place, therefore, at an individual, community, organizational and ultimately political level. This is a process now underway; it is a process of decolonization that, if it can continue to be rooted in traditional Aboriginal values of sharing and community, will be the foundation upon which healing and rebuilding are based.

This is a much different sense of "development" from that often taken for granted in the West. It is more consistent with a set of ideas and practices that have been critical of Western notions of development.

The post-Second World War initiatives that led to the idea of development have been widely criticized as exclusionary. Critics argue that development models premised upon the Western notion of modernization and capitalism have predominantly benefitted those who already have economic power (Hart-Landsberg and Burkett 2001; Sparr 1994). By attempting to generate prosperity within the framework of the capitalist market economy, development strategies have ignored the well-being of many (Sen 1999). Development has become a new colonialism, contributing to underdevelopment, which has turned the nations of the South into exploitable resources and dependent consumers (Zaoual 1999), and created barriers to human development and freedom (Sen 1999).

Many people have begun to question this concept of development — with its emphasis on profit and the pursuit of growth, and its enrichment of some and impoverishment of many — both in the "West" and in the "rest" of the world.

Marginalized groups in northern countries, like their counterparts elsewhere, have been the target of development strategies. What came to be labelled as the key characteristics of underdevelopment in southern countries, such as poverty and lack of access to education, health care and employment, for example, also exist among various groups of people in the North (Veltmeyer and O'Malley 2001; Labrecque 1991). Aboriginal people are a good example of people in the North who have been living in what came to be known as "underdeveloped conditions" and who have been the target of development policies (Loxley 1981, 2000; Silver 2003).

Community development has been advanced as an alternative. There are considerable differences between strategies, but in general, community development involves the continuous process of capacity building: building upon and strengthening local resources to generate well-being among community members (Dreier 1996; Fals-Borda 1992; Fisher and Shragge 2002; Perry n.d.: 1–21; Lewis 1994; Fortan et al. 1999). Community development is based on the premise that community members need to gain control of resources to generate economic well-being. The general goal of community development is to benefit those who have been marginalized from the current economic system.

In this chapter, we focus on Aboriginal community development in an inner-city setting. We draw upon the experiences of twenty-six Aboriginal people, men and women, young and old, who have been and remain active in Winnipeg inner-city community development. We use this case study to enter into the debate on development in general, and community development for Aboriginal people in particular. We show how Aboriginal people have been constructed as the "other" within Canadian society. Colonialism negatively affected, and continues to negatively affect, Aboriginal people: their economy, identity, culture, family, community and well-being. Despite difficulties, urban Aboriginal people have continued their struggles to reclaim their history and reconstruct their lives. The urban Aboriginal people who participated in this project provided us with strong evidence of the need to deconstruct the colonial project of development. In the final section of this chapter, those interviewed outline a workable model of community development by and for Aboriginal people. Non-Aboriginal people have a major role to play in ensuring these changes take place.

Two experienced Aboriginal interviewers, Joan Hay and Darlene Klyne, conducted the twenty-six interviews. They began by asking the participants to talk about their lives — their childhood and teen years, their education, work experiences and community involvement — and how they came to be where they are today. In general, the interviewers sought answers to the following questions: What kinds of obstacles to community involvement did you personally face? How did you overcome those obstacles and become actively involved in the community in Winnipeg's inner city? What do you consider appropriate forms of community development? And what would you like to see happening in the future in Winnipeg's urban Aboriginal community, or, what is your conception of an appropriate form of community development for the urban Aboriginal community? All interviews were concluded with basic demographic questions.

CONSTRUCTION OF ABORIGINAL PEOPLE AS THE "OTHER": COLONIZATION AND ITS IMPACT

The Canadian government's deliberate strategy from the late nineteenth and most of the twentieth century with respect to Aboriginal people was assimilation, which required the destruction of Aboriginal cultures. The justification for what can only be seen as a strategy of state-sanctioned violence against an entire people was that Aboriginal cultures were inferior to European-based cultures, and therefore the attempt to destroy Aboriginal cultures was a "civilizing" mission. Aboriginal people resisted this process and have clung tenaciously to their traditional ways of life, but the damage to individuals and to families from this campaign of cultural destruction has been massive.

Aboriginal people refer to the residential schools as their most painful encounter with colonialism. Those we interviewed expressed to us in a variety of ways that residential school was based on the idea that anything to do with Aboriginal people — knowledge, education, family, community, spirituality, language, their very way of being — had to be transformed. The residential schools did not prepare them for the outside world but put down their culture, broke their family ties and, worst of all, instilled a sense of shame. Former students rightly call themselves "residential school survivors." Residential school was a transformative experience for many Aboriginal people. Joseph[1] tells us:

> It produced individuals with new personalities. You never know who you are, there was a lost identity, and I speak really about myself, I didn't know who I was… consequently I was in no-man's land when I came out of residential school.

Jean spent fifteen years at the Pine Creek Residential School. She had been orphaned and went to the school at age three, with her five-year-old sister. When she left:

> There was nothing, no training, no preparation whatsoever in the school to prepare you for the outside world, so when I turned eighteen the principal said, "here's a dollar, and here's a change of clothes, now hit the road." That was the exact word, "hit the road".… I never went to a store, I never had

a dollar in my hand to go and buy myself something, and I didn't realize until after I left there that I knew nothing of the outside world.

This process did not stop when Aboriginal people began to arrive in the city in the 1960s and 1970s. Charles, who is in his late forties, describes the role of the church in defining Aboriginal families and cultures when he was growing up in Winnipeg's North End:

There was a bus that used to drive around every Sunday and pick kids up early in the morning and take them to different, sort of, ministries or churches, and I remember one, it used to be a Zion Church on Elgin. They would pick us up, and they would feed us, right, you know, feed us kinda snacks and stuff like that... and then they would take us into a room.... The minister or priest or whoever the person was then put down our families, eh, say all kinds of things, who our parents were... say they were drunks, they were lazy... and it was all Indian kids, eh, all Aboriginal kids... in that room.... I remember little kids, you know, just crying, literally crying, not just mildly crying, breaking-into-tears-crying, but emotionally breaking down.

Racism

Racism is an almost inevitable product of this process of colonization. All participants talk about racism and how it has affected, and continues to affect, their lives. Charles states: "I remember as a child, there was a lot of racism, eh, and like more openly.... We grew up in a really heavily racist time, and it was like, openly, you know." He describes the use of language:

common phrases like... called us Indians, call us things like "Chief," but like Indian was used like a swear word, it wasn't really used to describe a nation of people, it was used to describe, you know, people who were drunk, lazy, you know, all the sort of false images.

Racism continues to be a daily experience for Aboriginal people in Winnipeg. One of the things that most aggravates them is that non-Aboriginal people are so frequently oblivious to this. Maggie describes a recent high-level civic meeting, where an important city figure said, "I have tried everything for Aboriginal students just to stay in the programs, I think they just need to be encouraged."

And I just looked at her... and I was just like, speechless, and that doesn't happen often, but I didn't even know what to say other than to look at her, like, "are you for real? We just need to be encouraged?" How insulting.... It's all across the board, like, racism is very much alive in this city.

Destruction of Identity and Self-Esteem

The belief that Aboriginal cultures are inferior was constantly expressed by non-Aboriginal people. Some Aboriginal people have internalized those colonial beliefs, and they carry the pain of their supposed inferiority. It weighs them down because one needs a positive sense of oneself to cope with the world. (For a similar argument regarding African-Americans, see hooks 2003.) Charles tells us:

> *There was a lot of garbage that was going on around us, you know, like I said, a lot of violence, a lot of discrimination, a lot of racism.... What I sort of done, feeling and experiencing this racism and this discrimination and this violence.... I chose to, there was no help growing up for me... you know, getting things in life, eh, there was no major, major help.... There's no venue to talk about them.... You just see inequality all over the place.... And I don't know at what point, you know, growing up around here, that we began to sort of recognize that, you know, we were different.... Eventually these things really weigh heavy on a lot of people, they turn to drugs, they turn to alcohol... some of them become extremely violent, like extremely violent.... I remember being really violent as a kid. I just chose to sort of fight... but in a different way. I kind of fell on Main St. for a long time, you know, given up.*

Joseph comments:

> *I hated people, I hated white people, I hated churches, I hated God, I hated government. These things I hated because they destroyed my life, brought it to a standstill.... No hope, a useless existence with no future in mind and all I had was bitterness and anger.*

For some, the burden of internalizing colonialism manifests itself in a lack self-esteem and self-confidence. Ethel remembers when she was young and carrying "lots of shame." Another woman, Ingrid, describes her teenage years as feeling "very ashamed of who I was. I couldn't look anybody in the eye, you know, I walked half my life with my head down, very ashamed of who I was."

These are typical examples of the difficulties that these exceptionally gifted inner-city community leaders have experienced at different stages of their lives. Despite these difficulties, they have made remarkable changes in their lives and in their communities.

RECLAIMING THEIR LIVES

The Aboriginal people who are part of this study have experienced great difficulty convincing institutions of power to act in their interests. In response, they have developed their own, distinctly Aboriginal ways — conditioned in part by their age, class and other determinants of social status — of perceiving and understanding the situation and the possibilities for Aboriginal people in Winnipeg's inner city.

The twenty-six people in this study are working constantly to change their situation and that of urban Aboriginal people generally, and in so doing to challenge the existing relations of power. These individuals are part of, and leaders of, a culture of resistance. They are examples of what Antonio Gramsci (1978), the Italian political philosopher, called "organic intellectuals," in this case meaning Aboriginal people rooted in both traditional Aboriginal ways of thinking and the often harsh realities of Winnipeg's inner city. These are individuals who are using this intellectual framework to analyze and articulate the realities and the hopes and aspirations of inner-city Aboriginal people.

Part of their success story is the number of organizations built by and for Aboriginal people that exist in the city of Winnipeg. John states that there are now more than seventy Aboriginal organizations in the city — formed because urban Aboriginal people were committed to reconstructing their lives. There are differences between these organizations, but some of them are mentioned over and over again as having a tremendously positive impact on the lives of urban Aboriginal people. Among the Aboriginal-created organizations that have been successful in identifying problems and organizing and building to bring about change are: the Ma Mawi Wi Chi Itata Centre; the Aboriginal Centre; the Centre for Aboriginal Human Resource Development; the Indigenous Women's Network; the Native Women's Transition Centre; the Indian and Métis Friendship Centre; the Urban Circle Training Centre; the Urban Aboriginal Education Coalition; Thunder Bird House; the Native Addictions Council of Manitoba.

Each person has her or his own story of overcoming barriers and experiencing empowerment, but three distinct "paths" emerge. One is the crucial nature of adult education for Aboriginal people; a second is the importance of Aboriginal organizations run on the basis of Aboriginal culture; and a third is parenting as a source of empowerment, particularly for women. A combination of these "paths" helped Aboriginal people we interviewed to reclaim their lives and build on their strengths.

Empowerment: Education, Training and Public Investment

The role of education — in particular, post-secondary and adult education — in this process of personal transformation has often been a dramatic one.

For example, in the mid-1980s, Jack came to the city for health reasons and learned about the Métis Economic Development Program run by the Manitoba Métis Federation. "It was a real positive experience for me. Really opened a lot of doors for me," including eventually a bachelor's and a master's degree in social work and a senior position with one of the urban Aboriginal organizations mentioned above.

Ethel's experience was similar. She returned to school at age thirty after she and her partner had separated. She knew that, as a single parent, she had to make more money. This meant getting some education, despite "still feeling the shame of not having the strong foundation you get from your high school." She adds:

> And that's where the healing began, is when I returned when I was thirty years old, you know, started looking back at my life, and I was very lucky, you know, I was in the Core Area Initiative [a 1980s tri-level urban development program in Winnipeg that funded, among other things, a host of human resource programs] with a lot of other Anishinabe people so that environment was conducive to learning, you felt at home, there were other adult learners who were returning after being out of school for twenty years…. I quit at fifteen because I couldn't make it in the high school, so the shame… as soon as I turned sixteen, man, I was gone. So it was fifteen years of not being in school. But even prior to that, the school being so fragmented, and being on the run for all those years, there was never a foundation, a strong foundation. But I also know that as adult learners you choose to learn and I excelled.

Drawing on this experience, she went on to establish an Aboriginal adult education institute, which is now a leader in Canada in Aboriginal adult educational programming.

Three things should be noted here. One is the importance of adult education for Aboriginal people, of whom a larger proportion than non-Aboriginal people do not complete high school and have had very bad experiences in high school.

A second is the importance of designing Aboriginal educational initiatives on the basis of Aboriginal culture. Ethel says: "it was at that point, when I was thirty, that I first started identifying with who I was as an Aboriginal person… so returning to the culture was huge…. It was just, finally, a place of belonging." Doris, who experienced many difficulties as a teenager in Winnipeg, finally attended the Aboriginal high school, Children of the Earth. "That's where I started to figure out who I was and who my people were… that whole healing journey."

The third is the importance of public investment in the inner city. Ethel went to an adult education program created by the publicly funded Core Area Initiative. She subsequently played a lead role in developing the unique Aboriginal program at her adult education centre, which has had approximately a thousand Aboriginal students over the past fifteen years and has since its inception been funded in part by tri-level urban development agreements. So the initial investment in one adult education program that Ethel attended has generated a remarkable rate of return, considering the benefits to a thousand families, particularly since almost all of the program's graduates find jobs (see Chapter Three).

Another good example is Manitoba's ACCESS program, which provides a range of supports to Aboriginal and other disadvantaged students to enable them to attend and succeed at post-secondary education. Significant numbers of Aboriginal people, most attending as mature students, have now graduated with university degrees. As Agatha observes: "one reason that things are beginning to change too is that many Aboriginal people now have gone through post-second-ary education.... These people are often the spokespersons, you know, and they are very smart and they are very vocal and they are very articulate and they are demanding changes."

And as Aboriginal people have begun to attend university in growing numbers, their consciousness has been raised by the experience. Attendance at university enabled many of the people that we interviewed to see the bigger picture, to situate their personal grief in the historical process and impact of colonization. Richard, who grew up poor in Winnipeg's North End, puts it this way:

> One of the things that happened to me, and I think that happened to many of the people who started to go to university, we started to develop a stronger analysis or a stronger sense of who we were and a stronger sense of our rights and our responsibilities that went along with that, and so very early on we started to look at developing things that would be helpful for us and for our community.

Jean, who had only completed grade six at a residential school — "they only had up to grade six in the school, so I never went any further than that" — talked about being at the Indian and Métis Friendship Centre (IMFC) in the 1950s and 1960s. "I really admired the ones that had grade ten.... I think I only met about two or three people with grade twelve." But the IMFC began to work to change that. Talking about the early years of the IMFC, John said:

> We were organized because we wanted to see things happen, we wanted to see change take place and over the past thirty years there have been a lot of changes that have happened. Just one example, in education when we first

started out, I think we had only one university graduate: Verna Kirkness was one of the first graduates in Manitoba.

He described the IMFC role in making this happen:

When we created the BUNTEP [Brandon University Northern Teacher Education Program] and the ACCESS programs, that was a lot of work that people don't realize was done through the organizations, through the Friendship Centres, through pressure that was put on the government to do something about making university more accessible to the Aboriginal people.

Ironically, an education system that has failed so many Aboriginal students at the elementary and secondary levels has produced more successes for adult Aboriginal students — both at the post-secondary level and in adult education, including the outstanding adult learning centres in Winnipeg (see Chapter Three). The success of this "second chance" level of education is in large part attributable to its introducing Aboriginal students to an understanding of the process of colonization. In this way, students have been able to situate their own difficult circumstances in the broader historical context and then begin to rebuild their lives around their growing pride in their Aboriginal identity.

Aboriginal Organizations and Empowerment

For some of our respondents, it was not formal education but rather the education that comes with involvement in organizations created by and for Aboriginal people that played the key role in their renewed pride in Aboriginal identity.

Jean remembers attending an Indian-Métis Conference with her uncle in the early 1950s, shortly after the birth of her third child. She was a woman who, after fifteen years in the residential school, hardly spoke to anyone. She states: "My husband always said I was very shy and quiet, and I hardly said anything for the first three years we were married." But that would change with her introduction to a group of Aboriginal people dealing collectively with their issues.

I went with my uncle... and I got really interested, and you know the best part about that is I felt really good because here were my people, I'm talking to people that I know, I can talk to people that speak the same language, you know, and then I found out what they were going to be doing and I said, "I'd sure like to help," and that's how I got to be involved in the organizing of the first Friendship Centre in Winnipeg.... I helped organize the whole Friendship Centre, get it started, get it off the ground, encouraged other Aboriginal people.

John tells a similar story. He came from a small Métis community in

Manitoba's Interlake region, where there was a vibrant community life in which he was involved:

> *Well, I started getting involved when I was in my home town… and I remember the very first meeting, public meeting I ever went to. My mother dragged us to this meeting to listen to, of all people, John Diefenbaker, who came to our community to talk to the people and I remember going to the meeting there and that kind of stuck in my mind about getting involved in the community, and of course our community was very well organized in those days. We had Boy Scouts, Girl Guides, we had all kinds of activities, some of which we organized ourselves, a lot of which were organized through the school and the church. The church played a pretty big role in our community when I was growing up so we were always involved in some community activity or other… and we volunteered mostly, we never looked at it as volunteering, it was almost part of our responsibility to do stuff. So that's how I got my first taste of getting involved in community work.*

John came to Winnipeg in the 1960s and got involved with the Company of Young Canadians. The CYC started organizing the individual Friendship Centres into a provincial organization called the Manitoba Association of Friendship Centres, and in doing this he worked with a group of other young Aboriginal activists, including Louise Chippeway, Ovide Mercredi, Phil Fontaine, Moses Okimaw, Harold Harper, Dorothy Betz and Percy Bird. He describes things this way:

> *At that time they used to have Indian-Métis conferences here at the Royal Alexandra Hotel and they were run mostly by social workers, bureaucrats, church people, and so by attending these conferences we quickly realized that there was something wrong, because the white people were doing all the talking and the Indians were just sitting there. So we said "we better get organized."*

He adds: "what the Friendship Centre did is first of all it brought the community together, secondly it provided an environment in which leadership could develop, and then thirdly it provided a much-needed voice for people that had no voice."

Robert is a young participant whose experience exemplifies the importance of Aboriginal people creating opportunities to talk collectively about their issues. He got an opportunity in high school in the 1990s to work with a corporation as the result of an Aboriginal internship program.

> *They had this Aboriginal internship program and I went to work there. And they got all of us to go talk at this conference this one time, the AMC*

(Assembly of Manitoba Chiefs) Conference. We all got up front and chatted away and it didn't matter what we said. After we got off the stage everyone was like, "it's wonderful, you guys are leaders of the future, keep going," right? I just loved all that positivity.

This young man, who is in his early twenties, got a chance to work with the Indigenous Games and then returned to finish high school. "And then I started wanting to give back a little bit and so I started volunteering with different things. And then this job was available to work in my neighbourhood working with youth, and so I took it." One of the volunteer assignments he took was with Manitoba Youth Career Awareness Committee, where he worked closely with elders:

Like you are around elders or even just people who went through a little bit of roughness and now they are doing okay, they are trying to help you out. They drill it into your head, right? Like, "don't forget where you came from, you gotta help out other people" and, yeah, so they drill it into you, but at the same time they are really positive and they will do anything for you, right? They give you their home phone numbers, if you have any problems, you know that you are going to fall down, they tell really honest stories about their own problems. They drill it into you. You gotta give back.

Parenting and Empowerment

In the cases of several of the women we interviewed, when their children reached school age they were invited to become involved in their schools. Many women got involved around issues that directly affect them and matter to them — their children's lives.

Donna, for example, tried to register her son for the nursery program at William Whyte School in the city's North End and was devastated when she was told that the class was full. "But there was a CEDA (Community Education Development Association) worker there.... She was a community-school outreach worker and she came and started talking to me and she said 'well, you know what? If you volunteered in the nursery classroom, then maybe your kid could get in.'" At first Donna thought she had no skills. She had come to the city at age fourteen with her mother and fifteen siblings fleeing an abusive husband and father. But when the CEDA worker suggested volunteering, she took her up on it. "And of course the CEDA worker never left me alone, she got me involved in Parent Council, I became head of hot dog day, put me in charge of money collection and stuff, so there was a lot of trust given to me.... She made me believe in myself because I really felt I didn't have skills to offer." Before long she was "volunteering and being on boards all over the place."

Later she was encouraged to apply to the Winnipeg Education Centre

(WEC), the University of Manitoba's off-campus, inner-city social work program, to get her social work degree. After her first day at WEC, "I had to take the dictionary out to read, to understand five words out of the first sentence I read, so I, like, cried, and thought, you know, 'what am I doing, I can't do this,' you know, kind of thing. But I'm determined." She graduated with her bachelor's of social work degree and started working with CEDA at William Whyte Community School, where her transformation had started. She is now the executive director of an exemplary inner-city community development organization, operating in the William Whyte neighbourhood in Winnipeg's North End.

Linda's path was similar. "I first became involved when they were looking for teaching assistants at the school. I lived in Gilbert Park development, and they were looking for teaching assistants." In her case, it was a social worker who made the difference. "I was not going to apply for a job there, I dropped out in grade eight myself, I didn't really feel that I had anything to contribute, didn't have much self-confidence and those kinds of things, so she [the social worker] just wouldn't quit, eh, she brought me over the little form, the application form," and returned the day the applications were due and stayed with Linda's children while Linda took the form in. She got the job.

And then the transformation began. "It was just amazing to me, I wasn't making much money, but it was just amazing to me that I could contribute something, that I could work with the kids, I mean, within a short time I was actually... running a whole classroom while the teacher was away, I worked in two grade three classrooms and I did community work and I just loved the community work." And she was successful at working in the community. "I remember the first time I phoned welfare and said, you know, 'this is [so and so], and I'm a community worker from, you know, from Shaugnessey Park School, and blah blah blah, and yeah, this woman's got five kids and she needs a washing machine.' And like, they gave it to her, she couldn't get it, right? And I was just, like, so amazed." Eventually she, too, attended WEC and earned her bachelor of education degree. She became the executive director of a large and very effective Aboriginal community development agency that has increasingly adopted Aboriginal ways of operating.

This involvement led many to find their real abilities, which had been buried beneath the layers of racism, sexism and internalized shame. When they were presented with opportunities to become involved in the community and with the support of others who believed in them, those latent abilities came to the surface, and a remarkable transformation occurred.

COMMUNITY DEVELOPMENT
BY AND FOR ABORIGINAL PEOPLE

We have already discussed the devastating impact of colonization on Aboriginal people and their way of life. The twenty-six participants in this study fought back, rebuilt their lives and reclaimed their culture. All have become leaders in their communities. In particular, the older people in this group began doing "community development" long before the term became popular in Canada. For these "organic intellectuals," Aboriginal community development directly challenges Western models of development. It starts with decolonization; recognizes and builds on people's skills and empowers them; honours Aboriginal traditions, values and cultures; rebuilds a sense of community among Aboriginal people; goes beyond economic needs; and generates organizations and mechanisms for democratic participation. This approach to community development is holistic.

Decolonization

Through community development, people learn the true value of their work and how the dominant system excludes them (Freire 1973; Morgan 1996). Teaching the history of oppression to affected groups, so that community members can understand, articulate and recognize the forces that oppressed them, is essential (Okazawa-Rey and Wong 1997). This raises political consciousness and is part of the process of decolonization (Shor and Freire 1987; Freire 1973). For the participants in this study, Aboriginal community development requires, as a starting point, an understanding that colonization has had a devastating impact on the lives of Aboriginal people. By addressing the colonizing agenda and deconstructing the colonial discourse, Aboriginal people can reclaim their voices and their collective post-colonial identity can emerge. Healing is an outcome of this program and requires both an understanding of the historical process of colonization and an immersion in Aboriginal culture. We explored this in Chapter Three.

Josephine advocates that "we have to get to know ourselves," because the process of colonization took away her sense of identity. As she puts it, you "never knew who you are, there was a lost identity, and I speak really about myself, I didn't know who I was." The same is stressed by Walter: "Culture is a very big part of who we are as Aboriginal people.... Once our culture is in place, people are learning it, they are practising it, and eventually you are going to know who you are... and we have to know who we are to be able to succeed anywhere." Along the same line, Ethel believes that healing "begins first with the person and then it just floods out, it's like a pebble dropping; once that pebble drops, it just has an effect — self, family, jobs, community. For our people I think the first thing they have to do is do their own piece.... The next level isn't there until that piece is done with yourself." She adds that Aboriginal people won't become involved in community development "unless they've done their own work first. Because why would they be concerned about community if they're just surviving?" This process of cultural retrieval is a crucial part of inner-city Aboriginal people becoming involved in community development. They cannot do it without first *healing* themselves, and the process of healing involves the promotion of Aboriginal cultures, so that they can regain a positive sense of identity. In talking about a particular Aboriginal organization, for example, Agatha says that she follows traditional ways, although she is still learning:

> *And that's part of what we do at [the organization of which she is executive director] with the women and their children. Because a lot of them have lost their identity and the understanding of who they are, which really is critical in terms of when you do that healing work with people. You know it's very critical for them to have that sense of the roots and connection, and that's a really important piece in the work that we do in the community here.*

Again and again, in different ways, we were told that the first step in Aboriginal community development is rebuilding the sense of Aboriginal identity and the pride in being Aboriginal, and an understanding of the process and consequences of colonization. This is the foundation. As Jack states: "if people don't feel good about themselves as a person, as a Cree or Ojibwa or whatever person... they tend to have low self-esteem and tend to be more involved in negative coping... alcohol, drugs." Many problems that Aboriginal people face are rooted in their loss of identity. Ethel describes the sense of shame that she felt as a youngster, the product of both her institutionalization, first in residential school and then in the Manitoba Youth Centre, and the disconnection that she felt from her family and from mainstream institutions. She describes "acting out," and nobody in the school appearing to understand that she was a little girl carrying a huge burden of pain.

Non-Aboriginal people are disconnected from that Aboriginal reality. This is a part of the disconnection from the dominant culture, most members of which do not see the internalized consequences of colonization. They see the behaviour, the acting out, but they do not see that this is a product of the dominant culture, of the disruption caused by colonization. She says: "it wasn't until that point of healing that I started truly understanding what colonization meant, first of all to myself, and then to our family and then to our community." The process of healing, on a person-by-person basis, and the process of community-building are part of a holistic process of Aboriginal community development.

Agatha, the executive director of an important community-based inner-city Aboriginal organization, tells us that the women who come to her organization:

are totally disconnected from their sense of self, from their families, from their communities, from their nation. How do we now begin to remake those connections, that sense of belonging that brings some stability, that brings them that self-confidence, that voice...? To me community development work is looking at a healthy community... a community where there is ownership.... "This is part of me and I belong here and I have ownership of this community as well." That is critical for our women and children here because they didn't feel they belonged anywhere in those institutions. They had no voice, they had no sense of connection. So we have to re-instill that, and that's part of how we do community development, of how we build capacity.

Charles observed that at a recent conference lots of Aboriginal people talked about their personal lives. "One of the things that... every one of them said in different ways is that it was our community and being with Aboriginal people and being included and respected and valued that made the difference in their lives." *This* is community development.

Bringing Back the Sense of Community

Strong relationships and social ties are referred to as social capital. Community development, it is argued, entails building social relationships (Chapter Two). This empowers individuals, strengthens bonds and may also build a united political force. Aboriginal people need, Shirley believes, places and spaces to connect and to talk: "a long time ago in our communities there were always... places in the community... where you could sit and talk and listen. So we need to somehow recreate that in a way that fits the urban environment." Richard stresses the importance of establishing a sense of community:

A lot of people who grew up in the North End do community development by virtue of the fact that they come from conditions that are not always ideal, that is, they're poor, they come oftentimes from visible minorities, so they experience racism and discrimination and all of those sorts of things, so growing up in that kind of environment, you naturally tend towards a sense of community, so when I grew up as a little boy and onwards there was a real powerful sense of community in the North End. I grew up all of my life there, so I'm what's called an urban Indian, I guess. I can recall very, very clearly the strong sense of community that existed.

Lots of his relatives from outside Winnipeg have moved into his North End neighbourhood. They:

oftentimes gravitated to one area, and I think that even today that's probably very much the same... so that in a block radius, I had a couple of aunts, an uncle, some cousins, and then very familiar people who also became in some sense an extended family, and so there was a real closeness... and there was a real sense of sharing... with other people. I remember feeling very, very safe in my community... nothing could hurt me, there was nothing to be afraid of, I could walk the streets at night, could do anything I wanted to do and had no fear about that whatsoever, and that's because of that sense of community that existed.

This sense of belonging generates Aboriginal involvement in the community, states Maggie:

I think where people miss the mark on involving the Aboriginal community is really creating those opportunities just to get together and talk. I've seen that on a local level, just with our community care centres, people coming to our centres, sitting around, having a coffee, getting to know each other and saying, "hey, wouldn't it be nice if we put together a summer program for kids," and [her organization] can do that, can support that.

Others doing Aboriginal community development share these values; they talk about building human relationships. For instance, Maggie states, "building those relationships, going door-to-door, you know, knocking on people's doors, sitting around the kitchen table having a coffee and building that relationship." Ethel adds: "if you want community people involved, you've got to meet with your community... come right to your constituents, right to your neighbourhoods and get them involved." They are critical of the many people doing community development who spend much of their time in their offices. Says Robert:

I don't think it works that way, I think you need to find neighbourhood people and give them whatever supports they need.... When I... started working as the youth outreach worker with [a community organization in an inner-city neighbourhood], I was knocking on doors, right, and the kids open up and they're too ashamed to let me in the house because it's a big mess, right? I was like the same way, right? Walk right in, chat it up with the parents, and then the parents are like, "you're so and so's kid," right, "oh I dated your uncle," right. The little kids find out it's my house, that I live just down the street. So I think that's where it's at.

This idea is further stressed by Charles, who firmly believes that Aboriginal people need to build a sense of community in what others have called an "asset-based" fashion (Kretzmann and McKnight 1993):

So when we look at community... look at the value of people, you know, what do they have to offer, what is good about them, eh? You know, you go into the North End or you go into any sort of poor community, you make tea, and people organize around a cup of tea, they bring cigarettes out, and they share, and you know, those are community development things that we overlook... people helping each other out.

Starting Where People Are, Empowering and Creating Opportunities

Community development starts where people are and values local knowledge and people's understanding and aspirations for their lives and their communities. There is a conscious attempt made to identify and incorporate local knowledge in community development programs. By adopting such an approach, community development has the potential to foster cultural preservation and to weaken exploitative outside forces (Voyageur and Calliou 2003; O'Donnell and Karanja 2000).

Many of the participants in this study stressed the importance of starting where people are and patiently building from there. The damage done by colonization is not undone overnight. They support people in finding their own ways and making their own choices, in their own time. This may be a lengthy process. Donna states that people

come to the centre and they look like they are in crisis, and you just need to listen to them sometimes, and they just move, they are given options and they just fly on their own and some take years. But as long as there is that little movement on their part and stuff like that, we will support them if it takes twenty years. Because that is what it takes sometimes. You got to get them where they are at, where people are at.... You need to let them be at the point where they are ready, because why put them some place that they are not ready for it? Then they don't make it, and it is like, you know, because you get tired of failing, so you need to wait to see.

She adds:

And so long as they are growing and that is where their comfort level is then you stay, there is never any push.... Let the creator do his work, stop trying to do his work for him.... Just give the opportunities and when people are ready they will get the strength they need to do what they need to do. It may not be the choice I make, but it might be the choice they need to make.

Along the same line William sees community development as:

a matter of helping people look at their problems, or their challenges... eventually, I think it becomes a self-building process, and it is not so much you have an objective and you are here.... As I say, you have to begin where you are, you can't be anywhere else, but you want to do something and the processes, the process is the product, I think, like it's a journey not a destination.

ABORIGINAL ORGANIZATIONS, ABORIGINAL LEADERSHIP

Aboriginal organizations — those run by and for Aboriginal people in a way consistent with Aboriginal values — as we have seen earlier, have been a critical source of empowerment for all of the participants in this study. Therefore, for all of them, Aboriginal community development requires the building of Aboriginal organizations.

All participants reminded us that urban Aboriginal people have formed and run many Aboriginal organizations in Winnipeg. They also emphasized that much of this community development work, although not all, is being done by Aboriginal women. It is Aboriginal women who are, for the most part, the leaders in putting into practice an Aboriginal form of community development. Jack says:

Over the years I have found… a lot of women have been involved in all these projects, more women than men have been involved in all these projects…. Women in my experience, they've been the drivers of the child welfare initiative in the last few years, it's because of women the Ma Mawi Wi Chi Itata Centre was born, women have been a central part of community development in my experience. Men are on board too, but there are lower numbers of men… in order for men to become involved more we need to help them to participate in healing [his emphasis], also to regain their role, their identity, with the community.

Miles concurs: "The process that I've seen in Winnipeg is by strong leaders, and a lot of the strong leaders happen to be women."

Their organizing efforts reflect the movement toward enabling Aboriginal people to run their own affairs and creating an Aboriginal community development rooted in traditional Aboriginal values of sharing and community. This process has been going on for years in Winnipeg, at least since the 1960s, when Aboriginal people began coming to the city, but it is a story largely untold. Nonetheless, even the bare outline of the story reveals that building Aboriginal organizations has involved mobilizing Aboriginal people to challenge and to wrest power from those in control.

Indian Métis Friendship Centre

One of the first Aboriginal organizations in Winnipeg, indeed, perhaps the first, was the Indian Métis Friendship Centre (IMFC). John describes being part of the Company of Young Canadians in the early 1960s, charged with organizing Friendship Centres into the Manitoba Association of Friendship Centres. When the IMFC started, it was run by "a white board, and a white director... the intent was good." Within five years, the centre had elected an all-Aboriginal board and hired an Aboriginal director. This was not easy. There was considerable resistance to this change, because at that time it was believed that Aboriginal people could not run their own affairs. As Jean described it:

> Even in those days the government still did not believe that the Indian people could survive, you know, like they gave us a two-year pilot project... 1957–58 we opened the doors... and you know if you sit around and are waiting, you kind of hear what those white people are saying... they're saying that they're going to go into an agreement that is only going to be two years because they'll never make it.

They did make it, and the IMFC has had a significant impact on the development of other Aboriginal organizations in Winnipeg. As John puts it:

> I think when I started back in '65, there might have been about 5,000 Aboriginal people in the city of Winnipeg and the only organization that was doing anything representing their interests was the Friendship Centre. Actually the Friendship Centre was quite a prime mover and shaker in this whole area of development.... The Friendship Centres were meeting places because that's where everybody got together.... That was our connection to the community and the Friendship Centres were kind of at the forefront of all this stuff.

Now there are many Aboriginal organizations in Winnipeg: "there are about seventy organizations in the city now that have been formed over the last thirty years and most of them owe their being to the Friendship Centres."

Sometimes efforts to establish Aboriginal organizations did not succeed. John told us that the Main Street Project "was originally a native organization, [it was a] native group of people who were concerned that their relations were dying in the back alleys of the hotels there and freezing in the cold." One of our participants, Joseph, got involved with the Main Street Project and started looking for funding, but the federal government backed off because it was off-reserve, and the provincial government dismissed it, saying it was not responsible for Treaty Indians. Someone with the provincial government said: "Add some white people to the board, then we can consider funding, then it's not an Indian board." They did as suggested and the province of Manitoba funded the Main Street Project, and the federal government followed suit. "That's how it became funded, at the beginning, but then the Indian people got crowded out and it became a white board because the money started to flow.... People forget that it was a native initiative."

Children of the Earth High School

Children of the Earth High School, the Aboriginal high school in Winnipeg's North End, has its origins in the early 1980s in a series of meetings of urban Aboriginal people who had been active in the community, especially around education issues. As Richard describes it: "there was a strong sense that the schools were not providing the kind of education that our kids needed, that oftentimes they were very racist environments, that the content that was being taught in schools was very biased and very white mainstream Euro-Canadian information." The inner-city Aboriginal community mobilized large numbers in support of educational changes. Several meetings were held that drew hundreds of Aboriginal students and youth, who said their first priority was educational change.

There was considerable outside opposition to an approach that involved mobilizing large numbers of Aboriginal people and challenging such a powerful institution of the dominant culture — the Winnipeg School Division. There was even opposition from within the Aboriginal community by people who did not want to offend the system. One person active in this campaign says:

> When we began getting close to the prize, we began to notice that our own people… began not supporting us because we were starting to offend the larger system, and the larger system was starting to say things about us, eh, and these people… felt that there were other ways of creating change… we were doing social action…. They literally told us that we were doing it wrong and we were offending these people and who we were offending were white people. We were offending the Winnipeg School Division Number One, the senior staff, you know, the board.

Opposition from the School Division was intense:

> because they had their own agenda, they didn't want to see the kinds of significant changes we were suggesting because it would mean changes to their curriculum and changes to their administration and really those changes being untested. And mainstream systems have a hard time dealing with unknowns and they have a hard time dealing with untested kinds of theories or ideas about how things ought to be done. So there's always a great deal of hesitancy when Aboriginal people or other minority groups approach mainstream systems for changes.

Nevertheless, as the result of a very significant mobilization of urban Aboriginal people over a period of years, urban Aboriginal people in Winnipeg were successful in establishing the inner-city Aboriginal high school, Children of the Earth.

Ma Mawi Wi Chi Itata

Like education, child welfare is an area in which Aboriginal people have had many negative experiences. These experiences led, by a similar process of large-scale mobilization and confrontation, to the establishment of the Ma Mawi Wi Chi Itata Centre, the urban Aboriginal child welfare agency. As Richard explains it, the Ma Mawi movement:

> came from the Original Women's Network, and it came from the urban community, that whole initiative to make some changes in child welfare.... There was a whole coalition of Aboriginal organizations... to get some control over child welfare in Winnipeg and we were lobbying government to try and get some of the funding as well as some of the changes to the Child and Family Services Act so that it was more reflective of Aboriginal people and Aboriginal wants and needs. The people who were involved in this movement were people who were just from the community, you know.... There were some high-profile people, but high-profile people in terms of their involvement in community development already, people like Kathy Mallett, for example... and Linda Clarkson, who was also involved very strongly in community development in the late seventies, early eighties... and Wayne Helgason, when he was just beginning to, when he was actually working for Northwest Child and Family Services and he was beginning to get involved in community development and he didn't like what he was seeing and what was happening so he was one of the... first "system" people who was beginning to get involved. But this whole movement just, just escalated, just took off, it was a huge groundswell because obviously the issue that was at hand was one that affected the whole community, both urban and rural, because all of us had experiences that involved child welfare in one way or another, so people just jumped to the cause and put a lot, a lot, of pressure on government, which ended up in the changes to the Child and Family Service Act of 1984, and it also ended with the establishment of Ma Mawi Wi Chi Itata Centre. That was a community development initiative. That was a very purposeful agenda that was put together by grassroots people in the community to make some changes to a system.

The result is a completely Aboriginal organization, run according to Aboriginal values and deeply rooted in the inner-city Aboriginal community. But the creation of Ma Mawi, like the creation of Children of the Earth, required a form of community development that was mobilizing and challenging, and that was rooted in the community and the community's real needs, and in the Aboriginal values of community and sharing.

Without this kind of mobilizing and challenging political strategy, big gains like the establishment of Ma Mawi and Children of the Earth are not possible.

To Help One Another: The Story of Ma Mawi

The Ma Mawi Wi Chi Itata Centre is one of Winnipeg's most successful and innovative Aboriginal organizations. It was established in 1984, the result of the efforts of Aboriginal people, primarily Aboriginal women working through Aboriginal women's organizations. Since 1997, Ma Mawi has undergone a remarkable transformation, recreating itself as a genuinely Aboriginal organization, rooted in and responding to the needs of the Aboriginal community. What was a strong and important organization from the outset has developed into an exceptional agency whose mission is to provide culturally appropriate preventative and supportive programs and services for Aboriginal families.

The immediate spark for the creation of Ma Mawi was the bathtub drowning of an eighteen-month-old child in a non-Aboriginal foster home that was overcrowded and did not meet provincial standards. The broader concern was the number of Aboriginal children that were involved in the child welfare system. Aboriginal children continue to comprise 70 percent-plus of children in care in Manitoba. In fact, more Aboriginal children have passed through the child welfare system than ever went through the residential school system, leading some to describe the child welfare system as the modern equivalent of the residential school system.

By the mid-1990s, Ma Mawi was organized much like any other relatively large social service organization. The staff members were caring and they worked hard to help Aboriginal families, but the organization itself was structured as a bureaucracy. It conceived of its work as professionals tending to the needs of clients. The agency was located on Broadway Avenue, amid the insurance companies and government offices, far removed from those it sought to serve.

In 1997, some Ma Mawi workers began to realize that the organization had become so bureaucratic that it had lost touch with the community. At the Annual General Meeting of 1997, Ma Mawi began an intense process of consultations with members of the Aboriginal community. They found that most people didn't even know Ma Mawi existed.

In the three years of consultation with the Aboriginal community that followed, Ma Mawi found that many expected the organization to become more connected to and visible within the community, and to understand and work directly with the community. As a result, Ma Mawi dramatically changed the way that it did business.

This is a remarkable phenomenon. It is a case of a relatively big, bureaucratic organization re-imagining itself and then reconstructing itself on the basis of what its constituents said they wanted.

At the root of the change is the concept of community. Ma Mawi sought to reconnect with the urban Aboriginal community and to work with the community to build upon existing strengths and the capacity of the community to solve its own problems. The organization shifted from a deficit approach, which features "fixing" what is wrong in a community, to an asset-based approach to community development, which seeks to identify and build upon strengths. The underlying premise is that it is not professionals and so-called experts who will solve Aboriginal people's problems; it is Aboriginal people themselves, and Ma Mawi's role is to help the community to do so.

The office on Broadway was relocated to several sites in the inner city, where they were more easily accessible to those Ma Mawi sought to work with. The organization shifted from delivering 90 percent of its services in the form of responses to crises, to a capacity-building approach oriented to prevention and supports to families and communities, and accountable to the Aboriginal community. A new focus on building leadership in the community and in the organization itself was adopted. Ma Mawi became a learning organization, providing supports to staff to develop leadership skills within the organization. Programs were also developed to build leadership and capacity in the community. People in the community were no longer viewed as "clients," but as partners.

For example, each of the thirty or so programs at Ma Mawi is now delivered by a staff person, together with a community person who has gone through the program. Ma Mawi no longer plays the role of expert but rather of helper to the community. This is consistent with Ma Mawi's name, which translated into English means: "we all work together to help one another."

A crucial part of Ma Mawi's new approach is that its community-based, capacity-building work is all rooted in Aboriginal culture. Programs are intended to promote healing in the community, in large part by redeveloping pride in being Aboriginal. Ma Mawi runs pow wow clubs for Aboriginal youth and an Aboriginal Scouts program, and promotes traditional teachings and the learning of traditional ceremonies. Support groups are organized for women, men and children. There is a young fathers program, as well as a mentoring program for young women. Workshops are run regularly on leadership training and capacity building. Numerous programs exist to support young families and to promote healthy relationships and healthy lifestyles. These are all culturally appropriate, preventative and supportive services and programs.

Ma Mawi Wi Chi Itata now employs more than 120 people. All are Aboriginal. All twelve board members are Aboriginal. The way of working is Aboriginal.

There are growing numbers of successful Aboriginal organizations in Winnipeg, and in other urban centres in Canada. Ma Mawi is but one, albeit an important one. Such organizations are pointing the way to the future. They are reshaping the way things are done by responding creatively to the demands of the community.

The Aboriginal share of Winnipeg's and other cities' populations is going to continue to grow, and to grow rapidly, into the foreseeable future. This creates many exciting opportunities for all of us. To seize these opportunities, we will need to be open to new and innovative ways of doing things. The Ma Mawi Wi Chi Itata Centre is showing the way.

This is a revised version of Silver 2004a.

This is because non-Aboriginal people, as Miles says, "still have this view that they'll tell us what to do. With the growing confidence we have in the Aboriginal community, we want to do these things now ourselves, and there's a real kind of subtle undercurrent opposing that — giving the control to Aboriginal groups.... We want it now and I don't think they want to give it up." He adds that this process is "moving, oh, so slowly.... You can't even really see it's moving, but I think they know it's moving now." This is the almost subterranean process — invisible to most outside the inner city — that is now occurring. It is a struggle. It is a process of throwing off the urban shackles of colonialism. It is a crucial part of the process of Aboriginal community development.

ABORIGINAL ORGANIZATIONS
RUN BY AND FOR ABORIGINAL PEOPLE

There are, in Winnipeg's inner city, deeply held grievances about non-Aboriginal people delivering services to and for Aboriginal people, and thus earning good incomes from jobs built on Aboriginal people's grief. Central to the emergent Aboriginal form of community development is the belief that this is exploitative and ineffective, and must be replaced by Aboriginal organizations run by and for Aboriginal people in a fashion consistent with Aboriginal values. Alice says: "but really, like social work… it's a system of employment, eh… where you're not making a product but you are still administering people's pain, managing people's pain." Verna adds: "to non-Aboriginal people, we are a big commodity, you know, we're their bread and butter.... I've worked in agencies where, who are they servicing? All Aboriginal people. And that always upset me because… they don't understand them, they can't relate to them, so how are you gonna relate to somebody if you come from this big middle-class system… it's like talking a different language.... We need to have our own people servicing our own people." Alice adds: "a lot of community development… here is still all about imposing that Western, Euro-Western ideology as if it is the only way, the only system of operating, the only way of thinking." But "any system that's been imposed upon us, it has not worked. And that's because we are fundamentally different people, we have different value systems, and our value systems are just as good as anybody else's." She continues: "They've just got to get out of the business of Aboriginal people."

Genuine community development involves Aboriginal people solving their own problems through their own organizations. Alice says: "Having control over our own lives… it's the best community development you'll have." She argues that:

> Aboriginal people need to do it ourselves, in our way. And underline our values. I mean the paradox is that everyone wants a good life for themselves and their families… but we have different ways of getting there. And our

way of getting there is just as valid as a Western way of getting there....
If it is not "ourselves doing it," it becomes a form of "development" that is
tantamount to cultural imperialism.

"Non-Aboriginal people," Agatha says, need to be:

open to hearing new ways of doing things, and that hasn't always been the
case, you know. Because we've found in some situations that some of the
non-Aboriginal social workers that we've had experience with come here as
"experts" and they have that professional kind of demeanor and they knew
all the answers... and we had to quickly address that with them.

In fact, as Richard pointed out, unless they do so in non-Western ways, they
won't get to the root of the problem, which is the extent to which Aboriginal
people have absorbed and internalized colonial views of themselves. Thus, the
process of solving the problem must start at the level of the individual and must
involve the building of a positive sense of identity.

Today in the inner city there continues to be conflict between Aboriginal
and non-Aboriginal organizations over the issue of Aboriginal control. A lot of
inner-city money still goes to non-Aboriginal organizations working to meet
the needs of Aboriginal people, and in many cases the staff employed are non-
Aboriginal people. This creates a great deal of resentment. As Miles says: "if you
look at all those groups, the non-native groups, there's a lot of jobs there, there's
a lot of resources go there," but many Aboriginal people believe that soon they
are going to have to "transfer those organizations to the groups they work with."
Doug adds:

Previously, mainstream organizations felt that they had sort of the knowl-
edge and the experience and the know-how, of how to work with our people
but I think they have quickly come to realize that things are not changing,
they are going from worse to worse and that they need to allow Aboriginal
people ownership, right, of the resources and of the services, so that's begin-
ning to change now.

But this process of Aboriginal people taking control is slow. There is resistance. And although "the organizations that have helped us over the years have
not led to change," those who benefit from the system as it is now, according
to Doug, "have their teeth well-sunk into the status quo." But, as he correctly
observes, "good community development challenges the status quo."

Aboriginal Community Development is Not Just about Economics

Aboriginal community development is holistic. It focuses on the individual, the
family, the community, the cultures, the organizations. And it focuses on the

spiritual and emotional aspects of people's lives, not just on economic development. Thus Walter states:

> So for me, for Aboriginal people to truly succeed, and for the communities to get better... you need sort of a holistic approach to community development.... Community economic development is just a small part of it.... When I talk about holistic we are not just talking about education, training, or employment, we are talking about supporting the individual.

There is a danger, Richard says, when we equate community development with material needs. In an excellent example of "organic intellectualism," he tells us that the danger arises when:

> we begin to look at community development simply in terms of needs, material needs, and we think that the satisfaction of material needs is going to satisfy emotional, psychological and community kinds of needs. Well, initially it might, initially, but in the long term it probably won't, and in the long term it will probably lead to the eventual... colonization of our own people, because when you start looking at just simply the needs, well we need better housing and we need this and we need this and you attend to those things [but] you don't attend to the underlying issues about why we need more housing and why we need better health care and why we need these things. And why we need these things is because we have been put through a process that has changed us fundamentally, that has put us in a position where we no longer exercise our identity and no longer exercise who we are in a significant kind of way.... If we simply address it in a needs-based kind of thing, that larger system understands that and says "Okay, well better housing is good, right, so we'll do something about that." But if you say, "well, we need better housing with a co-operative strategy where community members share," that becomes a harder concept for them to understand, but that's a concept that's closer to an Aboriginal understanding of community, an Aboriginal understanding of sharing. And so it gets harder and harder to take the values and beliefs about who we are and incorporate them inside of our development if we simply address the community development from that needs-based perspective.... It's up to us to be able to look at why it is those things occur, why it is our community looks the way it does, and what it is we need to do to get back to the basic kinds of values about who we are so that now you're talking about the values that underlie the community itself, those basic kinds of values, and you're not identifying them as traditional values or Christian values or anything else, you're simply identifying them as Aboriginal values. But what you're also doing inside of that is beginning to make the connections... to some

sense of who we were historically and then you're beginning to make the connection to what happened to that group of people historically, and you're beginning to build an analysis within the community that understands that the conditions that exist are not conditions of their own but are conditions that were imposed from the outside. And when you do that... when you put the responsibility for that outside of them as opposed to inside of them, then they're able to attack that, they're able to deal with it, and they're able... to work to change that. As long as people have that sense of being wrong, or being marginalized inside of themselves, they can't exercise their own power, because all of those things that they've been told about who and what they are guide them.

Economic issues need to be dealt with, but they have to be put in the context of the Aboriginal reality. As Doug puts it: "I have a concern that all too often community development moves to community economic development too fast." Richard adds:

But those economic issues also need to be framed inside of our own under-standing of who we are and about our values and our sense of community and our sense of sharing and our sense of co-operation. [Otherwise,] the values get removed from the initiative, right? And they simply then begin to act as corporations that make profit and they lose this notion of the sharing that needs to happen inside of any economic activity in the community.[2]

But doing this, developing and maintaining a specifically Aboriginal community development process grounded in the Aboriginal values of sharing and community is a difficult challenge, because when one tries to maintain those values in an organizational form there is a danger, Doug argues, that one will:

get caught up or get sucked into that whole, larger sort of capitalist economic development notion... and it's going to continue to be a difficult challenge because as we more and more impact on those wider systems, we get pulled into them, we eventually become part of them, and when we become part of them, we sometimes simply adopt what's already in place rather than make changes to those systems ourselves. And when we do that we then begin to lose ourselves. And I speak from personal experience around that because I've been fortunate in that I've worked largely for Aboriginal organizations all my life but I've [also] worked for non-Aboriginal organizations... and when I've worked in those environments it's always been a struggle... to maintain my sense of who I am because a lot of the things that are done inside of those systems go against my own values base, personally and as an Aboriginal person, that whole sense of competitiveness and over-competitive-

ness that exists there is just totally inconsistent with the notion of community
and sharing, and so as an Aboriginal person you get lost in that.

Walter says much the same:

When you are looking at community development, you have to first of
all have that ability to work together and share resources but also have to
work to see the big picture, that you can't just work in one area.... Culture
is a very big part of who we are as Aboriginal people. Our ceremonies,
our traditional values... they have to become the foundation.... Once
our culture is in place, people are learning it, they are practising it, and
eventually you are going to know who you are, eventually.... We have to
know who we are to be able to succeed anywhere, whether it's business or
in the school system.

Most of our interviewees expressed the belief that Aboriginal values, particularly those related to community and sharing, must be the basis of Aboriginal
community development. This is a form of decolonization, in that, as Richard
says "we'd be strengthening who we are, we'd be reconstructing who we are."
    The use of traditional Aboriginal values as a fundamental part of Aboriginal
community development has grown dramatically in recent decades and is the
product of decades of work by urban Aboriginal people in Winnipeg's inner city.
Darlene Klyne, in interviewing Richard, mentions that the new Urban Circle
Training Centre building is Aboriginal-designed and features the Aboriginal
concepts of the four directions. Richard replies:

to hear that, to hear you say that, just makes my heart swell because what
it means is that the work that we did earlier, twenty years ago, twenty-five
years ago, makes it possible for you just to simply say, because you couldn't
have said that twenty-five years ago, "oh, we've got a building that has the
four directions." People would say: "What are you talking about, four direc-
tions, that doesn't sound like it makes any sense to me." You wouldn't be able
to have that conversation. You wouldn't even be able to build that building
unless somebody had established the groundwork. And that's not to say
that we did all that, because there were people before us that were already
establishing that groundwork anyway. I mean, we were simply part of a
wave of people who wanted to do something better in the community.

Even the language, the words, to enable Aboriginal people to talk about
rebuilding their culture and their community along Aboriginal lines had to be
retrieved and re-inserted into everyday discourse. This has been an important
creative process and a central feature of Aboriginal community development.
And Richard is saying that a part of this work is intellectual — building and

articulating and making into "common sense" the analysis of the decolonization process, for example. This suggests the importance to Aboriginal community development of "organic intellectuals" — Aboriginal intellectuals rooted in traditional Aboriginal ways of thinking as well as the realities of the inner city. Richard continues: "One of the things that we've learned, certainly that I've learned throughout all of that, is that there's still a tremendous amount of work that we need to do around community development, and part of that work relates to strengthening that decolonization process and to continue to build the analysis inside of the community." Organic intellectuals of the Aboriginal community have developed an analysis of the process of colonization and decolonization and of their relationship to Aboriginal people's often harsh inner-city lives. They interpret those lives through an Aboriginal lens, with an Aboriginal world view. It is the development of a "counter-hegemony" — an interpretation of Aboriginal people's lives that is counter to, alternative to, the largely colonial views of the dominant culture.

Thus Aboriginal community development requires that Aboriginal people heal and go through the process of decolonization. But healing is not just an individual process; it requires a community that is strong and healthy. That in turn requires an understanding and appreciation of Aboriginal culture and knowledge, and to achieve this requires the development of Aboriginal organizations — organizations run by and for Aboriginal people and operated in ways consistent with and respectful of Aboriginal culture. And all of this requires adherence to an ideology rooted in an understanding of the historical effects of colonization and the necessity for decolonization. This in turn requires the development of "intellectuals" — in at least some cases elders, but not only elders — capable of developing and articulating this ideology. So it is in this way that Aboriginal community development is holistic — it focuses on the individual, the family, the community, the cultures and the organization. And it focuses on the spiritual and emotional aspects of people's lives, not just on economic development.

A Future Full of Hope

Those active in inner-city Aboriginal community development face a number of challenges, but they are hopeful about the future. Up to the early 1960s, very few Aboriginal people lived in Winnipeg. As their numbers have grown and their urban experience has deepened, they have built their own, distinctive Aboriginal forms of community development. The gains that they have made have been substantial and important, and theirs is a sophisticated and holistic form of urban community development. But the challenges that remain are daunting.

New and Old Challenges

The participants in this study are proud of their communities' achievements and believe there is no turning back. However, they are aware of the challenges that continue to face them. They are concerned about persistent poverty, racism, violence, lack of direction among youth, emerging class divisions among Aboriginal people and the necessity for a collective voice.

Many talk about the difficulties that Aboriginal people are facing in Winnipeg. Alice believes that "racism is... deep in this culture." They remind us that many urban Aboriginal people are struggling with poverty, which affects their choices and life chances. James adds that the "vast majority of our people are in the lower income strata; I believe that is probably one of the reasons why people sort of have a hard time trying to do things for ourselves." He continues, "I live down in the inner city and I see a lot of challenges that the inner city faces, you know there is poverty, there are young families that are just trying to make ends meet.... There are people on social assistance, there are Aboriginal youth there that have no direction as to what they want to do." Agatha, who works with an inner-city Aboriginal women's organization, states:

> For our women here and our youth as well, who are really, really suffering right now and don't feel any sense of belonging and that's why we've been experiencing these rampant you know, violent assaults and also murders in the latest few months that have been popping up. The only sense of community that they are getting right now is the gangs, that is where they are getting a sense of belonging and we've got to change it.

She is very concerned about the high rate of illiteracy among Aboriginal people:

> There is still a lot of illiterate people, right, because they have never had the opportunity to really go beyond [grades] four, five, six or they have gone through, you know, some junior high and high school but they were kind of just pushed through. They did not receive the supports they needed to address their learning disabilities so they are still very much struggling with being illiterate, even.

Violence in Aboriginal communities is a grave concern for the people we have talked to. Verna says: "I wondered why is there still such a high suicide rate, why seven youth killed themselves in the past year in this community." Walter says: "what is happening out there, you know, youth violence seems to be increasing, you know every day you hear about a kid getting beaten or getting killed." John warns us:

> We've been very, very quiet and very, very silent, yet the problems in our

communities continue to escalate and ah, not so much in the cities but more in the reserves... and in the poverty stricken communities where a lot of our people are still languishing in poverty... drinking going on... gang problems and so on... absolute third world state.

The majority of Aboriginal people are struggling in their daily lives, but a small minority are succeeding, economically and otherwise. This growing polarization among Aboriginal people is expressed by Walter as he contemplates the future:

I think we will see a large group that is well educated in leadership positions and I think that we will see another group that will still be marginalized. People that are still in that cycle. I think I say that because that is kind of the trend right now. I think that the trend will continue until the Aboriginal leadership, you know, really sits down and starts working together [with the community].... The leaders have to listen to the messages these people are giving them... the message is strong.

Indeed class divisions are already emerging in the Aboriginal community (Hull 2001). And it is clear from our interviews that some Aboriginal leaders are ambitious in an individualistic sense, at odds with the Aboriginal values of community and sharing.

A gap is emerging between the "haves" and "have-nots" in Winnipeg's Aboriginal community because, John argues, Aboriginal organizations — community development and political organizations — are not rooted in Aboriginal values. He says: "our Aboriginal values and traditions and customs and beliefs are all different from the larger society.... Until we establish our own identity as a distinct group of people it's not going to make any difference." John believes that to undertake Aboriginal community development is to establish Aboriginal identity, and pride in it, as something different and then to build Aboriginal organizations rooted in that Aboriginal identity, in that differentness, in the traditional values of community and of sharing.

I mean the foundation for a lot of these organizations was community.... Until you live those beliefs, you're not going to make any progress, but the minute you start living them that means that you are going to spend a little more time talking to your people, a lot less time talking to bureaucrats and government people and right now the reverse is the case. We spend all our time talking to the government.... I know that if we would go back to our traditions and our beliefs and our practices of dealing with our community... we'd go a lot further.

NON-ABORIGINAL PEOPLE: WALK
BESIDE US, NOT IN FRONT, NOR BEHIND

Aboriginal people regularly experience the divide between themselves and a non-Aboriginal community that does not want to listen. As Alice states:

> To me that is all I call it, it's racism. There's a real divide between, I mean they don't hear us, we can say you know, jeez, we should have our own school and they don't hear us, they don't hear us. I mean... they got to fix themselves before they even begin to look at trying to help us. They really have to look at their own stuff.

People in this study genuinely believe, and have indicated in different ways, that they need non-Aboriginal people to be their allies in doing community development. They want non-Aboriginal people to be prepared to transfer some of their power and to operate on an equal footing with their Aboriginal allies. They want the non-Aboriginal community to listen to them and hear them, share their skills and experiences with them, without imposing their views and their ideas on Aboriginal people.

There is no doubt that non-Aboriginal people's involvement is needed. But only a particular kind of involvement is acceptable. Agatha puts it: "There definitely should be a relationship, we cannot do this alone. Our non-Aboriginal brothers and sisters have to be walking beside us, not in front of us, not behind us but beside us in this work. But also they have to be very respectful as well and open to hearing a new way of doing things, and that hasn't always been the case, you know." Similarly, Mary states: "I think the idea of partnership is good, but I think it must be a true partnership and I think that, you know, we really cannot become effective partners until we have some power."

Aboriginal people are asking for allies who respect their values and authority and will share with them their experience and skills and their power. Walter states: "I think the role of non-Aboriginal people should be... from my perspective, to help, you know, transfer knowledge and skills to the community, that ability to teach somebody and transfer those skills, so rather than helping people they should teach people to know how to help themselves." Another person, Robert, stresses the sharing of skill: "But it's got to be a hands-off role. And like, if it means that an organization takes longer to get up and running and doesn't get running as fast as it would otherwise, well that is what's got to happen." Along the same line, Richard believes that the non-Aboriginal community has a "huge responsibility" with respect to Aboriginal people, but that responsibility is different from telling people how to do things. It is the responsibility to be an ally.

To be an effective ally, non-Aboriginal people need to educate themselves. When they go into Aboriginal communities, they must be very sensitive and conscious of their position and their actions. This means being reflexive — being aware of white privilege and acting accordingly, acting supportively and co-operatively, with a full knowledge of one's position in the hierarchy. Alice stresses the need for education:

> *I know that there is a role for people that are non-Aboriginal people and it is in the role of allies. And really we need to know, we need to have a course on what an ally is. Allies are not fixer-uppers, allies are people that will support us, walk with us, walk beside us, supporting us in turning power over to us. That is the role of allies, is to turn over their power.... We really need them.*

It is through learning and un-learning that non-Aboriginal people can reflect upon themselves and their relationship or non-relationship with the Aboriginal community, and can understand their place within this process. Through reflexivity, non-Aboriginal people can learn to become the kind of allies that Aboriginal people are asking for: those who will walk beside Aboriginal people, not in front, not behind them.

AN ALTERNATIVE RELATIONSHIP WITH THE STATE

Aboriginal people have always had a contradictory relationship with the state. On the one hand, the participants in this study are very critical of state institutions. Although they recognize both the power and limitations of the state, one after another has told us that the educational system has failed Aboriginal people; that Aboriginal people do not trust the system; that the justice system is biased against Aboriginal people; that government programs and policies — particularly those associated with Indian Affairs — are not in touch with the reality of Aboriginal people, and repeatedly betray a lack of understanding of Aboriginal issues; that government has created an "Indian Industry"; that there are too many reports, too many programs, too many ineffective and costly big projects, as opposed to grassroots projects; that policies are short-sighted and do not have a long-term vision; and that government has created a culture of dependency among many Aboriginal people.

On the other hand, despite these and other criticisms, inner-city Aboriginal organizations depend on government and charitable organizations for their financial survival. They have to apply for funding, account for their spending and meet the expectations of the funders. This necessitates the creation and maintenance of good working relations with governments and others who control the flow of funds. These efforts deliver benefits, in the form of the maintenance and gradual growth of programs that assist inner-city Aboriginal people and the creation of jobs for inner-city Aboriginal people.

POLITICS OF ACCESS

The economic advantages of developing and maintaining these positive relationships with governments lead to what might be called a "politics of access." Community-based organizations need access to governments and other funders — those with money. In some cases this means a "don't bite the hand that feeds you" form of politics. John, for example, argues that:

> We've got so many organizations who have got complacent and comfortable... with the status quo, and nobody wants to rock the boat anymore. If you try to put the government... on the defensive, you know, people in our community say "oh we don't want to upset the bureaucrats, don't want to upset the government, because they are giving money," you know, so that's a real problem as I see it.

In other cases these economic realities lead inner-city Aboriginal activists to consider that they ought to join forces with those who allocate the resources. This strategy most often leads to developing close working relationships with, or even joining, the the Liberal Party of Canada. The Liberal Party has usually governed at the federal level, where the largest resources are located and where First Nations people have historically negotiated with the state.

The "politics of access" leads many of the best inner-city community development practitioners to refuse involvement at the broader political level. In some cases the lack of political involvement is attributable to a fear of offending potential funders. The majority of the Aboriginal people that we have interviewed see the importance of an *Aboriginal* community development rooted in the Aboriginal values of sharing and community, but do not for the moment see any way of expressing these values at the political level (see Chapter Four).

However necessary it may appear, given the financial dependency of community-based organizations, there are serious drawbacks to the "politics of access." Most importantly, it could be argued to lead, as Charles believes, not to "solving" the problems of the inner city but to "containing" them. By this he means that the dependency of community-based Aboriginal organizations on government funding may keep them silent and eliminate the political threat they might otherwise pose.

As well, the "politics of access" enables the dominant system to pay lip service to inner-city Aboriginal problems. Small amounts of money are doled out to community-based organizations that scramble constantly to get their share of an always-inadequate allocation. Charles refers disparagingly to this kind of politics as "this shopping spree, you know, getting a-hold of these programs when they're put out there for sale, you know, bargain basement sales." The "bargain basement" imagery implies the continued under-funding of inner-city community development initiatives despite the obvious needs.

So the needs go unmet because the political will is not there, and the political will is not there because the politics of access cannot put sufficient pressure on governments to force them to act.

It can be argued that governments and other funders do not really want to solve the problems of the inner city. Doing that would require public investment very far beyond what is now being committed to the inner city. Richard states: "There is also a very conservative trend that sets in place today, even with the NDP government that we have, the NDP government is very much a careful government right now." The current provincial government, for example, although more "inner-city-friendly" than its predecessor, is committed to reducing taxes and running a balanced budget and "inoculating" itself against criticism from its traditional foes (Flanagan 2003). This approach increases the likelihood of re-election. This necessitates responding positively to demands from the corporate community that taxes be cut and budgets balanced. It also necessitates responding positively to demands from the public and from powerful institutions that health and education be adequately funded. Once these demands have been met, there is little funding left for the inner city (Hudson 2004). This is a political strategy designed not necessarily to *solve* problems, but rather to *manage* them so as to ensure re-election. If there is pressure on the provincial government to cut taxes and increase spending on health and education, they will do so. And if there is little public pressure on the provincial government to increase funding to the inner city — and there is not because the "politics of access" practised by many inner-city community development organizations involves meeting the needs of funders to ensure continued funding — then they will not increase inner-city funding.

And to the extent that this is the case, the implicit strategy of governments — or at least the effect of government strategy — is simply to "contain" the problems of the inner city. The result is a constant shortage of funding. As Walter says: "Okay, government provides the resources but there is never enough, you know, to run a really effective program or programs… the resources are really spread thinly so there's never enough."

AN ALTERNATIVE APPROACH: THE POLITICS OF MOBILIZATION

To make real changes, significant and large changes that benefit the inner city, advocates require a different way of relating to the state, a different kind of politics, one built on mobilizing people and challenging systems. This alternative form of politics seeks power for Aboriginal people, but not power *over* others, rather power to enable all Aboriginal people to live in a healthy way in today's world and to do so as Aboriginal people.

This alternative way of relating to the state sees the virtues of and the necessity for the focus on healing and on community, but also sees its limitations.

It argues the case for a politics that includes mobilization and confrontation, to speed the process of Aboriginal people governing themselves through their own organizations. This is a politics that has been used by urban Aboriginal people and has been successful in securing big victories — the creation of the Ma Mawi Wi Chi Itata Centre and Children of the Earth High School, for example. As William puts it:

We have to get some power and... power is never given, you have to take it and you can only take it by building your knowledge, by organizing, and by doing things.... Then they begin to listen.... As long as you don't have power, you're going to be disadvantaged, so you have to organize.

Doug says much the same:

Fifty percent of what you'll achieve will be because there's really good people around... you know, wanting to help. But the other 50 percent, you have to take. You have to define it first, what is it you want... and demand it and challenge for it, take it.

Existing institutions resist change and are unlikely to change voluntarily. In the case of Children of the Earth School, for example, the existing school division and some powerful Aboriginal leaders opposed the creation of an Aboriginal school. But Aboriginal people mobilized and demanded change. The new Aboriginal school:

wasn't just handed over to us, as... popular opinion out there may have sort of said, "well, it's time for change and we'll give these Indians a chance." That's not how it really worked. We had to fight tooth and nail for that school, but we achieved getting the school, and it was only through resisting and fighting, fighting what was going on. That's the only reason they shifted it over to us, because we had numbers, eh, we had numbers of people.... It takes bringing people together, you know, to create change.

The politics of mobilization and confrontation, of collective and militant action, has a significant record of success in Winnipeg's inner city. In addition to Children of the Earth and Ma Mawi, the Aboriginal Centre might be seen as an example. Charles says:

After the Oka crisis, for example, the budgets for Aboriginal organizations shot up dramatically. In the city, here, they developed the Aboriginal Centre. All kinds of resources went there and again, you know, you could see it as a process to cool down the masses, eh, you know, a process to put the fire out, because they knew there was a movement occurring.

There is another form of politics, another way of relating to the state that emerges logically out of the financial dependency of Aboriginal community-based organizations. This is the demand for a form of urban Aboriginal self-governance that would give Aboriginal people the legal authority to control the allocation of resources. As John puts it:

> In the city here there is probably hundreds of millions of dollars going into the Indian industry, and I am talking about money going through the federal department... through the provincial departments, the municipal government, private industry, you name it, there is literally millions of dollars flowing into somebody's pockets. We [an Aboriginal organization] get a small portion of that through the grant we receive, but that is just a small portion and the difficulty we have is we don't have any legal authority to demand anything else. If we were to set up a government, our own government for example, in the city of Winnipeg, with a membership of 70,000 people and this government structure was legislated by parliament, then all the money that is going to all these different places would come together into our own hands and we would be able to control our own destiny, we would have the resources to control our own destiny.... I mean, there is enough money there right now that is flowing into the Aboriginal community from different sources to really set our people up in better houses, better jobs, better educational opportunities. We can't do that right now, because somebody else is running the show.

Those "running the show" are not likely to voluntarily relinquish their power and their control of resources. As a result, John argues:

> I think that we are at a point now where there has to be some kind of a movement towards getting more aggressive and more vocal again. I think the cities are in a position to make the loudest noise and to have the most impact because we have the largest [Aboriginal] populations here. And I know that it would scare the pants off the politicians if they realized that there were fifty or seventy thousand people ready to take them on and we're not at that stage yet, but ultimately that is where we would like to be so that we can have a stronger political presence and a stronger voice in issues that are of concern to our people.

A major part of the case for such a transfer of power and resources is that many, even most, of the bureaucrats who now make decisions about the allocation of resources do not really know Aboriginal people and their needs. William, who worked in Ottawa with the federal government for some years, says: "One thing that amazed me when I went to Ottawa was the number of very bright young people... who would sit in offices and dream up solutions for people out there... sometimes with very little relationship to reality." Walter says much the same:

> In Indian Affairs in the case of First Nations, the people that decide on financial resources don't know enough about their customers, so to speak... because the government system is so huge and the people that decide on this money are so far away that you don't really know what's happening at the grassroots level.

In all of these cases, what is being described is a process of decolonization. It has to do with Aboriginal people taking back control of their lives after many long decades of colonial domination. This is a process of rebuilding. It starts at the individual and local levels — healthy individuals require healthy communities, and vice versa; it means Aboriginal-controlled organizations; and as all of our participants have told us, it needs to be rooted in traditional Aboriginal values.

THERE IS NO TURNING BACK: THE FUTURE IS FULL OF HOPE

Although they expressed concerns about the future, our respondents are very optimistic and believe there is no turning back. Jack stresses the many positive things that are happening for the Aboriginal community and the momentum created. He states, "Oh, yeah, I am optimistic" and adds, "I see it already happening, a lot of training is going on, training and also employment initiatives are going on for our young people." Agatha notes the changes that are taking place: "I think things are changing because the mainstream organizations and government and funders have recognized that they need to include us, our voices at the table, and they need to hear our views of how things should be done. That wasn't always the case." As Miles puts it: "I was reading something about caterpillars, how they cocoon and then come out as butterflies. I think — maybe it is not a good analogy — but I think we are budding as a people; we are starting to bloom."

When asked about the future, most of the people that we spoke to responded in collective terms about the future of Aboriginal people *as a people*. Most also spoke about the future in terms consistent with the values of Aboriginal community development. Their responses were not about personal accumulation or consumption, but rather about community and sharing. For example, when asked what she hopes the future would bring, Verna replies: "Looking out for each other like they did years ago." Others talked about Aboriginal people being more in charge of their own affairs and having more hope. When asked what she would like the Aboriginal community to look like twenty years from now, Ethel replies: "my goal is... that our students are running their own organization. I want [her organization's] graduates running this program, people who've grown in this program." Shirley says: "We should be running the place! We should be running a lot of the mainstream organizations… [and] we need to be able to take our values with us, in there…. You really have to be able to come here and not check your belief system at the door in order to survive." Linda adds to this: "I'd like to see Aboriginal people taking the lead," and expresses the importance of "creating the opportunity for people to feel hopeful, to feel in control of their lives…. I mean community development to me is really human resource development, it's building people, providing opportunities for people, and standing by them when things fall, or being creative." This reference to creativity acknowledges the fact that Aboriginal people are different and some may not want to fit into pre-existing slots in the system. So an Aboriginal community development approach, Linda says, needs to "recognize who we are, and then build some economic opportunities around our situation and around who we are. You know, some of us are not going to be nine-to-fivers, and so you have to be creative about it."

Our respondents know what they want for themselves and for the urban Aboriginal community, but they also want to bring other people into their circle. They believe the Aboriginal way is the way of the future. Shirley describes her dream:

> You know, when I was a young girl I never thought it was possible but the elders told us that we are, we are the people that are going to bring other people out of their oppression, we are going to lead the way. A long time ago I would say, I would go, oh, that's never going to happen…. Now I could see it, you know, now I could see it. Now I go, "Wow," their prophesies are coming true… how much we have overcome and how much further we have to go.

CONCLUSION

We believe that by listening to the authentic voices of Aboriginal community leaders in Winnipeg's inner city, we have uncovered a story that is exciting and even inspiring. A process of decolonization is underway, and it is manifesting itself in a distinctive, Aboriginal form of urban community development.

This Aboriginal community development is rooted in the traditional Aboriginal values of community and sharing. Many of the people that we interviewed believe fervently in these values, and live and work in a way consistent with these values. They see Aboriginal community development starting with the individual, with the need for people to heal from the damage of colonization. Part of this involves rebuilding Aboriginal people's identity and creating pride in being Aboriginal. The process of people rebuilding themselves, recreating themselves, although it happens person by person, requires a strong sense of community — one in which Aboriginal culture flourishes — and this in turn necessitates the creation of Aboriginal organizations. Just as Aboriginal people need to reclaim their identity as individuals, so do they need to reclaim their collective organizational identity via the creation of Aboriginal organizations. This is a process that has been going on for more than thirty years in Winnipeg: the Indian and Métis Friendship Centre, the Ma Mawi Wi Chi Itata Centre, the Urban Circle Training Centre, the Native Women's Transition Centre, the Aboriginal Centre, and the Children of the Earth High School are just a few examples. The process of reclaiming an Aboriginal identity has to take place at the individual, community, organizational and political levels. This process is well underway.

All of this — at the individual, the community, the organizational and the broader political levels — is a process of decolonization, a process of Aboriginal people seeking to take back control of their lives after many decades of colonial control. Their lives have been badly damaged. They have to rebuild. This has to start at the individual and local community level — healthy individuals require healthy communities, and vice versa. It has to mean Aboriginal-controlled organizations. And perhaps most significantly, it needs to be rooted in traditional Aboriginal values. Why? There are two reasons.

One is that large numbers of Aboriginal people do not want to assimilate. They want to live with and take advantage of the dominant culture but they want to do so as Aboriginal people, in a way consistent with Aboriginal values.

The second is that adherence to Aboriginal values is likely to reduce the chances of an Aboriginal elite emerging and leaving others behind. An Aboriginal community development process rooted in Aboriginal values places a premium on community and sharing, and this is most likely to keep leaders in close contact with the people. Many of the individuals we interviewed adhere to these values, living and working in a way consistent with them. They grew up poor and lived rough. They have not forgotten their roots.

These organic urban Aboriginal intellectuals, as we described them earlier, are aware of the challenges they face. However, despite these challenges and difficulties, Aboriginal community development, with its strong emphasis on community and sharing, on respect for Aboriginal culture, is a reality in Winnipeg's inner city. Aboriginal people are building Aboriginal organizations in the inner city — run by and for Aboriginal people, and infused with Aboriginal values — to meet the needs of modern Aboriginal people. A process of healing and building is underway.

NOTES

1. We have used pseudonyms for each of the twenty-six people interviewed for this chapter.

2. This is an important observation. If relatively sophisticated community economic development (CED) initiatives are put in place before people in the community are ready to participate, then these CED organizations are likely to become just another external agency — disconnected from the community. They may become an outside force, acting *upon* rather than *with* the community. At the same time, however, it is important to acknowledge that the various Aboriginal community-based organizations that we are talking about are themselves central elements of an economic strategy. They employ hundreds, perhaps thousands, of Aboriginal people. They have been called "the invisible infrastructure," and Newhouse has recently calculated that there are approximately 3,000 such Aboriginal community-based organizations across Canada, most in urban centres (Newhouse 2003: 245). Not only do they deliver needed services, but they also employ Aboriginal people to deliver the services, and this makes them a central part of a community economic development strategy. Also, Aboriginal people themselves have developed sophisticated approaches to CED, and these have been described in detail by Loxley (2000), and Loxley and Wien (2003). It is important, we believe, to accept that sometimes "community development moves to community economic development too fast," while holding to the view that economic development is important and that the urban Aboriginal community has made important contributions to devising and implementing appropriate and effective forms of community economic development.

REFERENCES

Aboriginal Justice Inquiry (AJI). *Report of the Aboriginal Justice Inquiry of Manitoba, Volume 1: The Justice System and Aboriginal People* (Winnipeg: Queen's Printer, 1991).

Abu-Laban, Yasmeen. "Challenging the Gendered Vertical Mosaic: Immigrants, Ethnic Minorities, Gender, and Political Participation," in Joanna Everitt and Brenda O'Neill (eds), *Citizen Politics: Research and Theory in Canadian Political Behaviour* (Don Mills, Ontario: Oxford University Press, 2002).

Adams, Howard. *Tortured People: The Politics of Colonization*, Revised Edition (Penticton, BC: Theytus Books, 1999).

Adams, David Wallace. "Fundamental Considerations: The Deep Meaning of Native American Schooling, 1880–1900, *Harvard Educational Review*, 58, 1, 1988.

Alfred, Taiaiake. *Peace, Power, Righteousness: An Indigenous Manifesto* (Toronto: Oxford University Press, 1999).

Alia, Valerie. "Aboriginal People and Campaign Coverage in the North," in Robert Milen, *Aboriginal Peoples and Electoral Reform in Canada, Volume 9, Royal Commission on Electoral Reform and Party Financing* (Toronto: Dundurn Press, 1991).

Archer, Keith. "Representing Aboriginal Interests: Experiences of New Zealand and Australia," *Electoral Insight*, 5, 2, July 2003.

Barnsley, Jan, and Diana Ellis. *Research for Change: Participatory Action Research for Community Groups* (Vancouver: Women's Research Centre, 1992).

Barron, Laurie, and Joseph Garcea (eds). *Urban Indian Reserves: Forging the New Relationship in Saskatchewan* (Saskatoon: Purich Publishing, 1999).

Battiste, Marie, and Jean Barman (eds). *The Circle Unfolds: First Nations Education in Canada* (Vancouver: UBC Press, 1995).

Bedford, David. "Aboriginal Voter Participation in Nova Scotia and New Brunwick," *Electoral Insight*, 5, 2, July 2003.

Bedford, David, and Sidney Pobihushchy. "On-Reserve Status Indian Voter Participation in the Maritimes," *Canadian Journal of Native Studies*, 15, 2, 1995.

Behar, Ruth. *The Vulnerable Observer: Anthropology That Breaks Your Heart* (Boston: Beacon Press, 1996).

Betcherman, Gordon, Kathryn McMullen and Katie Davidson. *Training for the New Economy: A Synthesis Report* (Ottawa: Canadian Policy Research Networks, Inc., 1998).

Black, Jerome. "Representation in the Parliament of Canada: The Case of Ethnoracial Minorities," in Joanna Everitt and Brenda O'Neill (eds), *Citizen Politics: Research and Theory in Canadian Political Behaviour* (Don Mills, ON: Oxford University Press, 2002).

Blais, Andre. *To Vote or Not to Vote: The Merits and Limits of Rational Choice Theory* (Pittsburgh:

University of Pittsburgh Press, 2000).

Blais, Andre, Louis Massicotte and Agnieszka Dobrzynska. *Why is Turnout Higher in Some Countries than in Others?* (Ottawa: Elections Canada, March 2003).

Blais, Andre, Elisabeth Gidengil, Neil Nevitte and Richard Nadeau. *Anatomy of a Liberal Victory: Making Sense of the Vote in the 2000 Canadian Election* (Peterborough: Broadview Press, 2002).

Blais, Andre, Elisabeth Gidengil, Neil Nevitte and Richard Nadeau. "The Evolving Nature of Non Voting: Evidence From Canada." Paper presented at the Annual Meeting of the APSA, San Francisco, 2001.

Blake, Sherri. *Community-Based Measurement Indicators Resource Development Project* (Winnipeg: Province of Manitoba, 2003).

Bock, G., and S. James. *Beyond Equality and Difference: Citizenship, Feminist Politics and Female Subjectivity* (London: Routledge, 1992)

Boldt, Menno. *Surviving as Indians: The Challenge of Self-Government* (Toronto: University of Toronto Press, 1993).

Boothroyd, P., and C. Davis. "Community Economic Development: Three Approaches," *Journal of Planning Education and Research*, 12, 1993, pp. 230–40.

Borrows, John. *Recovering Canada: The Resurgence of Indigenous Law* (Toronto: University of Toronto Press, 2002).

_____. "'Landed' Citizenship: Narratives of Aboriginal Political Participation," in Alan C. Cairns, John N. Courtney, Peter MacKinnon, Hans J. Michelmann and David E. Smith (eds), *Citizenship, Diversity and Pluralism: Canadian and Comparative Perspectives* (Montreal and Kingston: McGill-Queen's University Press, 1999).

Bourdieu, Pierre. "From Rules to Strategies," *Cultural Anthropology* 1, 1, 1985, pp. 110–20.

_____. *Outline of a Theory of Practice* (Cambridge: Cambridge University Press, 1977).

Bourdieu, P., and L.J.D. Wacquant. *An Invitation to Reflexive Sociology* (Chicago: The University of Chicago Press, 1992).

Bowles, G., and R. Duelli Klein (eds). *Theories of Women's Studies* (London: Routledge, 1983).

Braden, Su, and Marjorie Mayo. "Culture, Community Development and Representation," *Community Development Journal*, 34, 3, 1999.

Brandt, B. *Whole life Economics: Revaluing Daily Life* (Gabriola Island, BC: New Society Publishers, 1995).

Braroe, Niels Winther. *Indian and White: Self-Image and Interaction in a Canadian Plains Community* (Stanford, CA: Stanford University Press, 1975).

Bridgman, Rae, Sally Cole and Heather Howard-Bobiwash (eds). *Feminist Fields: Ethnographic Insights* (Peterborough, Ontario: Broadview Press, 1999).

Brody, Hugh. *Indians On Skid Row* (Ottawa: Department of Indian Affairs and Northern Development, 1971).

Brookfield, Stephen. "Adult Learning: An Overview," in A. Tuinjman (ed), *International Encyclopedia of Education* (Oxford: Pergamon Press, 1995).

Bryant, C. "A Hard Look at 'Soft' Sociology: Rebuilding the Case for Qualitative Sociology." *Sociological Forum*, 3, 1980.

Burgos-Debray, E. *I... Rigoberta Menchu: An Indian Woman in Guatemala* (London: Verso, 1984).

Burt, Sandra. "The Concept of Political Participation," in Joanna Everitt and Brenda O'Neill (eds). *Citizen Politics: Research and Theory in Canadian Political Behaviour* (Don Mills, ON: Oxford University Press, 2002).

Cairns, Alan. "Aboriginal People's Electoral Participation in the Canadian Community," *Electoral*

Insight, 5, 2, July 2003.

_____. *Citizens Plus: Aboriginal Peoples and the Canadian State* (Vancouver: UBC Press, 2000).

_____. "The Fragmentation of Canadian Citizenship," in William Kaplan (ed), *Belonging: The Meaning and Future of Canadian Citizenship* (Montreal and Kingston: McGill-Queen's University Press, 1993).

Cairns, Alan C., John N. Courtney, Peter MacKinnon, Hans J. Michelmann and David E. Smith (eds). *Citizenship, Diversity and Pluralism: Canadian and Comparative Perspectives* (Montreal and Kingston: McGill-Queen's University Press, 1999).

Canada. *A Report on Adult Education and Training in Canada: Learning a Living* (Ottawa: Minister of Industry, 2001).

Canada. House of Commons, Standing Committee on Aboriginal Affairs. *"You Took My Talk": Aboriginal Literacy and Empowerment, Fourth Report of the Standing Committee on Aboriginal Affairs*, December 1990.

Canadian Centre for Policy Alternatives-Manitoba. *Alternative Provincial Budget 2003/04* (Winnipeg: CCPA-Mb., April 2003).

Cardinal, Harold. *The Unjust Society: The Tragedy of Canada's Indians* (Edmonton: M.G. Hurtig Limited, 1969).

Carter, Sarah. *Capturing Women: The Manipulation of Cultural Imagery in Canada's Prairie West* (Montreal: McGill-Queen's University Press, 1997).

Castellano, Marlene Brant. "Collective Wisdom: Participatory Research and Canada's Native People," *Convergence*, XIX, 3, 1986.

Chambers, Robert. *Whose Reality Counts? Putting the First Last* (London: IT Publications, 1997).

Clarkson, L., V. Morrissette and G. Regallet. *Our Responsibility to the Seventh Generation: Indigenous Peoples and Sustainable Development* (Winnipeg: International Institute for Sustainable Development, 1992).

Clatworthy, Stewart. *Factors Influencing the Migration of Registered Indians Between On and Off Reserve Locations in Canada* (Ottawa: Research and Analysis Directorate, Indian and Northern Affairs Canada, 2000).

_____. "The Migration and Mobility Patterns of Canada's Aboriginal Population," *Royal Commission on Aboriginal People: People to People, Nation to Nation* (Ottawa: Minister of Supply and Services Canada, 1996).

_____. *The Effects of Length of Urban Residency on Native Labour Market Behaviour.* Research and Working Papers 1 (Winnipeg: Institute of Urban Studies, 1983a).

_____. *Native Housing Conditions in Winnipeg.* Paper #81 (Winnipeg: Institute of Urban Studies, 1983b).

_____. *Patterns of Native Employment in the Winnipeg Labour Market* (Winnipeg: Institute of Urban Studies, 1981a).

_____. *Issues Concerning the Role of Women in the Winnipeg Labour Market.* Technical Study No. 5 (Winnipeg: Institute of Urban Studies, 1981b).

_____. *The Effects of Education on Native Behaviour in the Urban Labour Market* (Winnipeg: Institute of Urban Studies, 1981c).

_____. *The Demographic Composition and Economic Circumstances of Winnipeg's Native Population* (Winnipeg: Institute of Urban Studies, 1980).

Clatworthy, Stewart, Jeremy Hull and Neil Loughren. "Urban Aboriginal Organizations: Edmonton, Toronto, and Winnipeg," in Evelyn Peters (ed), *Aboriginal Self-Government in Urban Areas: Proceedings of a Workshop May 25 and 26, 1994* (Kingston, ON: Institute of Intergovernmental Relations, Queen's University, 1995).

Clatworthy, Stewart, and Jonathan Gunn. *Economic Circumstances of Native People in Selected Metropolitan Centres in Western Canada* (Winnipeg: Institute of Urban Studies, 1982).

Clifford, James, and George E. Marcus (eds). *Writing Culture: The Poetics and Politics of Ethnography* (Berkeley: University of California Press, 1986).

Cole, Sally, and Lynne Phillips (eds). *Ethnographic Feminisms: Essays in Anthropology* (Ottawa: Carleton University Press, 1995).

Comeau, Pauline. *Elijah: No Ordinary Hero* (Vancouver: Douglas and McIntyre, 1993).

Comeau, Pauline, and Aldo Santin. *The First Canadians: A Profile of Native People Today* (Toronto: James Lorimer and Company, 1990).

Cooke, Bill, and Uma Kothari (eds). *Participation: The New Tyranny?* (London and New York: Zed Books, 2001).

Culleton, Beatrice. *In Search of April Raintree* (Winnipeg: Pemmican Publishers, 1984).

Davis, Arthur K. *Edging Into Mainstream: Urban Indians in Saskatchewan* (Calgary: University of Alberta, 1965).

Deane, Lawrie, Larry Morrissette, Jason Bousquet and Samantha Bruyere. "Explorations in Urban Aboriginal Neighbourhood Development" (Winnipeg: unpublished paper, 2002).

Denton, T. "Migration From a Canadian Reserve," *Journal of Canadian Studies*, 7, 2, 1972.

Denzin, N. "The Epistemological Crisis in the Human Disciplines: Letting the Old do the Work of the New," in R. Jessor et al. (eds), *Ethnography and Human Development: Context and Meaning in Social Inquiry* (Chicago: University of Chicago Press, 1986).

Dickason, Olive Patricia. *Canada's First Nations: A History of Founding Peoples From Earliest Times* (Toronto: Oxford University Press, 1997).

Diehl, Claudia, and Michael Blohm. "Apathy, Adaptation or Ethnic Mobilization? On the Attitudes of a Politically Excluded Group," *Journal of Ethnic and Migration Studies*, 27, 3, 2001.

Dieter, Constance. *From Our Mothers' Arms: The Intergenerational Impact of Residential Schools in Saskatchewan* (Toronto: United Church Publishing House, 1999).

Distasio, Jino, et al. *First Nations/Métis/Inuit Mobility Study, Final Report* (Winnipeg: Institute of Urban Studies, 2004).

Dosman, Edgar. *Indians: The Urban Dilemma* (Toronto: McClelland and Stewart Limited, 1972).

Dreier, P. "Community Empowerment Strategies: The Limits and Potential of Community Organizing in Urban Neighborhoods," *Cityscape: A Journal of Policy Development and Research* 2, 2, 1996.

Dunaway, David, and Willa K. Baum (eds). *Oral History: An Interdisciplinary Anthology* (Nashville: American Association for State and Local History, 1984).

Dunning, R.W. *Social and Economic Change Among the Northern Ojibwa* (Toronto: University of Toronto Press, 1959).

Elections Canada. *2000 General Election Post-Event Overview*. Available at <www.elections.ca>.

Everitt, Joanna, and Brenda O'Neill (eds). *Citizen Politics: Research and Theory in Canadian Political Behaviour* (Don Mills, ON: Oxford University Press, 2002a).

_____. "Canadian Political Behaviour, Past and Present," in Joanna Everitt and Brenda O'Neill (eds), *Citizen Politics: Research and Theory in Canadian Political Behaviour* (Don Mills, ON: Oxford University Press, 2002b).

Falconer, Patrick. "The Overlooked of the Neglected: Native Single Mothers in Major Cities on the Prairies," in Jim Silver and Jeremy Hull (eds), *The Political Economy of Manitoba* (Regina: Canadian Plains Research Centre, 1990).

Fals-Borda, O. "Evolution and Convergence in Participatory Action Research," in J. Frideres (ed), *A World of Communities: Participatory Research Perspectives* (North York: Captus, 1992).

Ferguson, Ronald F., and William T. Dickens (eds). *Urban Problems and Community Development* (Washington, DC: Brookings Institution Press, 1999).

Fernandez, Walter, and Rajesh Tandon (eds). *Participatory Research and Evaluation: Experiments in Research as a Process of Liberation* (New Delhi: Indian Social Institute, 1981).

Ferris, Peter. *Challenges and Opportunities: Adult Learning Centres in Manitoba, A Discussion Paper* (Winnipeg: Manitoba Education, Training and Youth, 2000).

Fine, Michelle, Lois Weis, Linda C. Powell and L. Mun Wong. *Off White: Readings on Race, Power and Society* (New York: Routledge, 1997).

Fisher, R., and Shragge, E. "Organizing Locally and Globally: Bridging the Divides," *Canadian Dimension* 36, 3, 2002.

Flanagan, Donne. "Inoculating Traditional NDP Weaknesses Key to Doer's Success," unpublished paper, June 2003.

Fleras, Augie. "Aboriginal Electoral Districts For Canada: Lessons From New Zealand," in Robert A. Milen, *Aboriginal Peoples and Electoral Reform in Canada, Volume 9, Royal Commission on Electoral Reform and Party Financing* (Toronto: Dundurn Press, 1991).

Fleras, Augie and Jean Leonard Elliott. *Unequal Relations: An Introduction to Race, Ethnic, and Aboriginal Dynamics in Canada, Third Edition* (Scarborough, ON: Prentice Hall Allyn and Bacon Canada, 1999).

Fontan, J.M., P. Hamel, R. Morin and E. Shragge. "Community Economic Development and Metropolitan Governance: A Comparison of Montreal and Toronto," *Canadian Journal of Regional Science*, 22, 1–2, 1999.

Fordham, Signithia. "Racelessness as a Factor In Black Students' School Success: Pragmatic Strategy or Pyrrhic Victory?" *Harvard Educational Review*, 58, 1, 1988.

Fordham, Signithia and John Ogbu. "Black Students' School Success: Coping With the Burden of 'Acting White,'" *The Urban Review*, 18, 3, 1986.

Foucault, M. "The Order of Discourse," in R. Young (ed), *Untying the Text: A Lost Structuralist Reader* (London: Routledge and Kegan Paul, 1987).

_____. "The Subject and Power," in H.L. Dreyfus and P. Rabinow (eds), *Michel Foucault: Beyond Structuralism and Hermeneutics* (Chicago: University of Chicago Press, 1983).

_____. *Power/Knowledge: Selected Interviews and other Writings: 1972–1977* (New York: Collin Gordon Pantheon Books, 1980).

Freire, Paulo. *Education for Critical Consciousness* (New York: Seabury Press, 1973).

_____. *Pedagogy of the Oppressed* (New York: Herder and Herder, 1970).

Gage, S. and R. Hood. *The CED Tool Kit: A Step-by Step Manual of Community Economic Development* (Victoria, BC: International Development Education Association with the Greater Victoria CED Corporation, 1997).

Genovese, Eugene. *Roll, Jordan, Roll: The World the Slaves Made* (New York: Pantheon, 1974).

George, Priscilla. *Reaching the Rainbow: Aboriginal Literacy in Canada.* Video (Yorkton, SK: Parkland Regional College, 1997).

Ghorayshi, Parvin. "Women in Developing Countries: Methodological and Theoretical Considerations," *Women and Politics*, 16, 3, 1996.

Gibbons, Roger. "Electoral Reform and Canada's Aboriginal Population: An Assessment of Aboriginal Electoral Districts," in Robert A Milen (ed), *Aboriginal Peoples and Electoral Reform in Canada, Volume 9, Royal Commission on Electoral Reform and Party Financing* (Toronto: Dundurn Press, 1991).

Giddens, A. "Structuration Theory: Past, Present and Future," in C. Bryant and D. Jary (eds),

Theory of Structuration: A Critical Appreciation (London: Routledge, 1991).

_____. *The Constitution of Society: Outline of the Theory of Structuration*. (Cambridge: Polity Press, 1984).

Gidengil, Elizabeth, Andre Blais, Neil Nevitte and Richard Nadeau. "Turned Off or Tuned Out? Youth Participation in Politics," *Electoral Insight*, 5, 2, July 2003.

Gill, Sheila Dawn. "The Unspeakability of Racism: Mapping Law's Complicity in Manitoba's Racialized Spaces," in Sherene H. Razack (ed), *Space and the Law: Unmapping a White Settler Society* (Toronto: Between the Lines, 2002).

Graham, Katherine, and Evelyn Peters. "Aboriginal Communities and Urban Sustainability," in F. Leslie Seidle (ed), *The Federal Role in Canada's Cities: Four Policy Perspectives*, CPRN Discussion Paper No. F/27 (Ottawa: Canadian Policy Research Networks, 2002).

Graham-Brown, S. "Oral History," in T. Crowley (ed), *Clio's Craft: A Primer of Historical Methods* (Toronto: Copp Clark Pitman, 1988).

Gramsci, Antonio. *Selections from Political Writings 1921–1926* (Quentin Hoare, trans.) (New York: International Publishers, 1978).

Grant, Agnes. *No End of Grief: Indian Residential Schools in Canada* (Winnipeg: Pemmican Publications Inc, 1996).

Graveline, Fyre Jean. *Circle Works: Transforming Eurocentric Consciousness* (Halifax: Fernwood Publishing, 1998).

Guerin, Daniel. "Aboriginal Participation in Canadian Federal Elections: Trends and Implications," *Electoral Insight*, 5, 2, July 2003.

Guimond, Eric. "Fuzzy Definitions and Population Explosion: Changing Identities of Aboriginal Groups in Canada," in David Newhouse and Evelyn Peters (eds), *Not Strangers in These Parts: Urban Aboriginal Peoples* (Ottawa: Policy Research Initiative, 2003).

Haig-Brown, Celia. *Taking Control: Power and Contradiction in First Nations Adult Education* (Vancouver: UBC Press, 1995).

_____. *Resistance and Renewal: Surviving the Indian Residential School* (Vancouver: Tillicum Library, 1988).

Hall, B. "The Democratization of Research in Adult and Non-formal Education," in P. Reason and J. Rowan (eds), *Human Inquiry: A Sourcebook of New Paradigm Research* (Chichester: John Wiley and Sons, 1981).

Hallett, Bruce. *Aboriginal People in Manitoba* (Ottawa: Government of Canada, 2002).

Hammersley, M. "What is Wrong with Ethnography: The Myth of Theoretical Description," *Sociology*, 24, 4, 1990.

_____. "Using Qualitative Methods," *Social Science Information Studies*, 1981.

Hanselmann, Calvin. *Shared Responsibility: Final Report and Recommendations of the Urban Aboriginal Initiative* (Calgary: Canada West Foundation, 2003).

_____. *Urban Aboriginal People in Western Canada: Realities and Policies* (Calgary: Canada West Foundation, 2001).

_____. "Urban Aboriginals: Opportunities and Challenges," *Western Landscapes*, Canada West Foundation, Summer 2001.

Harrison, Bennett, and Marcus Weiss. *Workforce Development Networks: Community-Based Organizations and Regional Alliances* (Thousand Oaks, CA: Sage Publications, 1998).

Harrison, Lawrence, and Samuel P. Huntington (eds). *Culture Matters: How Values Shape Human Progress* (New York: Basic Books, 2000).

Harrison, Julia D. *Métis: People Between Two Worlds* (Vancouver: Glenbow-Alberta Institute, 1985).

Hart, Michael. *Seeking Mino-Pimatisiwin: An Aboriginal Approach to Helping* (Halifax: Fernwood Publishing, 2002).

Hart-Landsberg, M., and P. Burkett. "Economic Crisis and Restructuring in South Korea: Beyond the Free Market-Statist Debate," *Critical Asian Studies*, 33, 3, 2001.

Hawkins, Carol. *Urban Circle Training Centre: An English Language Program* (M.Ed. Thesis, University of Manitoba, Winnipeg, 1997).

Henderson, Hazel. *Creating Alternative Futures: The End of Economics* (West Hartford: Kumarian Press, 1996).

Hertz, Rosanna (ed). *Reflexivity and Voice* (Thousand Oaks, CA: Sage Publications, 1997).

Hill, Diane. *Holistic Learning: A Model of Education Based on Aboriginal Cultural Philosophy* (Master of Adult Education Thesis, Saint Francis Xavier University, Antigonish, NS, October 1999).

_____. *Aboriginal Access to Post-Secondary Education: Prior Learning Assessment and Its Use within Aboriginal Programs of Learning* (Deseronto, ON: First Nations Technical Institute, 1995).

hooks, bell. *Rock My Soul: Black People and Self Esteem* (New York: Washington Square Press, 2003).

Hudson, Ian. "The NDP's Dwindling Budget Options," *Fast Facts*. CCPA-Mb., May 12, 2004.

Hull, Jeremy. *Aboriginal People and Social Classes in Manitoba* (Winnipeg, Canadian Centre for Policy Alternatives, 2001).

_____. "Socio-Economic Status and Native Education in Canada," *Canadian Journal of Native Education*, 17, 1, 1990.

_____. *Native Women and Work*. Report 2 (Winnipeg: Institute of Urban Studies, 1984).

_____. *Natives in a Class Society* (Saskatoon: One Sky, 1983).

Hunter, Anna. "Exploring the Issues of Aboriginal Representation in Federal Elections," *Electoral Insight*, 5, 2, July 2003.

Imel, Susan. "Adult Learning in Cohort Groups, Practice Application Brief No. 24," ERIC *Clearinghouse on Adult, Career, and Vocational Education*, 2002.

_____. "Transformative Learning in Adulthood," ERIC *Digest* No. 200, 1998.

_____. "Adult Literacy Education: Emerging Directions in Program Development," ERIC *Digest* No. 179, 1996.

Jaccoud, Mylene, and Renee Brassard. "The Marginalization of Aboriginal Women in Montreal," in David Newhouse and Evelyn Peters (eds), *Not Strangers in These Parts: Urban Aboriginal Peoples* (Ottawa: Policy Research Initiative, Privy Council Office, 2003).

James, Alison, Jenny Hockey and Andrew Dawson (eds). *After Writing Culture: Epistemology and Praxis in Contemporary Anthropology* (London and New York: Routledge, 1997).

Jarvis, Peter. "Paulo Freire," in Peter Jarvis (ed), *Twentieth Century Thinkers in Adult Education* (London: Croom Helm, 1987).

Kahn, Si. *Organizing: A Guide for Grassroots Leaders* (Washington, DC: National Association of Social Workers Press, 1991).

Kastes, Wade. *The Future of Aboriginal Urbanization in Prairie Cities: Select Annotated Bibliography and Literature Review on Urban Aboriginal Issues in the Prairie Provinces* (Winnipeg: Institute of Urban Studies, 1993).

Kazemipur, A., and S.S. Halli. *The New Poverty in Canada: Ethnic Groups and Ghetto Neighbourhoods* (Winnipeg: University of Manitoba Press, 1999).

Keiffer, Charles H. "Citizen Empowerment: A Developmental Perspective," *Prevention in Human Services*, 3, 2–3, Winter–Spring 1984.

Keough, Noel. "Participatory Development Principles and Practice: Reflections of a Western Development Worker," *Community Development Journal*, 33, 3, 1998.

Key, V.O. *Southern Politics in State and Nation* (New York: A.A. Knopf, 1949).

Kingsley, Jean-Pierre. "Aboriginal Participation in Elections," Foreword to *Electoral Insight*, 5,

3, Nov. 2003, Special Issue on Aboriginal Participation in Elections.

Kinnear, Michael. "The Effect of Expansion of the Franchise on Turnout," *Electoral Insight*, 5, 2, July 2003.

Kirkness, Verna. "Aboriginal Education in Canada: A Retrospective and a Prospective," *Our Schools, Our Selves*, 10, 3, April 2001.

_____. *First Nations and Schools: Triumphs and Struggles* (Toronto: Canadian Education Association, 1992).

Kleymeyer, Charles D. (ed). *Cultural Expression and Grassroots Development: Cases from Latin America and the Caribbean* (Boulder, CO, and London: Lynne Rienner and Publishers, 1994).

Kohl, Herbert. *I Won't Learn From You* (New York: New Press, 1994).

Kothari, Uma. "Power, Knowledge and Social Control in Participatory Development," in Bill Cooke and Uma Kothari (eds), *Participation: The New Tyranny?* (London and New York: Zed Books, 2001).

Kretzmann, John P., and John L. McKnight. *Building Communities From the Inside Out: A Path Toward Finding and Mobilizing a Community's Assets* (Evanston, IL: Asset Based Community Development Institute, Institute for Policy Research, 1993).

Krosenbrink-Gelissen, Lilianne Ernestine. "The Native Women's Association of Canada," in James Frideres, *Native Peoples in Canada: Contemporary Conflicts, Fourth Edition* (Toronto: Prentice-Hall Canada, Inc., 1993).

Krotz, Larry. *Urban Indians: The Strangers in Canada's Cities* (Edmonton: Hurtig Publishers Ltd., 1972).

Kulchyski, Peter. "Forty Years in Indian Country," *Canadian Dimension*, November/December 2003.

_____. "Citizens Plus: Aboriginal Peoples and the Canadian State," by Alan C. Cairns, *The Canadian Journal of Native Studies*, xxii, 1, 2002.

Kymlicka, Will, and Wayne Norman (eds). *Citizenship in Diverse Societies* (Oxford: Oxford University Press, 2000).

Kymlicka, Will. *Multicultural Citizenship: A Liberal Theory of Minority Rights* (Oxford: Clarendon Press, 1995).

La Prairie, Carol. "Aboriginal Over-Representation in the Criminal Justice System: A Tale of Nine Cities," *Canadian Journal of Criminology*, 44, 2, 2002.

_____. *Seen But Not Heard: Native People in the Inner City* (Ottawa: Department of Justice, 1994).

La Prairie, Carol, and Philip Stenning. "Exile on Main Street: Some Thoughts on Aboriginal Over-Representation in the Criminal Justice System," in David Newhouse and Evelyn Peters (eds), *Not Strangers in These Parts: Urban Aboriginal Peoples* (Canada: Policy Research Initiative, Privy Council Office, 2003).

Labrecque, M.F. "Les femmes et le I: de qui parle-ton at juste?" *Recherches Féministes*, 4, 2, 1991.

Ladner, Keira. "The Alienation of Nation: Understanding Aboriginal Electoral Participation," *Electoral Insight*, 5, 2, July 2003.

Lance, David. "Oral History Project Design," in David K. Dunaway and Willa K. Braun (eds), *Oral History: An Interdisciplinary Anthology* (Nashville: American Association for State and Local History, 1984).

LeDuc, Lawrence, and Jon Pammett. *Elections and Participation: the Meaning of the Turnout Decline*. Paper presented at the Canadian Political Science Association, June 1, 2003.

Lee, Kevin. *Urban Poverty in Canada: A Statistical Profile* (Ottawa: Canadian Council on Social Development, 2000).

Levin, Ben, and William Alcorn. "Post-Secondary Education for Indigenous Populations," *Adult Learning*, 11, 1, 1999.

Lewis, M. *The Development Wheel: A Workbook to Guide Community Analysis & Development Planning*. The West Coast Series on CED, Second Edition (Vernon, BC: Westcoast Development Group, 1994).

Lezubski, Darren, Jim Silver and Errol Black. "High and Rising: The Growth of Poverty in Winnipeg," in Jim Silver (ed), *Solutions That Work: Fighting Poverty in Winnipeg* (Halifax and Winnipeg: Fernwood Publishing and the Canadian Centre for Policy Alternatives-Manitoba, 2000).

Liberal Party of Canada. Aboriginal People's Commission. Available at <http://www.apc-cpa.ca/> (accessed Feb. 2006).

Lithman, Yngve G. *The Community Apart: A Case Study of a Canadian Indian Reserve Community* (Winnipeg: University of Manitoba Press, 1984).

Little Bear, Leroy. "Jagged Worlds Colliding," in Marie Battiste (ed)., *Reclaiming Indigenous Voice and Vision* (Vancouver: UBC Press, 2000).

Loewen, Garry, Jim Silver, Martine August, Patrick Bruning, Michael MacKenzie and Shauna Myerson. *Moving Low-Income People in Winnipeg's Inner City Into Good Jobs: Evidence on What Works Best* (Winnipeg: Canadian Centre for Policy Alternatives-Manitoba, 2005).

Lopez, Mark Hugo. "Electoral Engagement Among Latino Youth," *Fact Sheet*, Circle, The Center for Information and Research on Civic Learning and Engagement, School of Public Policy, University of Maryland, March 2003.

Lopez, Mark Hugo, and Emily Kirby. "Voter Turnout Among Young Women and Men," *Fact Sheet*, Circle, The Center for Information and Research on Civic Learning and Engagement, School of Public Policy, University of Maryland, May 2003.

Loxley, John. "Aboriginal Economic Development in Winnipeg," in Jim Silver (ed), *Solutions That Work: Fighting Poverty in Winnipeg* (Winnipeg and Halifax: Canadian Centre for Policy Alternatives-Manitoba and Fernwood Publishing, 2000).

_____. "The 'Great Northern' Plan." *Studies in Political Economy*, 6, 1981.

Loxley, John, and Fred Wien. "Urban Aboriginal Economic Development," in David Newhouse and Evelyn Peters (eds), *Not Strangers in These Parts: Urban Aboriginal Peoples* (Ottawa: Policy Research Initiative, Privy Council Office, 2003).

MacKenzie, Michael. "Missing From the News," unpublished student paper, Department of Politics, University of Winnipeg, 2002.

Madariaga-Vignudo, Lucia, and Tatjana Miladinovska-Blazeus. "Refugee Housing in Winnipeg's Inner City," unpublished student paper, Department of Politics, University of Winnipeg, 2005.

Mamaday, N. Scott. "Confronting Columbus Again," in P. Nabakov (ed), *Native American Testimony: A Chronicle of Indian-White Relations From Prophecy to the Present, 1492–1992* (New York: Viking, 1991).

Manitoba. Office of the Provincial Auditor. *Investigation of an Adult Learning Centre in Morris- Macdonald School Division #19*, September 2001.

Manitoba. Department of Family Services and Housing. *Annual Report, 2003/04.*

Manitoba. Department of Education and Training. *Pathways for the Learner, A Strategy For Literacy For Manitobans: The Report of the Manitoba Task Force on Literacy* (Winnipeg: April 1989).

Manitoba. *Report of the Aboriginal Justice Inquiry of Manitoba*, Associate Chief Justice A.C. Hamilton and Associate Chief Judge C.M. Sinclair, (Winnipeg: Queen's Printer 1991).

Mansbridge, Jane. "What Does a Representative Do? Descriptive Representation in Communicative Settings of Distrust, Uncrystallized Interests, and Historically Denigrated Status," in Will Kymlicka and Wayne Norman (eds), *Citizenship in Diverse Societies* (Oxford: Oxford University Press, 2000).

Martin, Peter. "Considerations for Aboriginal Adult Education Program Planning," *Canadian Journal of Native Education*, 20, 1, 1993.

Maxim, Paul S., Carl Keane and Jerry White. "Urban Residential Patterns of Aboriginal People in Canada," in David Newhouse and Evelyn Peters (eds), *Not Strangers in These Parts: Urban Aboriginal Peoples* (Canada: Policy Research Initiative, Privy Council Office, 2003).

McCaskill, Don. *Migration, Adjustment, and Integration of the Indian Into the Urban Environment* (MA Thesis, Carleton University, 1970).

_____. "The Urbanization of Indians in Winnipeg, Toronto, Edmonton and Vancouver: A Comparative Analysis," *Culture*, 1, 1, 1981.

McDevitt, Michael, Spiro Kiousis, Xu Wu, Mary Losch and Travis Ripley. *The Civic Bonding of School and Family: How Kids Voting Enlivens the Domestic Sphere* (Circle: The Center for Information and Research on Civic Learning and Engagement, School of Public Policy, University of Maryland, Circle Working Paper 07, July 2003).

McFarlane, Peter. *Brotherhood to Nationhood: George Manuel and the Making of the Modern Indian Movement* (Toronto: Between the Lines, 1993).

McKenzie, Brad, and Vern Morrissette. "Social Work Practice with Canadians of Aboriginal Background: Guidelines for Respectful Social Work," in Alean Al-Krenawi and John R. Graham (eds), *Multicultural Social Work in Canada* (Don Mills, ON: Oxford University Press, 2003).

Mendelson, Michael. *Aboriginal People in Canada's Labour Market: Work and Unemployment, Today and Tomorrow* (Ottawa: Caledon Institute of Social Policy, 2004).

Mercredi, Ovide, and Mary Ellen Turpel. *In the Rapids: Navigating the Future of First Nations* (Toronto: Penguin Books Canada Ltd., 1993).

Mezirow, Jack. *Transformative Dimensions of Adult Learning* (San Francisco: Jossey-Bass Publishers, 1991).

Michelson, Melissa R. *Mobilizing the Latino Youth Vote*. Circle: The Center for Information and Research on Civic Learning and Engagement, School of Public Policy, University of Maryland, Circle Working Paper 10, August 2003.

Mies, Maria, and Veronika Bennholdt-Thomsen. *The Subsistence Perspective: Beyond the Globalized Economy* (London: Zed Books, 1999).

Milen, Robert A. *Aboriginal Peoples and Electoral Reform in Canada, Volume 9, Royal Commission on Electoral Reform and Party Financing* (Toronto: Dundurn Press, 1991).

Miller, J.R. *Shingwauk's Vision: A History of Native Residential Schools* (Toronto: University of Toronto Press, 1996).

Milloy, John. *A National Crime: The Canadian Government and the Residential School System, 1879–1986* (Winnipeg: University of Manitoba Press, 1999).

Milner, Henry. *Civic Literacy: How Informed Citizens Make Democracy Work* (Hanover and London: University Press of New England, 2002).

Mintz, Sidney. "The Anthropological Interview and the Life History," in David K. Dunaway and Willa K. Baum (eds), *Oral History: An Interdisciplinary Anthology* (Nashville: American Association for State and Local History, 1984).

Mohan, Giles. "Beyond Participation: Strategies for Deeper Empowerment," in Bill Cooke and Uma Kothari (eds), *Participation: The New Tyranny?* (London: Zed Books, 2001).

Mohanty, C., et al. (eds). *Third World Women and the Politics of Feminism* (Bloomington: Indiana University Press, 1991).

Monture-Angus, Patricia. "Women and Risk: Aboriginal Women, Colonialism and Correctional

Practice," *Canadian Woman Studies*, 19, 1 and 2, 1999.

_____. *Thunder in My Soul: A Mohawk Woman Speaks* (Halifax: Fernwood Publishing, 1995).

Morgan, M. "Working for Social Change: Learning From and Building Upon Women's Knowledge to Develop Economic Literacy," in P. Ghorayshi and C. Belanger (eds), *Women, Work and Gender Relations in Developing Countries, A Global Perspective* (Westport, CT: Greenwood Press, 1996).

Nagler, Mark. *Indians in the City: A Study of the Urbanization of Indians in Toronto* (Ottawa: Canadian Research Centre for Anthropology, Saint Paul University, 1973).

National Indian Brotherhood. *Indian Control of Indian Education* (Ottawa: NIB, 1972).

Newhouse, David. "The Invisible Infrastructure: Urban Aboriginal Institutions and Organizations," in David Newhouse and Evelyn Peters (eds), *Not Strangers in These Parts: Urban Aboriginal Peoples* (Ottawa: Policy Research Initiative, Privy Council Office, 2003).

Newhouse, David, and Evelyn Peters (eds). *Not Strangers in These Parts: Urban Aboriginal Peoples* (Ottawa: Policy Research Initiative, Privy Council Office, 2003).

Newhouse, David. "From the Tribal to the Modern: The Development of Modern Aboriginal Societies," in R.F. Lalberte, P. Settee, J.B.Waldrum, R. Innes, B.Macdougall, L.McBain and F.L. Barron (eds), *Expressions in Canadian Native Studies* (Saskatoon: University of Saskatchewan Extension Press, 2000).

Norris, Mary Jane. "Aboriginal Peoples in Canada: Demographic and Linguistic Perspectives," in D.A. Long and O.P. Dickason (eds), *Visions of the Heart: Canadian Aboriginal Issues, Second Edition* (Toronto: Harcourt Brace Canada, 2000).

Norris, Mary Jane, and Stewart Clatworthy. "Aboriginal Mobility and Migration Within Urban Canada: Outcomes, Factors and Implications," in David Newhouse and Evelyn Peters (eds), *Not Strangers in These Parts: Urban Aboriginal Peoples* (Canada: Policy Research Initiative, Privy Council Office, 2003).

Norris, Mary Jane, Martin Cooke and Stewart Clatworthy. "Aboriginal Mobility and Migration Patterns and Policy Implications," in J. Taylor and M. Bell (eds), *Population Mobility and Indigenous Peoples in Australasia and North America* (London: Routledge Press, 2002).

Norris, Mary Jane, Martin Cooke, Daniel Beavon, Eric Guimond and Stewart Clatworthy. *Registered Indian Mobility and Migration: Patterns and Implications* (Ottawa: Indian and Northern Affairs Canada, 2001).

O'Donnell, S., and S. Karanja. "Transformative Community Practice: Building a Model for Developing Extremely Low Income African-American Communities," *Journal of Community Practice*, 7, 3, 2000.

O'Neill, Brenda. "Examining Declining Electoral Turnout Among Canada's Youth," *Electoral Insight*, 5, 2, July 2003.

Okazawa-Rey, M., and M. Wong. "Organizing in Communities of Color: Addressing Interethnic Conflicts," *Social Justice*, 24,1, 1997.

Ontario Federation of Indian Friendship Centres. *Urban Aboriginal Child Poverty: A Status Report on Aboriginal Children and Their Families in Ontario* (Toronto: Ontario Federation of Indian Friendship Centres, October 2000).

Pammett, Jon H., and Lawrence LeDuc. *Explaining the Turnout Decline in Canadian Federal Elections: A New Survey of Non-Voters* (Ottawa: Elections Canada, March 2003).

_____. "Confronting the Problem of Declining Voter Turnout Among Youth," *Electoral Insight*, 5, 2, July 2003.

Patel, Sheela, and Diana Mitlin. "Sharing Experiences and Changing Lives," *Community Development Journal*, 37, 2, April 2002.

Perry, S. "Some Terminology and Definitions in the Field of Community Economic Development," *Making Waves*, 10, 1, n.d.

Peters, Evelyn. *Atlas of Urban Aboriginal Peoples*, available at <http://gismap.usask.ca/web_at-las/AOuap> (accessed Feb. 2006).

_____."Urban Aboriginal Peoples," in Caroline Andrew, Katherine Graham and Susan Phillips (eds), *Urban Affairs: Back on the Policy Agenda?* (Montreal: McGill-Queen's University Press, 2002a).

_____."Our City Indians: Negotiating the Meaning of First Nations Urbanization in Canada, 1945–1975," *Historical Geography*, 30, 2002b.

_____. "Developing Federal Policy For First Nations People in Urban Areas: 1945–1975," *The Canadian Journal of Native Studies*, 21, 1, 2001.

_____. "Aboriginal People in Urban Areas," in D.A. Long and O.P. Dickason (eds), *Visions of the Heart: Canadian Aboriginal Issues, Second Edition* (Toronto: Harcourt Brace and Company, 2000).

_____. "'Urban' and 'Aboriginal': An Impossible Contradiction," in J. Caulfield and L. Peake (eds), *City Lives and City Forms: Critical Research and Canadian Urbanism* (Toronto: University of Toronto Press, 1996).

Pettipas, Katherine. *Severing the Ties that Bind: Government Repression of Indigenous Religious Ceremonies on the Prairies* (Winnipeg: University of Manitoba Press, 1994).

Ponting, J. Rick. *First Nations in Canada: Perspectives on Opportunity, Empowerment and Self-Determination* (Toronto: McGraw-Hill Ryerson Limited, 1997).

_____."An Overview of First Nations' Empowerment and Disempowerment," in J. Rick Ponting, *First Nations in Canada: Perspectives on Opportunity, Empowerment and Self-Determination* (Toronto: McGraw-Hill Ryerson Limited, 1997).

_____."Historical Overview and Background: Part Two 1970–1996," in J. Rick Ponting, *First Nations in Canada: Perspectives on Opportunity, Empowerment and Self-Determination* (Toronto: McGraw-Hill Ryerson Limited, 1997).

Poonwassie, Deo H., and Anne Poonwassie (eds). *Adult Education in Manitoba: Historical Aspects* (Mississauga: Canadian Educators' Press, 1997).

Portes, A. "Conclusion: Towards a New World — the Origins and Effects of Transnational Activities," *Ethnic and Racial Studies*, 22, 2, 1991.

Putnam, Robert. "Social Capital Measurement and Consequences," *Isuma*, 2, 1, Spring 2001.

_____. *Bowling Alone: The Collapse and Revival of American Community* (New York: Simon and Schuster, 2000).

Rahman, MD Anisur. *People's Self-Development: Perspectives on Participatory Action Research* (London: Zed Books, 1993).

Razack, Sherene H. "Gendered Racial Violence and Spatialized Justice: The Murder of Pamela George," in Sherene H. Razack (ed), *Space and the Law: Unmapping a White Settler Society* (Toronto: Between the Lines, 2002).

Richards, John. *Neighbours Matter: Poor Neighbourhoods and Urban Aboriginal Policy* (Ottawa: C.D. Howe Institute, 2001).

Rodriguez, Carmen, and Don Sawyer. *Native Literacy Research Report* (Salmon Arm, BC: Native Adult Education Resource Centre, 1990).

Royal Commission on Aboriginal Peoples. *Report of the Royal Commission on Aboriginal Peoples, Volume 4, Perspectives and Realities* (Ottawa: Minister of Supply and Services, 1996).

_____. *Report of the National Round Table on Aboriginal Urban Issues.* (Canada: Minister of Supply and Services, 1993).

Rubin, H. *Renewing Hope Within Neighborhoods of Despair, The Community-Based Development Model* (Albany, New York: State University of New York Press, 2000).

Sabourin, Beverly Anne, and Peter Andre Globensky. *The Language of Literacy: A National*

Resource Directory of Aboriginal Literacy Programs (Winnipeg: Beverly Anne Sabourin and Associates, 1998).

Said, Edward. *Orientalism* (London: Penguin Books, 1978).

Saskatchewan Indian Institute of Technologies. *Aboriginal Literacy Action Plan: A Literacy Practioners' Guide to Action* (Saskatoon: Saskatchewan Indian Institute of Technologies, 1990).

Schouls, Tim. "Aboriginal Peoples and Electoral Reform in Canada: Differentiated Representation Versus Voter Equality," in *Canadian Journal of Political Science*, xxix, 4, December 1996.

Schumacher, E.F. *Small is Beautiful: Economics as if People Mattered* (New York: Harper Colophon Books, 1973).

Scott, J. *Weapons of the Weak: Everyday Forms of Peasant Resistance* (London: Yale University Press, 1985).

Scott, Sue M. "An Overview of Transformation Theory in Adult Education," in Sue M. Scott, Bruce Spencer and Alan M. Thomas (eds), *Learning for Life: Canadian Readings in Adult Education* (Toronto: Thompson Educational Publishing, Inc., 1998).

Selman, Gordon. "The Imaginative Training for Citizenship," in Sue M. Scott, Bruce Spencer and Alan M. Thomas (eds), *Learning for Life: Canadian Readings in Adult Education* (Toronto: Thompson Educational Publishing, Inc., 1998).

_____. "Stages in the Development of Canadian Adult Education," in Deo H. Poonwassie and Anne Poonwassie (eds), *Fundamentals of Adult Research: Issues and Practices for Lifelong Learning* (Toronto: Thompson Educational Publishing, Inc., 2001).

Selman, Gordon, Mark Selman, Michael Cooke and Paul Dempier. *The Foundations of Adult Education in Canada, Second Edition* (Toronto: Thompson Educational Publishing, Inc., 1998).

Sen, A. *Development as Freedom* (New York: Anchor Books, 1999).

Seshia, Maya. *The Unheard Speak Out: Street Sexual Exploitation in Winnipeg* (Winnipeg: Canadian Centre for Policy Alternatives-Manitoba, 2005).

Shor, I., and P. Freire. *A Pedagogy for Liberation: Dialogues on Transforming Education* (South Hadley, MA: Bergin & Garvey Publishers, Inc, 1987).

Shorten, Lynda. *Without Reserve: Stories From Urban Natives* (Edmonton: NeWest Press, 1991).

Shragge, E. "What is Left of Community?" *Canadian Dimension* 36, 2, 2002.

Shweder, Richard A. "Moral Maps, 'First World' Conceits, and the New Evangelists," in Lawrence Harrison and Samuel P. Huntington (eds), *Culture Matters: How Values Shape Human Progress* (New York: Basic Books, 2000).

Siggins, Maggie. *Bitter Embrace: White Society's Assault on the Woodland Cree* (Toronto: McClelland and Stewart Ltd., 2005).

Siggner, A.J. "Urban Aboriginal Populations: An Update Using the 2001 Census Results," in David Newhouse and Evelyn Peters (eds), *Not Strangers in These Parts: Urban Aboriginal Peoples* (Ottawa: Policy Research Initiative, 2003).

Silver, Jim. "To Help One Another: The Story of Ma Mawi," *Fast Facts*. (Winnipeg: Canadian Centre for Policy Alternatives-Manitoba, 2004a).

_____. "Winnipeg's Urban Aboriginal Strategy," *Outlook: Canada's Progressive Jewish Magazine*, 42, 2, 2004b.

_____. "The Spence Neighbourhood," *Fast Facts*. (Winnipeg: Canadian Centre for Policy Alternatives-Manitoba, 2003).

_____. "Persistent Poverty and the Push for Community Solutions," in L. Samuelson and W. Antony (eds), *Power and Resistance: Critical Thinking About Canadian Social Issues*

(Halifax: Fernwood Publishing, 2003).

_____. *Building On Our Strengths: Priorities and Principles For a Renewed Inner City Tri-Level Agreement* (Winnipeg: Canadian Centre for Policy Alternatives-Manitoba, 2002).

_____. *Solutions That Work: Fighting Poverty in Winnipeg* (Winnipeg and Halifax: Canadian Centre for Policy Alternatives-Manitoba and Fernwood Books, 2000).

Silver, Jim, Kathy Mallett, Janice Greene and Freeman Simard. *Aboriginal Education in Winnipeg Inner City High Schools* (Winnipeg: Canadian Centre for Policy Alternatives-Manitoba, 2002).

Skelton, Ian. "Residential Mobility of Aboriginal Single Mothers in Winnipeg: An Exploratory Study of Chronic Moving," *Journal of Housing and the Built Environment*, 17, 2002.

Sloane-Seale, Atlanta, Lori Wallace and Benjamin Levin. "Life Paths and Educational and Employment Outcomes of Disadvantaged Aboriginal Learners," *Canadian Journal of University Continuing Education*, 27, 2, Fall 2001.

Smith, Doug. *As Many Liars: The Story of the 1995 Vote-Splitting Scandal* (Winnipeg: Arbeiter Ring Publishing, 2003).

Smith, David. *First Person Plural: A Community Development Approach to Social Change* (Montreal: Black Rose Books, 1995).

Smith, Dorothy. "Institutional Ethnography: A Feminist Method," *Resources for Feminist Research*, 15, 1, 1986.

Sommer, D. "Not Just a Personal Story: Women's Testimonies and the Plural Self," in B. Brodski and C. Schenck (eds), *Life/Lines: Theorizing Women's Autobiography* (Ithaca: Cornell University Press, 1988).

Sparr, P. *Mortgaging Women's Lives: Feminist Critique of Structural Adjustment* (London: Zed Press, 1994).

Spence Neighbourhood Council. *Spence Neighbourhood Revitalization Strategy* (Winnipeg: Winnipeg Development Agreement, 1998).

Sprague, J., and M. Zimmerman. "Quality and Quantity: Reconstructing Feminist Methodology," *American Sociologist*, 20, 1, 1989.

Statistics Canada. "Labour Force Survey: Western Canada's Off-Reserve Aboriginal Population," *The Daily*, June 13, 2005.

_____. *Census of Canada*. Various years.

_____. "Aboriginal Peoples in Canada," *Canadian Centre for Justice Statistics Profile Series*, Catalogue No. 85F0033MIE, (Ottawa: Statistics Canada, June 2001).

Statistics Canada. *Adult Education and Training in Canada: Report of the 1994 Adult Education and Training Survey* (Ottawa: Statistics Canada, 1997).

Stymeist, David H. *Ethnics and Indians: Social Relations in a Northwestern Ontario Town* (Toronto: Peter Martin Associates Limited, 1975).

Tandon, R. "Participatory Evaluation and Research: Main Concepts and Issues," in W. Fernandes and R. Tandon, *Participatory Research and Evaluation: Experiments in Research as a Process of Liberation* (New Delhi: Indian Social Institute, 1986).

Tatum, Beverly Daniel. *Why Are All the Black Kids Sitting Together in the Cafeteria?* (New York: Basic Books, 1999).

_____. "Talking About Race, Learning About Racism: The Application of Racial Identity Development Theory in the Classroom," *Harvard Educational Review*, 62, 1, 1992.

Taylor, Charles. *Multiculturalism and the Politics of Recognition* (Princeton, NJ: Princeton University Press, 1992).

Thompson, E.P. "Time, Work-Discipline and Industrial Capitalism," *Past and Present*, 38, 1967.

Todd, Roy. "Between the Land and the City: Aboriginal Agency, Culture and Governance in

Urban Areas," *The London Journal of Canadian Studies*, 16, 2000/2001.

Togeby, Lise. "Migrants at the Polls: An Analysis of Immigrant and Refugee Participation in Danish Local Elections," *Journal of Ethnic and Migration Studies*, 25, 4, 1999.

Tough, Frank. *"As Their Natural Resources Fail": Native Peoples and the History of Northern Manitoba, 1870–1930* (Vancouver: UBC Press, 1996).

Tremblay, Manon, and Linda Trimble. "Women and Electoral Politics in Canada: A Survey of the Literature," in Manon Tremblay and Linda Trimble (eds), *Women and Electoral Politics in Canada* (Toronto: Oxford University Press, 2003).

Tremblay, Paulette, and Maurice Taylor. "Native Learners' Perceptions of Education Climate in a Native Employment Preparation Program," *Adult Basic Education*, 8, 1, Spring 1998.

Tully, James. *Strange Multiplicity: Constitutionalism in an Age of Diversity* (Cambridge: Cambridge University Press, 1995).

Turner, Bryan S. "Postmodern Culture/Modern Citizens," in Bart Van Steenbergen (ed), *The Condition of Citizenship* (London: Sage Publications, 1994).

Van Onselen, Charles. *Chibaro: African Mine Labour in Southern Rhodesia, 1900–1933* (London: Pluto Press, 1976).

Veltmeyer, H. and A. O'Malley. *Transcending Neoliberalism: Community-based Development in Latin America* (Bloomfield, CT: Kumarian Press, 2001).

Voyageur, Cora J. "Contemporary Aboriginal Women in Canada," in David Long and Olive Dickason (eds), *Visions of the Heart: Canadian Aboriginal Issues, Second Edition* (Toronto: Harcourt Canada, 2000).

Voyageur, C., and B. Calliou. "Aboriginal Economic Development and the Struggle for Self-Government," in L. Samuelson and W. Antony (eds), *Power and Resistance: Critical Thinking About Canadian Social Issues, Third Edition* (Halifax: Fernwood Publishing, 2003) .

Wallman, Sandra. "Appropriate Anthropology and the Risky Inspiration of 'Capability' Brown: Representations of what, by whom, and to what end?" in Alison James, Jenny Hockey and Andrew Dawson (eds), *After Writing Culture: Epistemology and Praxis in Contemporary Anthropology* (London and New York: Routledge, 1997).

Waring, Marilyn. *Counting for Nothing: What Men Value and What Women are Worth* (Toronto: University of Toronto Press, 1999).

_____. *Three Masquerades: Essays on Equality, Work and Hu(man) Rights* (Toronto: University of Toronto Press, 1998).

Welton, Michael R. "Mobilizing the People for Socialism: The Politics of Adult Education in Saskatchewan, 1944–45," in Michael R. Welton (ed), *Knowledge for the People: The Struggle for Adult Learning in English-Speaking Canada, 1828–1973* (Toronto: OISE Press, 1987).

Wharf, Brian, and Michael Clague (eds). *Community Organizing: Canadian Experiences* (Toronto: Oxford University Press, 1997).

Williams, Melissa. "The Uneasy Alliance of Group Representation and Deliberative Democracy," in Will Kymlicka and Wayne Norman (eds), *Citizenship in Diverse Societies* (Oxford: Oxford University Press, 2000).

Williams, A.M. "Canadian Urban Aboriginals: A Focus on Aboriginal Women in Toronto," *Canadian Journal of Native Studies*, 17, 1, 1997.

Wilson, William Julius. *The Truly Disadvantaged: The Inner City, the Underclass, and Public Policy* (Chicago: University of Chicago Press, 1987).

Yauk, Noah, and Tom Janzen. *Residential Back Taxes and Revitalization: A Study of Winnipeg's Spence Neighbourhood* (Winnipeg: Institute of Urban Studies, 2002).

Young, Lisa. "Can Feminists Transform Party Politics? The Canadian Experience," in Manon Tremblay and Linda Trimble (eds), *Women and Electoral Politics in Canada* (Toronto:

Oxford University Press, 2003).

Young, Iris. *Justice and the Politics of Difference* (Princeton, NJ: Princeton University Press, 1990).

Young, Doris. "Northern Manitoba Hydro Electric Projects and Their Impact on Cree Culture," in Y. Georg Lithman, Rick Riewe, Raymond Wiest and Robert Wrigley (eds), *People and Land in Northern Manitoba: 1990 Conference at the University of Manitoba* (Winnipeg: University of Manitoba Anthropology Papers 32, 1992).

Zaff, Jonathan F., Oksana Malanchuk, Erik Michelsen and Jacqueline Eccles. *Identity Development and Feelings of Fulfillment: Mediators of Future Civic Engagement*. Circle: The Center for Information and Research on Civic Learning and Engagement, School of Public Policy, University of Maryland, Circle Working Paper 04, March 2003.

_____. *Socializing Youth For Citizenship*. Circle: The Center for Information and Research on Civic Learning and Engagement, School of Public Policy, University of Maryland, Circle Working Paper 03, March 2003.

Zaoual, H. "The Maghreb Experience: A Challenge to the Rational Myths of Economics," *Review of African Political Economy*, 82, 1999.

Ziegahn, Linda. "Considering Culture in the Selection of Teaching Approaches for Adults," ERIC *Digest* No. 231, 2001.

Ziff, Bruce, and Pratima V. Rao (eds). *Borrowed Power: Essays on Cultural Appropriation* (New Brunswick, New Jersey: Rutgers University Press, 1997).